JOHN CAIRNEY, 'The Man Who [...] writer, lecturer and football fan.

After National Service 1948–5[...] College of Drama and the Unive[...] graduating in drama in 1953. In [...] he gained an MLitt from Glasgow University for a History of Solo Theatre and in 1994 a PhD from Victoria University, Wellington for his study of R. L. Stevenson and Theatre.

Cairney's professional association with Burns began in 1965 with the one man show, *There was a Man* by Tom Wright. In 1968 he wrote and starred in a six-part serial of the Burns story for Scottish Television, *Burns*. From 1975–79 his company Shanter Productions organised a Burns festival in Ayr. From 1974–81 he toured the world with his solo version of *The Robert Burns Story* and from 1981–85 he toured with his wife, New Zealand actress Alannah OSullivan, in *The Burns Experience*. In 1986 Shanter Productions presented the first full-length modern Burns musical *There Was A Lad*. In 1996 in commemoration of the Burns International Year a video, *Robert Burns: An Immortal Memory*, was issued, written and narrated by Cairney.

Prior to and interspersed between these performances he played a multitude of other characters on stage, radio, television and film. His films include *Jason and the Argonauts, Victim* and *A Night to Remember*. His theatre work includes *Cyrano de Bergerac* at Newcastle; C. S. Lewis in *Shadowlands* at the Court Theatre, Christchurch, as well as *Murder in the Cathedral* and *Macbeth* at the Edinburgh Festival. On television he played the lead in *This Man Craig*, as well as appearing in many other popular series.

Since 1990 Cairney has lived in Auckland, New Zealand. He has written two autobiographies and is still very much in demand as a lecturer, writer and consultant on all aspects of Burns.

The Luath
Burns Companion

JOHN CAIRNEY

Luath Press Limited

EDINBURGH

www.luath.co.uk

First published 2001
This edition 2008

ISBN 10: 1-906307-29-6
ISBN 13: 978-1-906307-29-5

The paper used in this book is acid-free, neutral-sized and recyclable.
It is made from low chlorine pulps produced in a low energy,
low emission manner from sustainable forests.

Printed and bound by
Bell & Bain Ltd., Glasgow

Typeset in 10.5 point Sabon by
3btype.com 0131 658 1763

To Mike Paterson,
who drove me to Burns again in 1996

'That I, for poor old Scotland's sake,
some usefu' plan, or book could make...'

Contents

A Letter from the Editor

Dear Reader,

Thank you for taking up this book. As you can see, it is not another Complete Works. These are available all over the place, and have been for more than 200 years. Burns has never been out of print since 1786, and I can't see what can be gained by adding yet another edition. This, however, is a Selected Works, and the selection is mine, which means it is a personal view of the poet and his life and work. This means that this book might best be regarded as a companion to Burns, an eclectic choice compiled by one who has virtually lived with the man in the study, on stage, and before the cameras for nearly 40 years.

You may not not agree with my choice, of course, but it's been made on the grounds of affectionate companionship, as he has been my professional companion for more than half of my acting and writing career. After all that time with the poet, I have come to know him, or at least my view of him. I have also come to respect, admire and like him as a man. Even his many faults I recognise as my own, and most every other man's, always bearing in mind his own comment, '*how many have been proof against the weaknesses of mankind, merely because they were never in the way of them?*'

What is more important, however, is that I have never tired of him. There is always something about the man, or his work, or his friends that takes me by surprise. A trick of rhyme, a turn of phrase, a striking thought, an unexpected attitude, you never know what is going to catch your eye as you turn the pages. He is alway interesting, even when he is not being very nice. How many people can you say that of after a 40-year relationship? A lot has been written about Burns since Robert Heron's *Memoir* of 1797, but I make no apology for adding to the pile. I think you can never get too much of a good thing and there are plenty of good things in Burns. This volume is an attempt to condense most of them.

The Contents are in four sections – an Introductory essay on the life of the man who was Burns, then his work is divided into three categories – The Poet, The Rhymer and The Songwriter. The selected items in each category are in chronological order except where a particular item is required to illustrate a theme or to introdce a new section. I start with some facts about him that might be useful and end with a complete chronology of his whole output. It is astonishing to see just how much he wrote in a very brief life, and to my knowledge it has not been laid out like this since Duncan McNaught's article in the *Burns Chronicle* of 1895. This is the complete canon. Everything is here in this summary, the good, the bad, and the wonderful. To use a modern word, correctly for once, it is awesome, but to put it *all* in a book would neither serve Burns nor the modern reader. Hence this selection.

To some, Burns was a poet first, and a songwriter second, but there are others who have exactly the opposite view. To me he is the ideal amalgam of both, having the ability to make poetry within a song, and make verse that almost sang. That ability is perhaps the hallmark of his genius. And even if he did write fewer poems as he grew in letters, he made up for that in his song industry both as collector and adaptor. He breathed new life into a song tradition that was thought dead and for that Scotland and music must be forever in his debt, but Robert Burns needs no apologist for his work. It speaks for itself, but he did enjoy his friends and his companions. Having made a lifetime journey with him, figuratively speaking, I feel I can offer this collection as from a friend and companion, in the hope that he will stimulate and delight as many in the new century as he had done in the last two.

I am highly indebted to Dr James A. Mackay for the use of his exemplary Burns scholarship as shown in the bicentenary volume of the Works published by the Burns Federation in 1986 and to W. E. Henley and T. F. Henderson for the same standard of research shown by them in the Centenary Edition of 1896. I must also acknowledge the Rev John G. Hill's 1961 book on the Love Songs which proved invaluable and I continue to be grateful to my on-going Burns mentors like Dr David Daiches and Dr Maurice Lindsay. However, most of all, I treasure the memory of the many, many nights I have shared Burns with an audience. This is where I really began to understand and appreciate him. I hope this book will help you, the reader, to do likewise.

So here you are then, a very personal view of my Robert Burns. Please share him with me in these pages.

Thank you.

John Cairney (Dr)
Auckland,
New Zealand

P.S.
One of the many sources to which I referred in writing this book was *Burns – A Study of his Poems and Songs* by Thomas Crawford (Oliver and Boyd Ltd, Edinburgh, 1960) which superseded John McVie's excellent *Some Poems, Songs and Epistles* of some years before. However, what I had not noticed before was that Dr Crawford's book was also written in Auckland, New Zealand in 1959. I just hope he enjoyed the process as much as I did, in the South Pacific sun 12,000 miles away from our mutual motherland, the Land o Burns.

Burns Facts

Born Alloway, Ayrshire, Scotland, 25 January 1759.

Worked as farm labourer for father in Ayrshire.

Founded Bachelors Club at Tarbolton, 11 November 1780.

First Commonplace Book, April 1783.

Elected Depute-Master, St James Lodge, Kilwinning, 27 July 1784.

First child born to Elizabeth Paton, 22 May 1785. A daughter.

Published *Poems, Chiefly in the Scottish Dialect*, at Kilmarnock, 31 July 1786 by subscription.

Twins born to Jean Armour, 3 September 1786.

Jean (d.1787) and Robert (d.1857).

Second Commonplace Book, April 1787.

Son born to May Cameron, Edinburgh, 26 May 1787.

William Creech publishes first Edinburgh Edition, 17 April 1787.

Thomas Cadell publishes first London Edition, 1787.

Works with James Johnson on *The Scots Musical Museum* 1787/88

Sets up Jean Armour in Mauchline house, 23 February 1788.

Twins born to Jean Armour, 3 March 1788. Both stillborn.

Enters marriage arrangement with Jean Armour, May 1788.

Buys farm at Ellisland, near Dumfries, 11 June 1788.

Commissioned in the Customs and Excise, 14 July 1788.

A son born to Jenny Clow, Edinburgh, November 1788.

First Dublin Edition of *Poems*, 1789.

Francis Wallace Burns (d.1803) born to Jean, 18 August 1789.

Writes *Tam o Shanter*, December 1790.

Daughter born to Anna Park, Dumfries, 31 March 1791.

William Glencairn Burns (d.1872) born to Jean, 9 April 1791.
Moves to the Wee Vennel in Dumfries, 11 November 1791.
Writes *Ae Fond Kiss* for Nancy McLehose, 27 December 1791.
Promoted to Dumfries Port Division, February 1792.
Elected to the Royal Company of Archers, 10 April 1792.
Begins work on Thomson's *Select Collection of Scottish Airs*,
    1792.
Elizabeth Riddel Burns (d.1795) born to Jean, 21 November 1792.
Second Edinburgh Edition of *Poems* published 18 February
    1793.
Moves to Millbrae Vennnel, Dumfries, 19 May 1793.
James Glencairn Burns (d.1865) born to Jean, 12 August 1794.
Joins Dumfries Volunteer Militia, 31 January 1795.
Writes *A Man's A Man*, December 1795.
Dies 21 July 1796 just after five o'clock in the morning, aged 37.
Maxwell Burns (d.1799) born to Jean, 25 July 1796.
Funeral procession of Burns from the Mid-Steeple to
    St Michael's Kirkyard, Dumfries, 25 July 1796.

Introduction

'There was a lad was born in Kyle...
'Twas a blast o Janwar win' blew hansel in on Robin...'

It may be said that Robert Burns was born in a thunderstorm and lived his brief life by flashes of lightning. The first flash revealed the poor, clay-walled, thatched cottage where he was born on the evening of 25 January 1759, and the last dwindling light showed through the rain of that day, the respectable stone-built Dumfries, house where he died on 21 July 1796. The thirty-seven and a half, tempest-filled years between were either bright with joyful creation, both physical and artistic, or dark with poverty, sickness or melancholy, all of which were to haunt him throughout his life. Things were always to be black or white with Robert Burns with little middle ground between. He was either very high up or very low down, and regrettably, he was down rather more than he was up. In addition, he was dogged throughout by money worries, more imagined than real, but he had known the bite of poverty from his earliest years and he was never to forget it. Even at his end, the last thing he wrote was a begging letter.

Yet he had his glorious hours in the sun, when poems and songs fell from him with a supreme ease and people flocked to hear him speak his rhymes, or just to have a look at him. Robert Burns was really two different people. His first person was the one who lived in a remote corner of 18th century Ayrshire until the publication of his only book, *Poems, Chiefly in the Scottish Dialect*. The book was published by subscription at Kilmarnock on 31 July 1786, and sold out in a matter of weeks. This phenomenon bred the other Burns who lived in Edinburgh and Dumfries, and to a large extent, on his meteor fame, for the final decade of his life. The poor ploughboy-scholar who grew up on his father's succession of failed farms seems little related to the literary dandy who made a royal progress throughout Scotland after the publication of the Edinburgh Edition in 1787, but they were one and the same man.

It was only for a handful of years, but this latter Robert Burns was arguably the most famous man in Scotland in his day, known to masters and servants across the land. He was as much at home in my lord's castle as he was in the cotter's but 'n' ben, for man and boy, he mirrored them exactly. The poet-artist in him was on a par with any peer, and the boy-Burns was of the same serf-soil as the most menial of farm labourers. This dichotomy is central to an understanding of the man he became and perhaps is at the core of his complexity as an individual.

It has always to be borne in mind how very young he was. He was never to grow old; he died before he was middle-aged, and his best work was done before he was 25. Given the quality of most of his poetry, this is hard to believe. What is more, it was largely written from 1785 to 1786, when masterpieces flew from his goosefeather like chaff from the thresher. In this golden year, and in the few months before and after, came all the great poetical works as well as many of the immortal songs, not to mention the verse epistles, epigrams, epitaphs and letters, and all in a copperplate hand that was his trade mark.

Everything seemed to come easily to his hand and with a fluency remarkable in one so young. At the very least it was proof of an astonishing industry and application. When one considers the fragmentary nature of his conventional education, it is remarkable, not that Burns wrote so well, but that he wrote at all. The credit for this undoubtedly belongs to his father.

My father was a farmer upon the Carrick border
And carefully he bred me in decency and order.

No real consideration of Robert Burns can be made, as Robert Louis Stevenson pointed out, without reference to the extraordinary man that was his father. William Burnes was born in the Mearns in the North East of Scotland, and had come down to the South West not long after after the troubles of the '45 Rebellion, to find a farm of his own and found a family. Burnes had his own claim to be unique. He was a Scottish peasant with a mind. Totally disregarding his given station in life, he made himself as

well read as he was able, and in so doing, developed an impreg-
nable sense of individual certitude founded on the Presbyterian
Bible and an unswerving trust in a just God. How this upright,
virtually Puritan man – by then a market gardener in Ayr – came
to marry Agnes Brown of Maybole is the first mystery of the
many that make up the Robert Burns story.

Nessie Brown was a short, vivacious, red-haired, black-eyed
bundle of energy, full of songs and stories. She was much sought
after in her own area, but turned down other offers to take the
sombre Burnes as her husband in 1757. This apparently ill-
matched couple produced six children in all, but they are only
remembered today by reason of Robert, their first-born. He is so
clearly a pattern of both, each imprinted on him in almost equal
degree. His character is the sythesis of two opposites, and this was
the basis of his seemingly contradictory nature. This was inevitable
given that the parents were so different from each other. Where
William was given to discourse, Nessie was given to song; where
he was grave, she was merry; where she was witty, he was wise.
In no area of personality did they seem to overlap, but they gave
to their son the best of each of them.

Even though he got his dark, gypsy good looks from his mother,
the maternal gift was almost entirely emotional. Thanks to her,
his feelings went deep but they as often dragged him down as lifted
him up. However his mother's contribution was also artistic.
From her came his sound musical instincts and a generous sensual
appetite. Fortunately, in his case, this was tempered by an easy
charm which was, by all accounts, irresistible – especially to
women. His gregarious and convivial side, his wit and love of the
social hour among other young fellows, all drew from his mother's
influence. Strange then that he never wrote one word about her
and only in the last days of his life did he send his regards to her.
All through the high days of his Edinburgh fame she lived with
her second son, Gilbert, in East Lothian but there is no record of
Robert's ever visiting her.

This reserve with his mother could be at the root of Burns's
ambivalent attitude to women generally. They were either socially

beyond his reach (as were many of the heroines in his songs) or under his feet. He was never able to meet with women as fellow-mortals. They were always to be different. There was an element of boyishness in his attitude to the other sex, and again this may have its roots in his attitude to his mother. He liked women as much as he loved them and he understood them. This was shown by how unerringly he was able to write in the voice of a woman in his songs. *John Anderson, my Jo*, for instance, is surely the finest-ever anthem to married love, and a wonderful, indirect compliment to his parents.

From his father came another kind of passion – a passion for words. To him, Robert owed his mind. This duality, the struggle between the man of feeling and the man of thought is at the base of his personality. In the future poet, the body was always at war with the soul. The opposite elements in his genes, contrasting and paradoxical, gave to his nature a two-sidedness that confused and complicated his attitudes and actions. The rigid philosophical spine connected to a considerable mind but it was always at odds with the generous and demanding animal. His character was a constant see-saw between these two extremes and it was this that gave him a life-long sense of guilt. We cannot begin to understand Burns unless we understand this.

The paternal legacy was compounded of integrity, compassion and a sturdy independence of mind. The boy is father to the man, but the father in this case was the boy's first companion, first teacher and, in every sense, his mentor. The father also passed on to his son the same love of the printed and spoken word he so enjoyed himself. He gave the boy all he would need to make his way in the world, but that included a very Scottish diffidence about self-seeking which, in this case, was hardly what an aspiring writer needed. Nevertheless, the moral ethic implanted gave Burns a spine of inherent decency which runs through all his work and informs the best of it. His sturdy independence, manly gaiety and love of the word, sung, spoken or on the page, are certainly the synthesis of his unique parentage and the manifestation of a pedigree that never suggested the emergence of a literary figure of any status, still less a genius.

Robert Burns may have had the best of each of his parents, but their very opposites occasionally brought out the worst in him. Nevertheless this imbalance was at the root of his genius. None of us can choose our parents. Similarly none of us can be a genius merely for the asking, but the fact remains that William Burnes and Nessie Brown produced the man we know as Robert Burns. By their very differences, as we have seen, they made him the two persons in one as already proposed above. This double identity appears to be a particlarly Scottish phenomenon. 'Two-facedness' or the duality of character within one nature is something which has concerned many Scottish writers, such as Stevenson and Hogg, and Burns himself in his work. This is not to say that hypocrisy is a hallmark of the Scottish character, but it does lend an insight to the two sides of Burns that were often in opposing action in his lifetime. It was this which caused him to seem at odds with himself and his environment. The man of thought versus the man of feeling, the cerebral scholar against the sensual role-player. The story of his life is the history of this on-going battle between his body and his soul. It was this vital aspect of his psyche made him the poet he became.

Nothing in his pedigree prepared him for poetry nor for the exceptional talent he was to have for it. The 'weary slave' who survived the grim boyhood, was an unlikely candidate for any kind of literary status, but, father-driven, with a book in one hand and a flail in the other, he won his way through a whole library of Augustan reading to become as well read as his temporary tutor, John Murdoch, and as fiercely book-based as his parent. Burns, in fact, was an auto-didact who gave himself, by almost constant reading, what amounted to an entirely English education. Apart from Blind Harry's *History of William Wallace*, he read very little of his native Scots as a boy, mainly because there was so little, if any, printed work in his own dialect available to him. His early reading was grounded in English authors but what better training in written language was there, and when this was added to the spoken absorption of his Scottish mother-tongue, one can see that a formidable wordsmith was in the making.

From the very beginning, the boy had an instinct to better himself. He knew somehow he wasn't destined to be broken on the land like his father before him. Something told him that he was different, and he prepared for fame with the sure knowledge that he would one day attain it, despite '*the unceasing moil of a galley slave*' that he knew growing up. Genius is nothing if not sure of itself. He took to rhyming as a way of life because life itself had so little to offer him. It was not only a respite, it was an escape. He was a peasant born to a peasant and he should have known his place, but both father and son knew there was something more and words were the key to it. Burns ate them up as greedily as he supped at the miserable crowdie that sustained them all. He was already in training for his future. The good father was aware of this. '*Who lives, will know that boy,*' he said to his wife. And Gilbert Burns was later to write of his older brother at this time, '*He was always panting after distinction.*'

In the meantime, he had first to survive. As long as there was light they would labour, and when darkness fell, they would fall in at the door, too tired to eat, too hungry to be refreshed by slumber. Robert Burns lived two lives as a boy. One, as a struggling farmer's son, was to break his body and help him to an early grave. The other, as an apprentice writer and reader, was to form his poetical skills and make him immortal. But for now, everything was directed to the daily, dreary drudgery of the kind of farming he and his family knew. Like them, he had one, simple, clear goal – to stay alive, and wait for the second flash of lightning. While he waited, he began to scribble his thoughts into a Commonplace Book. Commonplace thoughts perhaps but he had to start somewhere.

> *Observations, Songs, Scraps of Poetry etc, by Robert Burnes, a man who has little art in making money, still less of keeping it, a man, however, of some sense, a great deal of honesty and unbounded goodwill to every creature...*

The next lightning flash did not come in the writing, as it happened, or the reading, but in the winsome form of a young girl in the harvest field. The custom then was to partner the labourers in the field, man with woman, boy with girl, as the community joined to bring in the harvest. When he was 15, his partner was a young girl just one summer less than he, who, it appeared, had a song written about her by a laird's son. Young Burnes thought he could do as well as any laird's son, so for the 14-year old Nellie Kilpatrick, beside him in the field, he wrote his first song:

> O, once I loved a bonie lass, ay, and I love her still,
> And while that virtue warms my heart, I'll love my hand-
> some Nell...

The words were silly, by his own admission, but he was on his way. From this time on, Robert Burns was to be in a permanent state of being in love. It was vital for his muse that he was in love with somebody. As he had said, '*I never thought to turn poet till I got heartily in love*', but what he really meant was not love but sex. Fresh, disturbing, exciting, young sex but that didn't matter. The important thing was that lightning had struck again, and by it, poesy was opened up to him via the young female.

> There's nought but care on ev'ry han',
> In ev'ry hour that passes-O.
> What signifies the life o man,
> An twere na for the lassies-O!

He had grown into a handsome youth, and his reading had given him an extensive vocabulary, unusual to say the least, for an Ayrshire tenant-farmer's son. And he was not afraid to use it. It was no accident that he founded the Tarbolton Bachelors Club which was open to all '*professed admirers of the female sex*'. He was assiduously rehearsing the future role he was to play, and with his saffron plaid, tied hair and buckled shoes, he was certainly dressed for the part. He cut a dashing figure in the parish and was loud in his admiration for most of the local girls, although truth was he could only talk a good seduction. He was as innocent as they all were, but there was no doubt he was

caught by a few of them, especially one whom he chose to call
Mary Morison.

> *Tho this was fair, and that was braw,*
> *And yon the toast o a' the town,*
> *I sigh'd and said, 'Amang them a'*
> *Ye are na Mary Morison.'*

The limpid directness of that last line contains the secret of high
art. By being honest to himself and his situation in the poem, he
had stumbled on poetry. This boy was no mean rhyming hack; he
had found his voice early and he had found it through women,
and he was to be true to both till life did them part. This thrilling
economy with a line was to make him near the end of his life one
of the greatest songwriters of all time, but first he had to write a
great deal of verse.

Ironically, he couldn't begin properly with his life, or his life's
work, until he was free of his father, the man who had done so
much to make him the artist he would become. William Burnes
died at Lochlea Farm on 13 February, 1784, aged 63, and worn
out by hard toil and *'the snash of cruel factors'*. Legal action he
had taken against a greedy landlord had gone all the way to the
High Court of Session in Edinburgh which found in William's
favour, but the case had bankrupted the family and the victory
came to the father on his death-bed. His last words were for his
first son, *'It's only you I fret for'* – then he was *'carried off to*
where the wicked cease from troubling and the weary are at rest.'

Robert and Gilbert quickly moved the family over the hill to
Mossgiel, another farm near Mauchline, to avoid further credi-
tors, and start all over again on their own. This time, Burns left
the running of the farm to his brother and took up his pen as if it
were a sword. He would cut himself free from farming and he
would do it in verse. He was 25 years old and raring to go. He
had nothing to lose but his head. Rab Mossgiel was born and
ready to take his place as the Ayrshire Bard.

> *Beware a tongue that's sweetly hung,*
> *A heart that warmly seems to feel,*

> *That feeling heart but acts a part,*
> *Tis rakish art in Rab Mossgiel!*

If the death of his father released his muse to soar, the same loss of restraint allowed for other explorations in another direction. As a further precaution against litigation both brothers changed their names officially from Burnes to Burns. Robert was free to be himself at last. Almost the first thing he did was to enjoy the freedom of a young serving girl in the house, Bess Paton, and the natural result in the following year was his first child – a 'misbegotten child' or bastard wean. Being Burns, he could do no less than trumpet his pride to the world in the first poem in literature to celebrate the tangible result of love. A child was a child and this was his child. His first.

> *Welcome my bonie, sweet, wee dochter!*
> *Tho ye come here a wee unsought for,*
> *And tho your comin I hae fought for,*
> *Baith kirk and queir;*
> *Yet, by my faith, ye're no unwrought for –*
> *That I shall swear!*

Needless to say, this paean to parenthood was not among his published works in his lifetime. Like so many of his greater works, it was thought to be indelicate and unfit for gentle consumption, but this particular poem has long outlived its first prissy detractors and exists today for what it was, and still is, the spontaneous outpouring of a young father's feelings on seeing his child for the first time...

> *What tho they ca' me fornicator,*
> *And tease my name wi kintra clatter,*
> *The mair they talk I'm kenn'd the better,*
> *E'en let them clash;*
> *An auld wife's tongue's a feckless matter*
> *To gie ane fash.*

Bess Paton left the district soon afterwards leaving Burns holding the baby. He promptly gave it up to his mother and sisters, to

bring up as one of their own. The which they did, until she was
married herself. Burns hardly mentioned the matter again.

Auld Nature swears, the lovely dears
Her noblest work she classes, O:
Her prentice han' she try'd on man,
An then she made the lasses, O.

His mother had wanted him to marry Bess but he couldn't. He
didn't love her. Bess had understood, but his mother hadn't. She
never spoke to her son again, leaving him to his own devices.
Burns, however, having been given a taste of women, wanted
more. The serious-minded Tarbolton bachelor gave way to the
young Mauchline bull, who now proceeded to run wild among
the startled maidens of the parish, but in reality, making more
noise than mischief.

It was upon a Lammas night when corn rigs are bonie
Beneath the moon's unclouded light I hied awa to Annie.
The time flew by wi tentless heed, till tween the late and
early
Wi sma' persuasion she agreed to see me through the barley.

He became known in the town as a maker of rhymes – and for
much else. Freed from his father at last, he could now do more or
less as he pleased. And it pleased him most to make love and verses,
and generally, in that order.

Miss Miller is fine,
Miss Markland divine,
Miss Smith, she has wit
And Miss Betty is braw,
There's beauty and fortune
To get with Miss Morton,
But Armour's the jewel for me o them a'.

Jean Armour was the first serious love of his life and was to be his
last. This particular Mauchhline belle, favourite daughter of the
local stone-mason, was to become the wife of Burns, and the

mother of their nine children, only three of whom would survive into adulthood. She was the rock on which he would build his family and she stood firm no matter how the winds blew around them. Jean Armour was to remain the constant, the only factor that was to be common to both halves of his life – that is, the Burns before the publication of his poems and the Burns after it. They were to prove two quite different people but they were both the same Burns to Jean.

In 1785, however, they were very young, and Robert was rampant – in every sense. Poems flew from his hand as fast as seed from his body, and both with the same fervour. Almost at once, Jean was in her first pregnancy and Burns was in consternation. Coming hard as it did after the scandal of Bess Paton, it was the beginning of the thunder and lightning that typified the meteorological complexities of his love life. A whirlwind now blew around them from all sides. Burns tried to appease Jean and her father by writing a paper declaring themselves married in the eyes of God, but her father declared that he knew his own daughter better than God did and packed her off to Paisley.

But not before they both had to suffer three Sundays running on the cutty stool before all the congregation and take their reprimand from the Minister. The Kirk ruled in rural Scotland and the Kirk elders ran the parish, ever on the look-out for transgressions, especially '*ye sin of fornication*'. William Fisher, one of the elders, was especially assiduous in seeking out those who '*sinned against the flesh*' and Robert Burns was a ready target. His retort was to '*puzzle Calvinism with much heat and indiscretion*' and write his shattering satire on Fisher – *Holy Willie's Prayer*.

> *O Thou that in the Heavens does dwell*
> *Wha, as it pleases best thysel,*
> *Sends ane to Heaven an ten to Hell,*
> *A' for they glory,*
> *And no for any guid or ill*
> *They've done before Thee.*

In the months that followed, deprived of Jean, he took his solace

where he found it – at Freemason meetings, drinking sessions and
any occasion at all that allowed him to take a girl in his arms. He
was on the rebound and it landed him in places like Poosie
Nansie's Tavern where he could enjoy the company of tinkers and
trollopes, soldiers and beggars, all the low life of the road, met to
sing and dance, but mostly to drink. Burns watched and listened,
and as a result, produced *The Jolly Beggars*, a brazenly bawdy
song scena, and his first masterpiece. It was an unkempt hymn to
love and liberty and he delighted in it as he delighted in the free
spirits of the derelict and down-and-out.

> *What is title? What is treasure?*
> *What is reputation's care?*
> *If we lead a life of pleasure*
> *Tis no matter how or where.*
> *Life is all a variorum*
> *We regard not how it goes*
> *Let them cant about decorum*
> *Who have character to lose.*

He lived only for the moment and for the making of verses, short
and long, verse-letters, epigrams, epitaphs, songs – and scraps of
poetry. He made his verses and rhymes the way he made his chil-
dren – spontaneously and naturally, but he was inching nearer
and nearer poetry with every line.

The notion of seeing his words '*in guid, black prent*' had been
planted just a few years earlier when, during a walk in Leglen
Woods near Irvine with Richard Brown, the future sea-captain
suggested that the 22-year old Burns's verses were good enough
to print in a newspaper, even a book. Even a book? The young
rhymer was caught, even though at first thought, the idea seemed
preposterous. Who would buy a book of ploughboy scribbles?
Yet the idea persisted, and in 1785 it all came to a head.

1785 was *annus mirabilis* and his heart was in everything he
did. Everything that was later to make his name was written in
and around this one tremendous year. He was driven forward in
a white heat of creativity and nothing could stop it – or him.

Everything in his life up till that time had prepared him for this moment. All the silent hours of stolen boyhood reading, all the earnest discourse with his pedagogic father, all the songs he had heard at the hearth, the stories round the frugal table, it was all grist to this mill, which now ground out at full tilt the first harvest of all his artistic instinct.

The posturing and bravado of his innocent youth was set aside as he touched on real feeling for the first time, and he couldn't believe what he found he could do with words. It was an amazing tide and it almost swept him off his feet but he kept his head as his local fame as a bard grew by the hour, and what was, in effect, his life's work, apart from the late songs, was written in the nine months between July 1785 and April 1876. Nine months. In the time it took to make a child, he created a corpus of poetic work that would prove to be timeless. And he was only 26 years old.

He was at the very height of his physical and mental powers. He could have done anything it seemed. And what he wanted to do, apparently, was emigrate. He had suddenly decided that he would become what he called '*a negro-driver*' in Jamaica. Everyone was astonished. And puzzled. But he seemed determined. This far-fetched plan to emigrate had arisen out of a desperation about his affairs at home. He was no further forward with Jean Armour and had now become involved with a Highland nursery-maid, Mary Campbell. He wanted out of farming, he wanted out of Scotland. There was nothing to hold him to either. So he gave up his share of Mossgiel to his brother, Gilbert, and concocted a scheme with his lawyer friend, Gavin Hamilton, to buy a passage to the West Indies for Mary Campbell and himself.

Then Farewell Scotland, I shall never see you more.

But how to raise the money for the voyage? Other friends, like Robert Aiken and John Ballantyne, suggested that he publish some – not all – of his poems in a book and raise the cash through sales. Sell a book of poems? *His* poems? Why not? It was his fate to be a poet, and he knew it. But a whole book? Could he do it?

Of course he could. He had no doubt. He reasoned that if even if the book failed,

> *the roar of the Atlantic would drown out the voice of censure.*

This was to be the third lightning flash. The first had found him in a cottage, the second had shown him women and poetry, and now, the third, revealed the prospect of paid authorship. This prospect had been opened up by the Freemasons. His Masonic contacts were now to prove invaluable. Undoubtedly, without the Freemasons in Scotland at that time, there would have been no book, and, therefore, no Robert Burns, at least as we know him today.

Significantly, his own initiation in the Craft came in July 1781, the same year as he was given the idea of printing his own work by Captain Brown. He had been proposed at his local Lodge, St David No 24, Tarbolton, (later to become the St James, Kilwinning), by Gavin Hamilton. Within months he had passed to the Fellowship Degree, and before the end of the year he had been raised to the Degree of Master. By the time he began to think seriously about putting out a book he had been elected Depute Master. In unusually quick time, he was to became a Mark Mason, a Royal Arch Mason and a Knight Templar, a rare level indeed, but then suddenly, in the last year of his life, like Mozart just before *his* death, he gave up the Masons, or they gave up on him.

However, at the beginning, there were many reasons why Burns enjoyed being a Freemason. The first was the opportunity it gave him to revel in easy male company. It was a natural step up from the Tarbolton Bachelors' Debating Society. Secondly, its principles of brotherly love and the betterment of mankind by intellectual development were entirely in accord with his own views. Thirdly, its egalitarian structure, where titles meant little, and '*a man's a man for a' that*', were exactly in line with the new sense of freedom being promulgated in the late 18th century by the European Enlightenment, with its return to classical and rational principles. This might have been seen to be subversive and therefore dangerous in Burns's day, and no doubt that would have appealed to him too.

However, it was the Masons who came to Burns's aid, and just when he needed them. Gavin Hamilton took Burns to the St John's Lodge in Kilmarnock, where he persuaded some of the members to open a subscription for the publication of '*Poems, Chiefly in the Scottish Dialect*' by Robert Burns. The cost of the paper, estimated at twenty seven pounds, had to be met before any work could be started. John Wilson, the Kilmarnock printer, was also a Mason, so it must be supposed that Burns got a good deal. Even so, it was much more than he or Gavin Hamilton could afford, so help was needed and that came from nine good men of Killie – Will Parker, Tam Samson, Robert Muir, John Goldie, Gavin Turnbull and Doctors Moore, Hamilton and Paterson – who pledged between them 350 of the 612 volumes projected. With this assurance, the printing of the subscription sheets was put in hand and Burns had taken the first step to becoming a printed poet. For the first time in Lodge records, he was referred to as '*Poet Burns*', a legend that was to apply to him for the rest of his life.

It might have been expected, then, that he was a happy man, but happy he certainly was not, and the reason was Jean Armour, or rather her father. Seemingly, when he was first informed that Jean, his favourite daughter, was pregnant, he fainted. On being revived with the best Ne'erday brandy, and being told that Burns was the father, he fainted clean away again. Now Jean returned from Paisley with twins, a boy and a girl, and proudly admitted that Burns was the father. This time, Armour slapped a warrant on Burns for his arrest by the Sheriff's officers for failure to pro-vide Jean with maintenance for herself and any child – or chil-dren. The Kirk also fined him for fornication. In addition, Mary Campbell had gone to the port of Greenock to await him and had died there. '*Of a malignant fever*,' it was said. The Campbell fam-ily were supposed to be after his blood. Things did not look good for the putative poet. He went into hiding at one of his aunt's farms until he could escape to Jamaica, but then, on 31 July 1786, the book came out – and suddenly everything changed.

Poems, Chiefly in the Scottish Dialect by Robert Burns. One volume, octavo, price stitched, three shillings. It is worth more than three thousand pounds today. The Kilmarnock Edition. One little book of verse. But it changed his life forever. Every copy printed was sold within a week. Almost every household in Ayrshire had one except the Burns family at Mossgiel. They had never thought to subscribe. Not that it mattered, the first son of the house was now a poet in print, and with a book in his hands to prove it. How he must have wished his father could have seen it. Not only would he have been proud, he would have felt justified. Burns was now called for on all sides, and in the the taverns was proclaimed the Ayrshire Bard. Suddenly, he was famous. Armour withdrew his warrant and the Campbells retreated to Campbeltown, so that Poet Burns could have his local hour.

Every line he had ever written was a determined step to win his way out of farming and a life of drudgery. From being a parochial rhymer he had made a huge step into print. National fame now beckoned as a Scottish poet. Everything had to be re-thought – emigration, marriage, career – but the first priority was, without doubt, a second edition. However, Mr Wilson could not be persuaded that Ayrshire wanted another book of poetry so soon, and if it did, he would have to be paid in full up front. Burns packed his trunk again for the Indies. It was already on its way to Greenock by the carter when he got a letter from a Dr Blacklock suggesting that he try for a second edition in Edinburgh. Edinburgh? Why not? Burns was charged by this time and nothing was going to stop him now. As far as he was concerned, Edinburgh was just as foreign and far away as Jamaica. It was as good an escape as any. Let another ship sail without him, he hired a horse and set out for the capital.

> Then out into the world, my course I did determine,
> Tho to be rich was not my wish, yet to be great was
> charming...

He was completely overawed by the big city and didn't move out of his lodging for two days. When he did, it was to attend a meeting of the Canongate Lodge, Kilwinning. Here, Burns was hailed as the Ayrshire Bard by influential fellow-countymen resident in the capital and introduced by them to his new patron, the Earl of Glencairn. The good lord arranged a quick visit to a tailor for his new *protege* so that Burns might appear in the familiar buff waistcoat and blue top-coat which was to become his bardic uniform. And so, at the St Andrew's Lodge, in a great company of gentlemen and distinguished visitors from abroad, Burns was proclaimed '*Bard of All Scotland*'. What a situation for a poor country lad. Fortunately, he made an effective reply and sat down to great applause.

It must be understod at this point just how far Burns had come in his 27 years. A man born in a poor station in a remote corner of an even poorer country which at the time was trying to adjust to becoming North Britain after being shamefully sold as a nation only eighty years before. An old Scotland was being lost before the new Scotland could be realised and now a young poet had arisen and was being proclaimed Scotland's Bard. It was heady stuff. It was as if he were meant to arise just at this time to remind the ordinary people of Scotland, who read him first, who they were and where they had come from before they were lost in the furnaces and manufactories of the new industrial age that were already growing up around them.

Janus-like, Burns pointed both ways, backwards to the old Scotland of the Makars and forward to the Enlightenment and the begininng of Modernity. He stood at the watershed of a new tide of change that was sweeping all of Britain. Revolution may have been in the air but prejudice was still thick on the ground, and Burns soon found himself uncomfortably with a foot in each camp. All his new patrons, and most of his new acquaintances were of the gentry and the landed class, while his old friends were of the land. That is, they were peasant-bound to it and tied for life, unless they could break away to schoolmastering or the law. Burns escaped to letters. His book also marked a watershed in his own life, for after it, he was never to be the same man again.

He began to feel he had been born to the wrong parents, as much as he loved and respected them both. Lines of social demarcation were clear in Scotland in his lifetime. The Divine Right, which had sustained a whole line of Stuart kings, had filtered down the class ladder only gradually and those on the higher rungs were convinced that God had made them from a finer kind of dust, and were sure that the quality lessened as it descended through the pre-ordained pecking order to what they called the lower orders. The trouble was that those at the base, at actual ground level, believed this too, and felt that theirs was a coarser grain than the gentry, but no one had told Burns this. His father had seen to it that he knew his place, and that it certainly was not with those who fatalistically accepted their lot as part of God's plan for the human race.

In his time, too, there was no aristocracy of the arts. There was no way in which his talents would have carried him far for their own sake. His gifts of social ease and his conversational skills, not to mention his writing, would have stood him in good stead in today's arts market place, but in 1787, he was still, as far as Edinburgh society was concerned (and that meant, in effect, Scottish society) firmly fettered to the farmyard. One might make one's way out of one's station, but only so far it would seem, and then the barrier came down – even to genius. One had to be born to greatness, it would appear, and certainly to privilege. It was small wonder that Burns bristled at his first contact with this unreal world inhabited by the few. And yet, had he known, he could have entered Edinburgh with palms under his feet. Be that as it may, the Robert Burns Story, as the world knows it, could now begin.

My Lord Glencairn proved an efficient patron and thanks to his efforts, and the support of the gentlemen of the Caledonian Hunt, a second edition of the Poems was put in hand almost at once with Mr Creech, the bookseller in the High Street. He had struck lightning again. Thanks to Creech, he also met with the formidable William Smellie, printer and founder-editor of the *Encyclopaedia Britannica*. Smellie was also founder-President of the Crochallan Fencibles, a company of wits and rakes who met regularly in Dawny Douglas's tavern in the Anchor Close for sessions of jocular talk and serious drinking. Burns soon became one of its most popular members and made new friends like Woods, the actor, Clarke, the musician, and Naysmith, the painter. He came into his own in such convivial company and he revelled in their companionship.

He also enjoyed that other kind of companionship offered by May Cameron, a serving-girl at Mrs Carfrae's, where he lodged. But if he played hard by night, he worked as hard all day. He had a book to get out and most of his waking hours were spent on a high stool in Smellie's print shop correcting proofs. When these were completed, and the second book came out to the same rapturous reception, invitations poured into Baxter's Close. Every door was open to him. Every table had a place set. Every hand was offered. He refused no one. By the new lightning light, he saw that he was indeed famous. This wasn't Ayrshire, this was the world. And a whole new world it was, this candle-lit world of Edinburgh celebrity and he relished it. No one enjoyed being famous more. Who wouldn't? He was 27 years of age, in good health for once, and for the first time in his life, he had leisure and the money to enjoy it.

He resolved to take a holiday tour through his native land. Besides, he had new contacts to make, and book monies to collect *en route*. It was a triumphal progress. Crowds flocked to gaze on the famous Bard as he passed through village and town on the way. With various friends at various stages, he made a detour around the Borders, being given honours and freedoms at every stopping place. His book had gone before him. Eventually, he pointed his horse towards Mauchline. He could have entered the village like a king. What a difference a year had made. Even James Armour made his obeisance, and, as a gesture of his new goodwill, he offered his daughter as an earnest of his change of mind. There was no talk now of writs or Sheriff's officers. Burns accepted the ransom in as much as it allowed him to meet with Jean again – and the twins – but he was in no hurry to marry. Not while he had the whole of Scotland at his feet. He had his fame to enjoy as much as Jean Armour and, in any case, there were other

beauties met with on the way, to flatter and make songs upon.
There was Peggy Chalmers, for instance.

This was the first woman of quality and education who had
looked on Burns as an equal, if not in rank, then in brains and
attainment. She was also good-looking. Each flattered the other,
and he even went so far as to propose to her during a visit to her
relatives at Harvieston House, near Stirling. She, however, being
more practical, turned him down in favour of an Edinburgh
banker. A year later, writing to her from Ellisland, (and by now,
married to Jean) he wrote:

> *When I think I met with you, and lived more of real life*
> *with you in eight days than I could do with almost any-*
> *body else I met with in eight years – when I think of the*
> *improbability of meeting you again in this world – I could*
> *sit down and cry like a child.*

There was no doubt, he loved her – if only for eight days. She her-
self went off to India with her husband and eventually retired to
live in France, but she never forgot her poet, and said that she
might have given a different answer had he asked her again.
Meantime, he continued his tour by travelling into the Highlands
by coach with Willie Nicol, the school master, to visit Aberdeen
and meet with Burnes cousins at Stonehaven. He had come into
his fatherland in every sense, but he found nothing lovelier in this
stern countryside than the Duchess of Gordon who invited him to
dinner – but not Nicol. Burns had to leave the table in a hurry, to
prevent Nicol running off with the coach, and the two friends
returned to Edinburgh in a huff.

By this time, Burns was a national figure, a status he was to
retain till the end of his life. His popularity fluctuated naturally,
but from here on he was known to rich and poor alike through-
out the land in a manner which is hardly paralleled even today,
with fame being available at five minute's notice. Without the
benefit of TV, radio or even a reliable post, Burns was genuinely
nationally famous inside a year. He had his detractors, even then,
but they were powerless against the *éclat* which greeted this

young man, when, between 1887 and 1889, he walked across Scotland like a god.

All he had done was bring out a little book of poems, but he had done so in a strong, bold, Scottish voice and the country loved him for it. Scottish letters, at that time wilting under the weight of snobbish Anglified gentility, was in urgent need of his unashamed, native, natural style, and when he was able to ally this with a dashing appearance and a romantic, pastoral aura, the combination was devastating. He could also talk, and in good English. Those early 'conversations' with his father, brother and John Murdoch were now paying off. Although he still *pretended the peasant* he was not at all overawed by the nobility, whatever obsequious noises he made on paper. He made such a strong impression on the ordinary people of Scotland that they came to believe they might have in him a champion, and a new hero. They were sadly in need of one. Had he had political ambitions, this would have been his time, but he had none, and the time passed.

Meantime, he made the best of it. Back in Edinburgh, he went to the theatre, attended concerts, was a special guest at lunches, dinners and suppers, and dutifully 'sang' at all of them. He also attended the new tea-parties which were almost as much of a craze in the capital as he was. He was sought after by every hostess, each eager to show off the Ploughboy Poet to her guests. He accepted, although he knew the game they were all playing. He was as *'novel as the balloon ascent or the performing pig in the Grassmarket'*. He played up because it was a way of meeting people and making contacts. Networking, it would be called today. He had, after all, to look to his future, despite the giddy present. He was well aware of his passing novelty.

It was at a tea-party, given by Miss Mirren, sister to an important man in the Excise Service, that he met with a certain Edinburgh grass-widow, unhappily married to a Glasgow man by the name of McLehose, who was absent in the Indies. Her name was Agnes, but friends called her Nancy and for Burns, she was to become 'Clarinda'. She was actually a Glasgow girl herself, exactly the same age as Burns, and just his kind of catch, young,

blonde, articulate – and unattainable. Being Burns, this might have
been her greatest attraction. A meeting between the two at her house
in the Potter Row was quickly arranged, but before the night, he
was thrown from a coachload of drunken theatricals and wrenched
his knee. He was forced to sit in his room at St James Square with
his leg up on a stool. He wrote to Clarinda to explain:

> *I can say with truth, Madam, I never met a person I was
> more anxious to meet again, but an unlucky fall has put
> out my knee, and I am forced to correspond...*

She replied politely, and he replied to her reply:

> *Some unnamed feeling, yet stronger than a whim, carries
> me on...*

She replied again, and he replied by the same messenger (Jenny
Clow, her maid):

> *Let me but see your eyes and hear your voice –*

Clarinda replied this time in just a little alarm. Burns was
unfazed:

> *I beg your pardon. I fear I go wrong in my usual unguarded
> way...*
> *You say we cannot talk of love – then put 'respect',
> 'esteem' or any other tame, Dutch expression you like in
> its place.*

Soon they were writing six letters a day to each other. At first, his
were delivered by the penny porter, but soon Jenny Clow was the
solitary courier, flying between each of them. Sometimes, she had
to wait for Burns to write his. This proximity to the young man
in his own room had its dangers, as was realized in due course
when Jenny had a son and claimed Burns as the father.
Meantime, he only had his pen, and not his penis, for Clarinda:

> *All I ask you to believe, sweet lady, is how much store I
> set by our future friendship. I look back sadly on my loss
> in not knowing you sooner...*

They had whipped each other into a frenzy of passion by proxy. One of them had to take action soon. Burns, or Sylvander, as she insisted on calling him, acted:

> *I shall come to you on Sunday. I mean to take a chair and be with you at five.*

She replied at once, asking to come a little later when the neighbours' curtains would be closed. She didn't realize she was dealing with a master.

> *Fear not, lady; my heart has ever run before my head, which consequence has been that I now boast a luckless troop of my own follies. But rascals are they that would not let me do a dishonest or dishonourable thing –*
> *Forgive me, I am interrupted –*

The interruption here may be considered as episodic intensification. The mere facts of the matter are that during this dainty courtship of Clarinda he had gone back to Mauchline on a visit and saw Jean again as a matter of course – with the inevitable results. She was thrown out into the street by her own father for persisting in breeding with Poet Burns. Now word had come to Edinburgh that she had had twins again – and both had died within a matter of days.

Since he was, by his own admission, incapable of a 'dishonest or dishonourable thing', he was left with no alternative. He must go to Jean. There was no sporting with human misery. He must leave Nancy McLehose. There is no trifling with another's happiness. And so, at the White Hart Inn in the Grassmarket, Robert Burns took farewell of his Clarinda, now restored as Mistress Mac. No one knows what they said at that last meeting. All we know is that he walked her home. Who knows how they said goodbye. Certainly, it was not in the brittle artificiality of their letters. All we do know, is that when he got back to the West again, he penned to her a card from Sanquhar Post Office. On it he had written his real farewell – a tender song of parting love which came directly from the heart:

I'll ne'er blame my partial fancy,
Nothing could resist my Nancy!
But to see her was to love her,
Love but her, and love forever.
Had we never lov'd sae kindly,
Had we never lov'd sae blindly,
Never met – or never parted –
We had ne'er been broken-hearted.

Nancy McLehose lived to be an old lady in Edinburgh, but she never forgot her year of love for Robert Burns, and on the evening of its first anniversary she wrote in her diary,

> *This day parted from Burns, never to meet again in this world.*
> *O, may we meet in Heaven.*

Six years later, when Burns himself came to die in Dumfries, he was buried in his best shirt, and under the collar, Jean stitched the cameo of Nancy McLehose which her husband had received from Clarinda during his Edinburgh year. It was the act of a wife who not only loved her husband, but understood him.

> *BE IT KNOWN – that Jean Armour is installed in all the*
> *rights and privileges, immunities, franchises and paraphernalia that at present do, or at any time may, belong to the*
> *name, title and designation – WIFE – of Robert Burns, Poet.*

It was time to start life in earnest. His days in the sun were over – or so he thought – and with a firm resolve he took up his triple responsibilities as part-time Exciseman, part-time Farmer and full-time Father of a family. His Edinburgh follies were put aside. It was time now to put down roots, but the soil at Ellisland, the farm near Dumfries which his book had bought him, was as unyielding as any his father had known in three farms in Ayrshire. The Excise commission committed him to ride 200 miles a week around Nithsdale for a scant salary and even less leisure. What little he had, he gave to Jean and the children. Poetry was almost forgotten, but he wasn't.

Every other day brought either a visitor to the door, or the public chaise to the road-end where the passengers would alight for the chance of seeing the Poet Burns at work in his field or at his desk. He tried not to oblige them but his was an insistent fame and it would not let him go. In that summer of 1789 he was to write his greatest work. The final lighting flash hovered over Ellisland in late autumn and it struck with a vengeance on a wet November day – resulting in a work he entitled: *Tam o Shanter – A Tale.*

But here, my Muse, her wing maun cour,
Sic flights are far beyond her pow'r...

If Burns had written nothing else other than this work, it would have earned him a place in the front rank of world writers. Not since *The Jolly Beggars* five years earlier, had his dramatic instinct emerged so clearly as it does in this brilliant scenario of one man's drunken adventure. Every one of its 229 octosyllabic lines surges with linguistic certainty, both in Scots and English, and the unerring rythmic detail conjures up those pictures in the mind that are the mark of narrative artistry. The work flows with an ease that underlines the seeming spontaneity his careful workmanship so cunningly conceals. It is a seamless garment of words that cloaks a series of events that are both comical and horrifying.

Tam may have escaped his devils but Burns himself was not so lucky. His own devils were the social hour and the sins of the flesh. He had thought that marriage to Jean would have dealt with the latter and his increasing work-load in the Excise the former, but almost the opposite was true. His work forced him away from home for days at a time. His stays at inns and taverns drew company around him and his own gregariousness saw that he was rarely out of reach of a bottle. As he said himself,

There are men here who would not give me their company
if I did not drink with them, so I give to each a slice of
my constitution.

This was so true. He did not have the stomach for drink. His boyhood had seen to that. The legacy of long, cold, wet, gruelling days of labour on a poor diet when he was little more than a growing boy took its later dividend in rheumatoid arthritis, colic fever, headaches, night sweats and fits of depression. His intestinal weakness, despite a sturdy physique, made him no match for the five-bottle-a-night gentry, so he found his company in the taverns and inns. Particularly at the Globe Inn, Dumfries, where there were other consolations:

Yestreen, I had a pint o wine, a place where body saw na
Yestreen, lay on this breast o mine, the gowden locks o
Anna.

Anna Park was the niece of the Globe Inn proprietor, Mrs Hyslop, who had befriended Burns during his many visits to her hostelry. She provided him with his own chair near the fire and a bed for the night. She also, I'm sure quite unwittingly, provided her niece. Anna, of course, was blonde. Burns had a predeliction for blondes. In time, Anna was delivered of a daughter in Edinburgh at the same time as Jean gave birth to her third son. Unfortunately, Anna did not survive the birth and Jean sent for the baby and took her into her house as her own. Her only comment was

Oor Robin should hae had twa wives.

Who are we to say more?

It is salutary to consider that while many men have gone on record to deplore the poet's attitude to women and conduct with them, not one woman has. Except his own mother. She refused to talk of him at all, even though she survived him for 24 years, preferring to live with her other son, Gilbert – on an annuity provided by Robert.

14 July 1792. Juillet Quatorze! The Bastille had fallen and the whole of Europe rang with Liberte! Égalite! Fraternite! Thomas Paine had published *The Rights of Man* and every heart had leapt to the surge of the new Republicanism – except in Dumfries. And it was to that douce, smug little town that Burns had moved in the previous year having been promoted to the Dumfries Port

Division with a rise in salary of a pound a week. Ellisland had been sold at public auction – '*a ruinous affair all round*' – and he and his growing family were now installed in what was called the Glasgow or 'Stinking' Vennel in a low part of the town.

Despite his making no secret of his French sympathies, Burns was greeted as a great man by the worthy citizens. He was allowed to use his Burgess Ticket to secure free education for his sons at the local academy, and as an Honorary Member of the Royal Company of Archers, he had access to every drawing-room in the county. He seemed set fair for a whole new respectability, but only as long as he played the game by their rules, and Burns was a poor games player. Not only did he lack the head for it – his heart was in the wrong place.

> *And the heart's ay the part ay*
> *That maks ye right or wrong.*

In the time of widespread political ferment, his heart went out to the people instead of to the 'people who mattered'. The poor are ever with us, so the Book says, and they were everywhere in Scotland, even in the streets of comfortable Dumfries where they rioted for bread. In Paris, they had been told to eat cake, but Burns gave them something more digestible. He gave them a song – an anthem for the underprivileged. He spoke for the poor man the world over and in words that rang like a trumpet:

> *Is there for honest poverty*
> *That hangs his head, an a' that,*
> *The coward slave, we pass him by –*
> *We daur be poor, for a' that!*
> *For a' that, an a' that,*
> *Our toils obscure, an a' that,*
> *The rank is but the guinea stamp,*
> *The man's the gowd for a' that.*

He also gave them that other staple of the under-privileged – hope.

> *Then let us pray that come it may,*
> *(As come it will, for a' that),*

That sense and worth
oer a' the earth,
Shall bear the gree, for a' that.
For a' that, an a' that,
It's comin' yet for a' that,
That man to man, the world oer,
Shall brothers be – for a' that.

The brotherhood of man is an ideal all men hope for, a few strive
for and even fewer die for, but for Burns it was something he saw
little evidence of, in his own life and times, and only a small expe-
rience of it in the brotherhood of Freemasonry. The Masonic
Order was important to Robert Burns. Without it, as has already
been said, we would have no Kilmarnock or Edinburgh Editions.
It was the Masons who put Burns in print and we must ever be
grateful to them for that, but where were these same Masonic
friends during the later Dumfries days when he needed them
most? Like his contemporary, Mozart, the Masonic tie frayed
somewhat at the end.

Admittedly, times were difficult. Britain was now at war with
France and Burns was in a dilemma. He could not, and would
not, retract his Republican views, but his upholding of Paine's
Rights of Man while worthy, was also foolhardy. He had to
remember that for all his fame he was a man *'wi' wife an weans'*.
He had to tread carefully. But he found it as hard to mince his
steps as mince his words. And when he tried saying nothing at all,
he found himself at the heart of a riot in the stalls of the Dumfries
Theatre. He had refused to take his hat off for the National
Anthem, or so it looked, for others were singing *Ca Ira*, the
French rebel song at the same time, so Burns took no chance of
seeming to stand for that, and therefore couldn't win either way.
He was hauled over the coals for his conduct by his superiors and
reminded that he was now a mere *'placeman'* – a minor civil ser-
vant – whose job was not to think but to do as he was told. Burns
knew that he faced emigration again, although it was now called
transportation. He shut his mouth and, for appearance's sake,

moved to a better house on the Mill Brae and, as a gesture, he joined the local volunteer militia.

His last years were a dwindling down of all outside activities and a fevered concentration on the final songs for the George Thompson collections. 1796 ushered him into his fatal illness. Whether it was rheumatoid or arthritic, or 'flying gout' or 'acute myocarditis in conjunction with auricular fibrillation', it matters little now. All he knew was that his body, still bursting with songs, simply began to waste away. And what a waste. He was 37, at an age when he should have been in the prime of his life and the peak of his powers. Instead, he had been carried to the Brow Well to immerse himself in sea-water on doctor's orders – thus effectively killing him. Elizabeth Riddell, an English beauty and an admirer, visited him there at sunset.

> *The sun still shines,* he said. *'It will not, alas, shine long for me.'*

She said later that she had never seen him so calm, almost serene.

'Who would wish for many years?' he had written to his old friend, Mrs Dunlop of Dunlop. He knew his life work had been done, most of it before he was 25, when he wrote of things like male friendship, love of women, babies, daisies – and mice:

> *But Mousie, thou art no thy lane*
> *In proving foresight may be vain;*
> *The best-laid schemes of mice and men*
> *Gang aft agley*
> *And leave us nought but grief and pain*
> *For promis'd joy!*

As Elizabeth Riddell left on that summer evening in 1796, he said to her, quietly,

> *Well, Madam – have you any commands for the next world?*

She went home in her carriage. He came home in a cart, and took to his bed for the last time. So did Jean, who was expecting their next child at any moment. Virtually ignored in that provincial, self-important little town, he rose above their apathy, for he knew, like all great artists, he would face posterity on his own terms. There was no looking for lightning now, only the waning light of a lingering star.

His strength of personality had carried him far, but his weakness of nature had brought him down. This was not a weakness of character, but of the flesh. The demands of a stringent boyhood had to be met, and a lifetime of slow wastage through malnutrition, headaches, fevers, colic, night sweats and poor teeth had to be paid for by an early death. He had only survived this by finding respite in writing, by the joy in rhyme, by discovering that he had the knack of arranging words on paper with unerring felicity. In the end, however, an attractive if flawed body cracked, his winning way became warped by continued frustration, his spirit broke before the petty demands of inferior superiors. Yet he died singing, at the very height of his artistic powers, and as a direct result of a well-meaning doctor's guesses.

On the evening of 20 July 1796, a crowd began to gather outside the poet's house on the Mill Brae as the news began to spread that Poet Burns was at his end. Not a word was said as they continued to assemble during the night. They somehow knew that their hero would not see the morning. The ordinary folk gathered to pay their silent respect to his final hours. There were no gentry here, no lords, no 'superiors', just poor, plain folk who had their own troubles, but felt for one whom they regarded as one of themselves, and for his wife and for his family.

He never fought a battle, or signed a treaty, or discovered a great cure, or was supreme in sport, or did any of those things that make a public man a hero to his country, yet Burns was, in his day, every bit as much a hero to ordinary Scots as Wallace, for he touched a chord in them that has resonated down the ages ever since. No other writer in any country has attained this supra-literary level in the consciousness of a nation. He has gone beyond mere posthumous fame, and through the haze of dubious legend, until he has become a continuing dynamic in the contemporary Scottish psyche and an undisputed national icon.

Burns did see the morning of 21 July, even if it were only through delirium. Just after five oclock, he rose up then fell back, and Jessie Lewars slowly pulled down the white blind at the upstairs window. A voice from the street called out piteously,

Wha'll be oor poet noo?

A great wail went up from those standing on the cobblestones, and the noise of it evolved into a murmured singing which kept low and tender as if afraid it might wake him up. But then it grew louder as other people nearby took it up and soon the whole street and perhaps all of Dumfries, all of Scotland, began to sing it too in his honour.

Should auld acquaintance be forgot
And never brought to mind?
Should auld acquaintance be forgot
And days o lang syne?

Auld Lang Syne – his song, or rather, an ancient fragment which he had worked into a new song that was to become the world's anthem. 'Auld Lang Syne', meaning literally 'a long time since' but meaning much more to anyone who sings it as a song of family, of friendship, of memory and of time past. We all have our own families, friends, memories. And when we sing this song that's what we sing about. In the end it is all we have left – memories. Perhaps all we are is only what we can remember...

For auld lang syne, my jo,
For auld lang syne,
We'll take a cup of kindness yet
For all lang syne.

What we remember best of Burns was that he was the singer of the parish who became the bard of the nation and a poet for the world. He told of ordinary things in an extraordinary way that still gives us new insights into who and what we are. He spoke with the voice he was born with for he knew that voice to be true and he knew it would be heard. He spoke of life as he found it, but he spoke with the wisdom of the ages. For every line he wrote had something in it of the human condition. For he wrote with truth, and humour, understanding and love. And it is this that keeps him in our memory to this day and makes him immortal.

In his great year of 1786, Burns was lifted up by the Kilmarnock Edition and swept out of Ayrshire in a great wave of acclaim. The Edinburgh Edition continued the tide of applause so that he might have drowned in acclamation, but he always knew his essential self, and never allowed it to be completely carried away. It says much for his durability as a poet and song-maker that he has survived the outgoing and incoming tides of literary fashion, the reaction and counter-reaction to celebrity, and even more the hagiography of those who would make him a saint or the vilification of those who only see him as the devil. He was neither a saint nor a devil, but a bit of both at different times. He was a man. A Scotsman. Yes, there was a man, and he was in all he wrote, and the best of it – and him – may be found in the pages of this book. I wish you joy of both.

PART ONE

The Poet

TWENTY SELECTED POEMS

The Death and Dying Words of Poor Mailie

A Poet's Welcome to his Love-begotten Daughter

Holy Willie's Prayer

Death and Doctor Hornbook

Halloween

To a Mouse

The Jolly Beggars

The Cotter's Saturday Night

The Auld Farmer's New-Year's Morning Salutation to his
Auld Mare Maggie

The Twa Dogs

Address to the Unco Guid

To a Mountain Daisy

To a Louse

The Holy Fair

Address to a Haggis

On Meeting with Lord Daer

On Seeing a Wounded Hare

To Collector Mitchell

On the Late Captain Grose's Peregrinations through Scotland

Tam o Shanter

The Poet and the Poems

In his Preface to the Kilmarnock Edition of his Works, Burns claims not to have *'the advantages of learned art'* and yet, two lines later, mentions Theocrites and Virgil. He knew exactly what he was doing. This was the first lie Burns was to tell about himself in order to sell his book. He perpetrated another in his Dedication to the Gentlemen of the Caledonian Hunt for the Edinburgh Edition of his Poems in 1787, when he wrote

> *The Poetic genius of my country found me, as the*
> *prophetic bard Elija did Elisha, at the plough and threw*
> *her inspiring mantle over me.*

This is so much rubbish, and he knew it, but he was not above any ruse or ploy or sycophantic phrase if it meant he could see his work in print. Certainly, this is a ruthlessness that belongs to any artist in any medium faced with the challenge of selling himself and his work to a paying public. The working artist has to resort to any means he has in order to sell. Burns was not alone in this. Down through history, the correspondence of most artists is inevitably about money first and art second. Of course, the proper noises must be made, and Burns was merely giving his subscribers what they wanted. He knew that the gentry wanted to see him as a 'Heaven-inspired rustic', so he obliged, and thus saddled himself with an image he was never to shake off completely.

Had they been able to see his work as a whole, they would have seen that he had painstakingly trained himself in letters, first by omniverous reading and then by trying his hand right away in his Commonplace Books. It is noticeable that his output was meagre to begin with but as he went on, year by year, his youthful self-consciousness was replaced by a manly self-confidence in his pen which was never to leave him. Once he found his true voice he never lost it and he was still 'singing' on his death-bed.

Not everything he wrote was memorable, but a lot of it was. In 25 years of writing, he had made himself the complete professional in words, both in speech and on the page, and there is very little he couldn't have done in literature had he really applied himself, but the novel was too new at his time, and the theatre just a little out of his experience, although he did toy with the idea of writing a play. As a wordsmith, he worked on a small scale (apart from *The Jolly Beggars* and the epic *Tam o Shanter*) but he worked to big effect. He used what was immediately at hand, the world of nature all around him and the interplay of ordinary character and the human personality as he saw it. As he said to John Murdoch, '*I seem to be one sent into the world to watch and observe.*'

His playing the agricultural oaf to various aristocratic ninnies was only another of his several 'performances'. There could have been nothing further from the truth that '*Coila tuned his wild, artless notes*'. Nobody worked harder on revisions than he did. No hand could have been less untutored, nor was his verse anything other than considered, well-worked and painstakingly revised as holographs and transcripts will show.

The Reverend John Logan was the Scots-born editor of the *English Review* in London when the Edinburgh Edition came out in February 1787, and he wrote,

> *Robert Burns, though represented as an ordinary plough-*
> *man, was a farmer, or what they call a tenant in Scotland,*
> *and he rented land which he cultivated with his own*
> *hand. He is better acquainted with the English poets than*
> *most English authors under review.*

This was proved when at a breakfast party Burns met with another clergyman, a pompous individual who was violently attacking Gray's *Elegy* without knowing a single line of it. Yet he opposed Burns's defence of the poem with continual quibbling and fastidious criticism, until Burns turned on him. '*Sir,*' he said, '*I now perceive a man may be an excellent judge of poetry, and after all, be a damned blockhead.*'

All the various aspects of Burns, poet, politician, patriot and poser, all show as if on a prism, each face showing a different side

of a complex and gifted man troubled at times by his own genius
with words. In the end, it is the results of this genius that matter.
Everything else is immaterial. Only the work stands. It is signifi-
cant that one magnificent mausoleum erected in his memory is
inscribed 'To the Works of Burns'. Or was it that they were still
uncertain about the man? Be that as it may, the work is done, and
remains immortal. How he came to begin on this work is better
shown by what he said in a letter to Dr Moore in 1787.

> *I never thought to turn poet till I got heartily in love, then*
> *rhyme and song were, in a manner, the spontaneous*
> *language of my heart.*

The Death and Dying Words of Poor Mailie

The author's only pet yowe
An unco mournfu' tale

1783

This was the sixth entry in the Kilmarnock Edition, but could be said to be the first poem of any consequence in his output. He was in the ninth year of his writing and had done nothing in the verse line of any size apart from *The Ronalds of the Bennels* and a couple of *Prayers in the Prospect of Death* but neither of these could be said to carry any real poetic weight. Gilbert Burns, who was with his brother during the incident which inspired the poem, explained in its genesis in a letter to Dr Currie (Burns's official biographer) in April 1798, almost 15 years after the event. Gilbert wrote,

> *Robert had, partly by way of frolic, bought a ewe and two lambs from a neighbour, and she was tethered in a field adjoining the house at Lochlie. He and I were going out with our teams, and our two younger brothers to drive for us, at mid-day, when Hugh Wilson, a curious-looking, awkward boy, clad in plaiding, came to us with much anxiety on his face, with the information that the ewe had entangled herself in the tether, and was lying in the ditch. Robert was tickled with Hugh's appearance and posture on the occasion. Poor Mailie was set to rights and when he returned from the plough in the evening he repeated to me her **Death and Dying Words** pretty much in the way they now stand.*

As Mailie, an her lambs thegither,
Was ae day nibbling on the tether,
Upon her cloot she coost a hitch,
An owre she warsl'd in the ditch;

There, groaning, dying, she did lie,
When Hughoc he cam doytin by.

Wi glowrin een, and lifted han's
Poor Hughoc like a statue stan's;
He saw her days were near-hand ended,
But, wae's my heart! he could na mend it!
He gaped wide, but naething spak,
At langth poor Mailie silence brak.

'O thou, whase lamentable face
Appears to mourn my woefu' case!
My dying words attentive hear,
An bear them to my Master dear.'

'Tell him, if e'er again he keep
As muckle gear as buy a sheep –
O, bid him never tie them mair,
Wi wicked strings o hemp or hair!
But ca' them out to park or hill,
An let them wander at their will:
So may his flock increase, an grow
To scores o lambs, an packs o woo'!'

'Tell him, he was a Master kin',
An aye was guid to me an mine;
An now my dying charge I gie him,
My helpless lambs, I trust them wi him.'

'O, bid him save their harmless lives,
Frae dogs, an tods, an butcher's knives!
But gie them guid cow-milk their fill,
Till they be fit to fend themsel;
An tent them duly, e'en an morn,
Wi taets o hay an ripps o corn.'

'An may they never learn the gaets,
Of ither vile, wanrestfu pets –
To slink thro slaps, an reave an steal

At stacks o pease, or stocks o kail!
So may they, like their great forbears,
For mony a year come thro the shears:
So wives will gie them bits o bread,
An bairns greet for them when they're dead.'

'My poor toop-lamb, my son an heir,
O, bid him breed him up wi care!
An if he live to be a beast,
To pit some havins in his breast!'

'An warn him – what I winna name –
To stay content wi yowes at hame;
An no to rin an wear his cloots,
Like ither menseless, graceless brutes.'

'An neist, my yowie, silly thing,
Gude keep thee frae a tether string!
O, may thou ne'er forgather up,
Wi ony blastit, moorland toop;
But aye keep mind to moop an mell,
Wi sheep o credit like thysel!'

'And now, my bairns, wi my last breath,
I lea'e my blessin wi you baith:
An when you think upo your mither,
Mind to be kind to ane anither.'

'Now, honest Hughoc, dinna fail,
To tell my master a' my tale;
An bid him burn this cursed tether,
An for thy pains thou'se get my blather.'

This said, poor Mailie turn'd her head,
And clos'd her een amang the dead!

Even as early as this, Robert was quick to turn the folly of teth-
ering a silly sheep into an allegory of family concern and obligation.
The device of an animal's supposed death had been used before
by Hamilton of Gilbertfield in the *Last Dying Words of Bonny*

Heck and by Alan Ramsay in *Lucky Spence's Last Advice*, but Burns was never one to spurn a good model. Similarly, when it came time to include the poem in the Kilmarnock Edition in 1786, he added *Poor Mailie's Elegy* in a six-line stave. This form came to be known as a 'Standart Habbie' after Habbie Simson, whom Sir Robert Sempill of Beltrees had depicted in *The Piper of Kilbarchen*. This was a form of mock-elegy which Burns was to make especially his own in other poems, like the *Elegy for Tam Samson* in the same year. It is pleasant to think of Burns's musing on Mailie at the plough and then coming home to write it up in his Commonplace Book and then reciting it to the family – *that same night.*

A Poet's Welcome to his Love-begotten Daughter

The first instance that entitled him to the venerable appellation of father

1785

This is something of a singular piece in literature in that the poet unashamedly hymns his pride in siring a 'bastard wean', but the phrase in the original title says it all – 'love-begotten', and for Burns, that was the salient point. Yet the irony was that while he loved the child and cared for her upbringing in his mother's house, he did not love her mother, Elizabeth Paton, the serving-girl at Lochlea. 'Love-begotten' according to Burns meant at the time of the procreative act and not to any intention of a life-partnership in marriage. Miss Paton was less put out than Burns's mother, and leaving her baby happily in the family's care, she left the district and later married a farm servant called Andrew by whom she had four children.

The birth of Elizabeth Paton Burns on 22 May 1785 was the first recorded confirmation of Burns's sexual activity. He was 26 years of age and just coming into his male maturity. It is my opinion that he lost his virginity to Bess Paton, and, significantly, only after his father died. Although in this poem he might seem to revel in fornication, and risk the strictures of the Kirk and the 'Unco Guid', his kindness was shown by his reference to the child as the *'wee image of my bonie Betty'* and all his essential morality is in the admission at the end of the poem –

> *I'll ne'er rue my trouble wi thee,*
> *The cost nor shame o't,*
> *But be a loving father to thee,*
> *And brag the name o't.*

One can be sure he was relieved that his own father had died early in the year before.

Thou's welcome, wean; mishanter fa' me,
If thoughts o thee, or yet thy mamie,
Shall ever daunton me or awe me,
My bonie lady,
Or if I blush when thou shalt ca' me
Tyta or daddie.

What tho now they ca' me fornicator,
An tease my name in kintry clatter,
The mair they talk, I'm kent the better,
E'en let them clash;
An auld wife's tongue's a feckless matter
To gie ane fash.

Welcome! my bonie, sweet, wee dochter,
Tho ye come here a wee unsought for,
And tho your comin I hae fought for,
Baith kirk and queir;
Yet, by my faith, ye're no unwrought for,
That I shall swear!

Sweet fruit o mony a merry dint,
My funny toil is now a' tint,
Sin thou came to the warl' asklent,
Which fools may scoff at;
In my last plack thy part's be in't
The better ha'f ot.

Tho I should be the waur bestead,
Thou's be as braw and bienly clad,
And thy young years as nicely bred
Wi education,
As ony brat o wedlock's bed,
In a' thy station.

Wee image o my bonie Betty,
As fatherly I kiss and daut thee,
As dear, and near my heart I set thee

Wi as gude will
As a' the priests had seen me get thee
That's out o hell.

Gude grant that thou may aye inherit
Thy mither's person, grace, an merit,
An thy poor, worthless daddy's spirit,
Without his failins,
Twill please me mair to see thee heir it,
Than stockit mailens.

And if thou be what I wad hae thee,
And tak the counsel I shall gie thee,
I'll never rue my trouble wi thee,
The cost nor shame o't,
But be a loving father to thee,
And brag the name o't.

The girl whom Burns called his 'Dear-bought Bess' was brought up in Lochlea and Mossgiel until her father's death when she went to live with her natural mother. At 21, she received £200 from the Burns Fund after the poet's death. She married John Bishop of Polkemmet in 1817, but sadly, it is thought that she died giving birth to her own child. Needless to say, this poem was not included in the first edition and was not published until 1799 when it was issued by Stewart in Glasgow.

Holy Willie's Prayer

1785

This was, without doubt, Burns's first masterwork in verse, although, it too, was denied a place in the famous first edition, and also had to wait for the Stewart and Meikle Glasgow edition of 1799. The manuscript shows the heading motto from Pope – '*And send the Godly in a fret to pray.*' The poem was provoked by Gavin Hamilton's being hauled before the Kirk Session after being accused by the chief elder, William Fisher, of playing cards on a Sunday. In this unerring satire which never lost its aim, the poet was certain of his target from the start. In Burns's own words, the subject was –

> *a rather oldish bachelor in the parish of Mauchline and much, and justly, famed for his polemical chattering which ends in tippling orthodoxy, and for that spiritualized bawdry which refines to liquorish devotion. In a sessional process with a gentleman in Mauchline – a Mr Gavin Hamilton [to whom the poem is dedicated] – Holy Willie, and his priest, Father Auld, came off but second best, owing partly to the oratorical powers of Mr Robert Aiken, Mr Hamilton's counsel; but chiefly to Mr Hamilton's being one of the most irreproachable and truly respectable characters in the country. On losing his process, the muse overheard him at his devotions as follows –*

O Thou, who in the heavens does dwell,
Wha, as it pleases best Thysel,
Sends ane to Heaven an ten to Hell,
A' for Thy glory,
And no for ony gude or ill
They've done afore Thee!

I bless and praise Thy matchless might,
When thousands Thou hast left in night,
That I am here afore Thy sight,

For gifts an grace
A burning and a shining light
To a' this place.

What was I, or my generation,
That I should get sic exaltation,
I wha deserve most just damnation
For broken laws,
Sax thousand years ere my creation,
Thro Adam's cause?

When frae my mither's womb I fell,
Thou might hae plunged me in hell,
To gnash my gums, to weep and wail,
In burnin lakes,
Where damned devils roar and yell,
Chain'd to their stakes.

Yet I am here a chosen sample,
To show thy grace is great and ample;
I'm here a pillar o Thy temple,
Strong as a rock,
A guide, a buckler, and example,
To a' Thy flock.

But yet, O Lord! confess I must,
At times I'm fash'd wi fleshly lust:
An sometimes, too, in wardly trust,
Vile self gets in:
But Thou remembers we are dust,
Defil'd wi sin.

O Lord! yestreen, Thou kens, wi Meg –
Thy pardon I sincerely beg,
O! may't ne'er be a livin plague
To my dishonour,
An I'll ne'er lift a lawless leg
Again upon her.

Besides, I farther maun avow,
Wi Leezie's lass, three times I trow –
But Lord, that Friday I was fou,
When I cam near her;
Or else, Thou kens, Thy servant true
Wad never steer her.

Maybe Thou lets this fleshly thorn
Buffet Thy servant e'en and morn,
Lest he owre proud and high shou'd turn,
That he's sae gifted:
If sae, Thy han' maun e'en be borne,
Until Thou lift it.

Lord, bless Thy chosen in this place,
For here Thou hast a chosen race:
But God confound their stubborn face,
An blast their name,
Wha bring Thy elders to disgrace
An public shame.

Lord, mind Gaw'n Hamilton's deserts;
He drinks, an swears, an plays at cartes,
Yet has sae mony takin arts,
Wi great and sma,
Frae God's ain priest the people's hearts
He steals awa.

An when we chasten'd him therefor,
Thou kens how he bred sic a splore,
An set the warld in a roar
O laughing at us;
Curse Thou his basket and his store,
Kail an potatoes.

Lord, hear my earnest cry and pray'r,
Against that Presbyt'ry o Ayr;
Thy strong right hand, Lord, make it bare
Upo their heads;

Lord visit them, an dinna spare,
For their misdeeds.

O Lord, my God! that glib-tongu'd Aiken,
My vera heart and flesh are quakin,
To think how we stood sweatin, shakin,
An pish'd wi dread,
While he, wi hingin lip an snakin,
Held up his head.

Lord, in Thy day o vengeance try him,
Lord, visit them wha did employ him,
And pass not in Thy mercy by 'em,
Nor hear their pray'r,
But for Thy people's sake, destroy 'em,
An dinna spare.

But, Lord, remember me an mine
Wi mercies temp'ral an divine,
That I for grace an gear may shine,
Excell'd by nane,
And a' the glory shall be thine,
Amen, Amen!

This work did much to loosen the grip that the Presbyterian Kirk of Scotland, through its local Sessions and its elders, had on the peasantry at that time. The church was at the centre of all their communal activities and the arbiter of their civil interests as much as of their spritual welfare. The minister was almost as powerful as the laird and the elders were his henchmen. Willie Fisher was especially prominent for his pursuit of all offences 'against the flesh'. He was later dismissed for drunkenness and found one morning in February 1809 frozen to death in a ditch.

Death and Doctor Hornbook
1785

'Doctor Hornbook' was really John Wilson, the parish school-master at Tarbolton, between 1781 and 1789. A horn book was a children's aid to learning consisting of a paper showing the alphabet, numbers, the rules of spelling and the Lord's Prayer, which was mounted on a wooden board and protected by a thin plate of transparent horn. The name would then be familiar as a school artifact. Wilson eked out his meagre teacher's salary by opening a small grocer's shop, to which he added the sale of a few medicines and also 'advice in common disorders, gratis'. In the spring of 1785, Burns overheard Wilson airing his 'medical skill-s' at a Masonic meeting, and walking home, the poet was 'visited by one of those floating ideas of apparitions' at the very place he descibed in the poem. He linked this 'spectre' to schoolmaster Wilson's medical pretensions, and before he had reached Mossgiel he had the satire fixed and most of the poem in his head. He turned it in the favoured Habbie Simson six-stop metre and developed it in the form of a conversation piece which was almost a little playlet in itself.

> Some books are lies frae end to end,
> And some great lies were never penn'd:
> Ev'n ministers they hae been kenn'd,
> In holy rapture,
> A rousing whid at times to vend,
> And nail't wi Scripture.

> But this that I am gaun to tell,
> Which lately on a night befell,
> Is just as true's the Deil's in hell
> Or Dublin city:
> That e'er he nearer comes oursel
> 'S a muckle pity.

The clachan yill had made me canty,
I was na fou, but just had plenty;
I stacher'd whiles, but yet too tent aye
To free the ditches;
An hillocks, stanes, an bushes, kenn'd eye
Frae ghaists an witches.

The rising moon began to glowre
The distant Cumnock hills out-owre:
To count her horns, wi a' my pow'r,
I set mysel;
But whether she had three or four,
I cou'd na tell.

I was come round about the hill,
An todlin down on Willie's mill,
Setting my staff wi a' my skill,
To keep me sicker;
Tho leeward whiles, against my will,
I took a bicker.

I there wi *Something* did forgather,
That pat me in an eerie swither;
An awfu scythe, out-owre ae shouther,
Clear-dangling, hang;
A three-tae'd leister on the ither
Lay, large an lang.

Its stature seem'd lang Scotch ells twa,
The queerest shape that e'er I saw,
For fient a wame it had ava;
And then its shanks,
They were as thin, as sharp an sma
As cheeks o branks.

'Guid-een,' quo I; 'Friend! hae ye been mawin,
When ither folk are busy sawin!'
It seem'd to make a kind o stan'

But naething spak;
At length, says I, 'Friend! whare ye gaun?
Will ye go back?'

It spak right howe, – 'My name is Death,
But be na fley'd.' – Quoth I, 'Guid faith,
Ye're maybe come to stap my breath;
But tent me, billie;
I red ye weel, tak care o skaith
See, there's a gully!'

'Gudeman,' quo he, 'put up your whittle,
I'm no designed to try its mettle;
But if I did, I wad be kittle
To be mislear'd;
I wad na mind it, no that spittle
Out-owre my beard.'

'Weel, weel!' says I, 'a bargain be't;
Come, gie's your hand, an sae we're gree't;
We'll ease our shanks an tak a seat –
Come, gie's your news;
This while ye hae been mony a gate,
At mony a house.'

'Ay, ay!' quo he, an shook his head,
'It's e'en a lang, lang time indeed
Sin' I began to nick the thread,
An choke the breath:
Folk maun do something for their bread,
An sae maun Death.'

'Sax thousand years are near-hand fled
Sin I was to the butching bred,
An mony a scheme in vain's been laid,
To stap or scar me;
Till ane Hornbook's taen up the trade,
And faith! he'll waur me.'

'Ye ken Hornbook i' the clachan,
Deil mak his king's-hood in spleuchan!
He's grown sae weel acquaint wi' Buchan
And ither chaps,
The weans haud out their fingers laughin,
An pouk my hips.'

'See, here's a scythe, an there's dart,
They hae pierc'd mony a gallant heart;
But Doctor Hornbook, wi his art
An cursed skill,
Has made them baith no worth a f-t,
Damn'd haet they'll kill!'

Twas but yestreen, nae farther gane,
I threw a noble throw at ane;
Wi less, I'm sure, I've hundreds slain;
But deil-ma-care,
It just play'd dirl on the bane,
But did nae mair.

'Hornbook was by, wi ready art,
An had sae fortify'd the part,
That when I looked to my dart,
It was sae blunt,
Fient haet ot wad hae pierc'd the heart
Of a kail-runt.'

'I drew my scythe in sic a fury,
I near-hand cowpit wi my hurry,
But yet the bauld Apothecary
Withstood the shock;
I might as weel hae tried a quarry
O hard whin rock.'

'Ev'n them he canna get attended,
Altho their face he ne'er had kend it,
Just-in a kail-blade, an sent it,

As soon's he smells 't,
Baith their disease, and what will mend it,
At once he tells 't.

'And then, a' doctor's saws an whittles,
Of a' dimensions, shapes, an mettles,
A' kind o boxes, mugs, an bottles,
He's sure to hae;
Their Latin names as fast he rattles
as A B C.'

'Calces o fossils, earths, and trees;
True sal-marinum o the seas;
The farina of beans an pease,
He has't in plenty;
Aqua-fontis, what you please,
He can content ye.'

'Forbye some new, uncommon weapons,
Urinus spiritus of capons;
Or mite-horn shavings, filings, scrapings,
Distill'd per se;
Sal-alkali o midge-tail clippings,
And mony mae.'

'Waes me for Johnie Ged's Hole now,'
Quoth I, 'if that thae news be true!
His braw calf-ward whare gowans grew,
Sae white and bonie,
Nae doubt they'll rive it wi the plew;
They'll ruin Johnie!'

The creature grain'd an eldritch laugh,
And says 'Ye needna yoke the pleugh,
Kirkyards will soon be till'd eneugh,
Tak ye nae fear:
They'll be trench'd wi mony a sheugh,
In twa-three year.'

'Whare I kill'd ane, a fair strae-death,
By loss o blood or want of breath
This night I'm free to tak my aith,
        That Hornbook's skill
Has clad a score i' their last claith,
        By drap an pill.'

'An honest wabster to his trade,
Whase wife's twa nieves were scarce weel-bred
Gat tippence-worth to mend her head,
        When it was sair;
The wife slade cannie to her bed,
        But ne'er spak mair.'

'A country laird had taen the batts,
Or some curmurring in his guts,
His only son for Hornbook sets,
        An pays him well:
The lad, for twa guid gimmer-pets,
        Was laird himsel.'

'A bonie lass-ye kend her name –
Some ill-brewn drink had hov'd her wame;
She trusts hersel, to hide the shame,
        In Hornbook's care;
Horn sent her aff to her lang hame,
        To hide it there.'

'That's just a swatch o Hornbook's way;
Thus goes he on from day to day,
Thus does he poison, kill, an slay,
        Ans weel paid for't;
Yet stops me o my lawfu prey,
        Wi' his damn'd dirt!

'But, hark! I'll tell you of a plot,
Tho dinna ye be speakin o't;
I'll nail the self-conceited sot,

As dead's a herrin;
Neist time we meet, I'll wad a groat,
He gets his fairin!'

But just as he began to tell,
The auld kirk-hammer strak the bell
Some wee short hour ayont the twal',
Which rais'd us baith:
I took the way that pleas'd mysel,
And sae did Death.

The poem was one of the first additions to the Edinburgh Edition
of the Works in 1787. The publication caused considerable
embarrassment to Wilson when it came out but it caused him to
close his shop and discontinue his sale of quack medicine. Once
again, Burns had caused a change for the better by virtue of his
verse. Wilson soon afterwards accepted promotion to a school in
Glasgow where he became Session Clerk to the Gorbals parish in
that city. He died there in 1839.

Halloween

Yes! let the rich deride, the proud disdain,
The simple pleasure of the lowly train;
To me more dear, congenial to my heart,
One native charm, than all the gloss of art.

1785

This poem featured in the first edition and with a forward quatrain by Oliver Goldsmith which hails '*simple pleasure of the lowly train*' as being preferable to '*the gloss of art*'. This would have been very much in Burns's ostensible way of thinking although he made every attempt to put a gloss on everything he did. In this instance, he looked back to his own childhood and the tales told him by his mother and her kinswoman and help about the house, Betty Davidson, who had a fund of tales about '*devils, ghosts, witches, warlocks, spunkies, elf-candles, deadlights, wraiths and apparitions*'. He matched these with his own reading of Celtic pagan festivals like Samhuinn which merged with the Christian ritual of All Saints on the first day of November to create the playful feast of Hallowe'en – or 'Holy Evening', that is, the night before All Souls Day on November 2 – when the souls of those in Purgatory have a night on earth in disguise to frighten sinners and encourage the faithful to hold out for Heaven. The ancients placated the wandering spirits with gifts and this survives today in the guisers who come to the door for Halloween 'treats'. The Feast Burns described was already ancient in his day but there were many then who still believed in fairies. Many today still do.

Upon that night, when fairies light
On Cassilis Downans dance,
Or owre the lays, in splendid blaze,
On sprightly coursers prance;
Or for Colean the rout is taen,
Beneath the moon's pale beams;

There, up the Cove, to stray an rove,
Amang the rocks and streams
To sport that night;

Amang the bonie winding banks,
Where Doon rins, wimplin, clear;
Where Bruce ance rul'd the martial ranks,
An shook his Carrick spear;
Some merry, friendly, countra-folks
Together did convene,
To burn their nits, an pou their stocks,
An haud their Halloween
Fu' blythe that night.

The lasses feat, an cleanly neat,
Mair braw than when they're fine;
Their faces blythe, fu' sweetly kythe,
Hearts leal, an warm, an kin':
The lads sae trig, wi wooer-babs
Weel-knotted on their garten;
Some unco blate, an some wi gabs
Gar lasses' hearts gang startin
Whiles fast at night.

Then, first an foremost, thro the kail,
Their stocks maun a' be sought ance;

They steek their een, and grape an wale
For muckle anes, an straught anes.
Poor hav'rel Will fell aff the drift,
An wandered thro the bow-kail,
An pou't for want o better shift
A runt was like a sow-tail
Sae bow't that night.

Then, straught or crooked, yird or nane,
They roar an cry a' throu'ther;
The vera wee-things, toddlin, rin,
Wi stocks out owre their shouther:

An gif the custock's sweet or sour,
Wi joctelegs they taste them;
Syne coziely, aboon the door,
Wi cannie care, they've plac'd them
To lye that night.

The lassies staw frae 'mang them a',
To pou their stalks o corn;
But Rab slips out, an jinks about,
Behint the muckle thorn:
He grippit Nelly hard and fast:
Loud skirl'd a' the lasses;
But her tap-pickle maist was lost,
Whan kiutlin in the fause-house
Wi him that night.

The auld guid-wife's weel-hoordit nits
Are round an round dividend,
An mony lads' an lasses' fates
Are there that night decided:
Some kindle couthie side by side,
And burn thegither trimly;
Some start awa wi saucy pride,
An jump out owre the chimlie
Fu' high that night.

Jean slips in twa, wi tentie e'e;
Wha twas, she wadna tell;
But this is Jock, an this is me,
She says in to hersel:
He bleez'd owre her, an she owre him,
As they wad never mair part:
Till fuff! he started up the lum,
An Jean had e'en a sair heart
To see't that night.

Poor Willie, wi his bow-kail runt,
Was brunt wi primsie Mallie;

An Mary, nae doubt, took the drunt,
To be compar'd to Willie:
Mall's nit lap out, wi pridefu fling,
An her ain fit, it brunt it;
While Willie lap, and swore by jing,
Twas just the way he wanted
To be that night.

Nell had the fause-house in her min',
She pits hersel an Rob in;
In loving bleeze they sweetly join,
Till white in ase they're sobbin:
Nell's heart was dancin at the view;
She whisper'd Rob to leuk for't:
Rob, stownlins, prie'd her bonie mou',
Fu' cozie in the neuk for't,
Unseen that night.

But Merran sat behint their backs,
Her thoughts on Andrew Bell:
She lea'es them gashin at their cracks,
An slips out-by hersel;
She thro the yard the nearest taks,
An for the kiln she goes then,
An darklins grapit for the bauks,
An in the blue-clue throws then,
Right fear't that night.

An ay she win't, an ay she swat –
I wat she made nae jaukin;
Till something held within the pat,
Good Lord! but she was quaukin!
But whether twas the deil himsel,
Or whether twas a bauk-en',
Or whether it was Andrew Bell,
She did na wait on talkin
To spier that night

Wee Jenny to her graunie says,
'Will ye go wi me, graunie?
I'll eat the apple at the glass,
I gat frae uncle Johnie':
She fuff't her pipe wi sic a lunt,
In wrath she was sae vap'rin,
She notic't na an aizle brunt
Her braw, new, worset apron
Out thro that night.

'Ye little skelpie-limmer's face!
I daur you try sic sportin,
As seek the foul thief ony place,
For him to spae your fortune:
Nae doubt but ye may get a sight!
Great cause ye hae to fear it;
For mony a ane has gotten a fright,
An liv'd an died deleerit,
On sic a night.'

'Ae hairst afore the Sherra-moor,
I mind't as weel's yestreen –
I was a gilpey then,
I'm sure I was na past fyfteen:
The simmer had been cauld an wat,
An stuff was unco green;
An eye a rantin kirn we gat,
An just on Halloween
It fell that night.'

'Our stibble-rig was Rab M'Graen,
A clever, sturdy fallow;
His sin gat Eppie Sim wi wean,
That lived in Achmacalla:
He gat hemp-seed, I mind it weel,
An he made unco light o't;
But mony a day was by himsel,

He was sae sairly frighted
That vera night.'

Then up gat fechtin Jamie Fleck,
An he swoor by his conscience,
That he could saw hemp-seed a peck;
For it was a' but nonsense:
The auld guidman raught down the pock,
An out a handfu' gied him;
Syne bad him slip frae 'mang the folk,
Sometime when nae ane see'd him,
An try't that night.

He marches thro amang the stacks,
Tho he was something sturtin;
The graip he for a harrow taks,
An haurls at his curpin:
An ev'ry now an then, he says,
'Hemp-seed I saw thee,
An her that is to be my lass
Come after me, an draw thee
As fast this night.'

He wistl'd up Lord Lennox' March
To keep his courage cherry;
Altho his hair began to arch,
He was sae fley'd an eerie:
Till presently he hears a squeak,
An then a grane an gruntle;
He by his shouther gae a keek,
An tumbled wi a wintle
Out-owre that night.

He roar'd a horrid murder-shout,
In dreadfu' desperation!
An young an auld come rinnin out,
An hear the sad narration:
He swoor twas hilchin Jean M'Craw,

Or crouchie Merran Humphie –
Till stop! she trotted thro them a';
And wha was it but grumphie
Asteer that night!

Meg fain wad to the barn gaen,
To winn three wechts o naething;
But for to meet the deil her lane,
She pat but little faith in:

She gies the herd a pickle nits,
An twa red cheekit apples,
To watch, while for the barn she sets,
In hopes to see Tam Kipples
That vera night.
She turns the key wi cannie thraw,
An owre the threshold ventures;
But first on Sawnie gies a ca',
Syne baudly in she enters:
A ratton rattl'd up the wa',
An she cry'd Lord preserve her!
An ran thro midden-hole an a',
An pray'd wi zeal and fervour,
Fu' fast that night.

They hoy't out Will, wi sair advice;
They hecht him some fine braw ane;
It chanc'd the stack he faddom't thrice
Was timmer-propt for thrawin:
He taks a swirlie auld moss-oak
For some black, grousome carlin;
An loot a winze, an drew a stroke,
Till skin in blypes cam haurlin
Aff's nieves that night.

A wanton widow Leezie was,
As cantie as a kittlen;
But och! that night, amang the shaws,

She gat a fearfu' settlin!
She thro the whins, an by the cairn,
An owre the hill gaed scrievin;
Whare three lairds' lan's met at a burn,
To dip her left sark-sleeve in,
Was bent that night.

Whiles owre a linn the burnie plays,
As thro the glen it wimpl't;
Whiles round a rocky scar it strays,
Whiles in a wiel it dimpl't;
Whiles glitter'd to the nightly rays,
Wi bickerin, dancin dazzle;
Whiles cookit undeneath the braes,
Below the spreading hazel
Unseen that night.

Amang the brachens, on the brae,
Between her an the moon,
The deil, or else an outler quey,
Gat up an gae a croon:
Poor Leezie's heart maist lap the hool;
Near lav'rock-height she jumpit,
But mist a fit, an in the pool
Out-owre the lugs she plumpit,
Wi a plunge that night.

In order, on the clean hearth-stane,
The luggies three are ranged;
An ev'ry time great care is taen
To see them duly changed:
Auld uncle John, wha wedlock's joys
Sin Mar's-year did desire,
Because he gat the toom dish thrice,
He heav'd them on the fire
In wrath that night.

Wi merry sangs, an friendly cracks,

I wat they did na weary;
And unco tales, an funnie jokes –
Their sports were cheap an cheery:
Till butter'd sowens, wi fragrant lunt,

Set a' their gabs a-steerin;
Syne, wi a social glass o strunt,
They parted aff careerin
Fu' blythe that night.

Burns added his own notes to the poem:

...The passion of prying into futurity makes a striking part of the history of human nature in its rude state, in all ages and nations; and it may be some entertainment to a philosophic mind, if any such should honour the author with a perusal, to see the remains of it among the more unenlightened in our own...[Halloween] is thought to be a night when witches, devils and other mischief-making beings are all abroad on their baneful, midnight errands; particularly those aerial people, the fairies...

He may have known of Montgomerie's Flyting which had the couplet,

In the hinder end of haruest on Alhallow euen
When our good neighbours doe ryd, gif I read right...

And also Halloween by John Mayne which appeared in Ruddiman's *Weekly Magazine* in November 1980.

To a Mouse

On turning her up in her nest with the plough

NOVEMBER 1785

This little gem of a poem requires little introduction. It speaks so perfectly for itself in its heading and in its eight exact verses.

Wee, sleekit, cow'rin, tim'rous beastie,
O, what a panic's in thy breastie!
Thou need na start awa sae hasty,
Wi bickering brattle!
I wad be laith to rin an chase thee,
Wi murd'ring pattle!

I'm truly sorry man's dominion,
Has broken nature's social union,
An justifies that ill opinion,
Which makes thee startle
At me, thy poor, earth-born companion,
An fellow-mortal!

I doubt na, whiles, but thou may thieve;
What then? poor beastie, thou maun live!
A daimen icker in a thrave
'S a sma request;
I'll get a blessin wi the lave,
An never miss't!

Thy wee bit housie, too, in ruin!
It's silly wa's the win's are strewin!
An naething, now, to big a new ane,
O foggage green!
An bleak December's winds ensuin,
Baith snell an keen!

Thou saw the fields laid bare an waste,
An weary winter comin fast,
An cozie here, beneath the blast,
Thou thought to dwell –
Till crash! the cruel coulter past
Out thro thy cell.

That wee bit heap o leaves an stibble,
Has cost thee mony a weary nibble!
Now thou's turn'd out, for a' thy trouble,
But house or hald,
To thole the winter's sleety dribble,
An cranreuch cauld!

But, Mousie, thou art no thy lane,
In proving foresight may be vain;
The best-laid schemes o mice an men
Gang aft agley,
An lea'e us nought but grief an pain,
For promis'd joy!

Still thou art blest, compar'd wi me
The present only toucheth thee:
But, Och! I backward cast my e'e.
On prospects drear!
An forward, tho I canna see,
I guess an fear!

This work may be of extra interest in that it is the source of the phrase '*the best-laid schemes*' and also '*Of Mice and Men*' which became the title of a famous novel by American author, John Steinbeck, in 1937.

The Jolly Beggars

or

Love and Liberty – A Cantata

1785

This sprawling, lively, unkempt work ought to have been a play. Indeed, it has been staged in recent times by various groups as a theatrical piece as it lends itself so easily to characterisation and group presentation. It is the first indication of what he might have done in the dramatic line for all the play ingredients are there, but he chose to call it a cantata and interspersed songs rather than linking dialogue. The influence of John Gay's *The Beggars' Opera* of 1728 are obvious, but Burns has succeeded in catching a particularly Scottish atmosphere in a tavern environment which must have been so like Poosie Nansie's, the tavern run by Agnes Gibson in the Cowgate, Mauchline. The whole opus here is an irresistible picture of low life caught in the act, as it were. It is as full of life as the tinkers, soldiers, whores and vagabonds of the cast must have been to Burns's watching eye in 1785, as he sat with his friends, Jock Richmond and Jamie Smith, watching, wide-eyed,

> *those who sorn and thieve, and pilfer and extort alms from*
> *the weak and timid, to the disgrace of the police, the terror*
> *of the inhabitants, and discredit of humanity.*

Burns was fascinated by the scene, and only a few days later, he recited to Richmond excerpts from the work in progress. In doing so, he reproduced, for the first time in Scots verse, the tradition of the Gaberlunzie Man and The Jolly Beggar which date from the time of James V (1512–1542). This was part monachal and part goliardic, but since Burns was neither monk nor wandering scholar, he did it in his own way.

RECITATIVO

When lyart leaves bestrow the yird,
Or wavering like the bauckie-bird,

Bedim cauld Boreas' blast;
When hailstanes drive wi bitter skyte,
And infant frosts begin to bite,
In hoary cranreuch drest;
Ae night at e'en a merry core
O randie, gangrel bodies,
In Poosie-Nansie's held the splore,
To drink their orra duddies;
Wi quaffing an laughing,
They ranted an they sang,
Wi jumping an thumping,
The vera girdle rang,

First, neist the fire, in auld red rags,
Ane sat, weel brac'd wi mealy bags,
And knapsack a' in order;
His doxy lay within his arm;
Wi usquebae an blankets warm
She blinkit on her sodger;
An aye he gies the tozie drab
The tither skelpin kiss,
While she held up her greedy gab,
Just like an aumous dish;
Ilk smack still, did crack still,
Just like a cadger's whip;
Then staggering an swaggering
He roar'd this ditty up –

AIR
Tune: 'Soldier's Joy.'

I am a son of Mars who have been in many wars,
And show my cuts and scars wherever I come;
This here was for a wench, and that other in a trench,
When welcoming the French at the sound of the drum.

Lal de daudle, &c.

My prenticeship I past where my leader breath'd his last,

When the bloody die was cast on the heights of Abram: and
I served out my trade when the gallant game was play'd,
And the Morro low was laid at the sound of the drum.

I lastly was with Curtis among the floating batt'ries,
And there I left for witness an arm and a limb;
Yet let my country need me, with Elliot to head me,
I'd clatter on my stumps at the sound of a drum.

And now tho I must beg, with a wooden arm and leg,
And many a tatter'd rag hanging over my bum,
I'm as happy with my wallet, my bottle, and my callet,
As when I used in scarlet to follow a drum.

What tho with hoary locks, I must stand the winter shocks,
Beneath the woods and rocks oftentimes for a home,
When the other bag I sell, and the other bottle tell,
I could meet a troop of hell, at the sound of a drum.

RECITATIVO

He ended; and the kebars sheuk,
Aboon the chorus roar;
While frighted rattons backward leuk,
An seek the benmost bore:
A fairy fiddler frae the neuk,
He skirl'd out, encore!
But up arose the martial chuck,
An laid the loud uproar.

AIR
Tune: 'Sodger Laddie.'

I once was a maid, tho I cannot tell when,
And still my delight is in proper young men;
Some one of a troop of dragoons was my daddie,
No wonder I'm fond of a sodger laddie,
Sing, lal de lal, &c.

The first of my loves was a swaggering blade,

To rattle the thundering drum was his trade;
His leg was so tight, and his cheek was so ruddy,
Transported I was with my sodger laddie.

But the godly old chaplain left him in the lurch;
The sword I forsook for the sake of the church:
He ventur'd the soul, and I risked the body,
Twas then I proved false to my sodger laddie.

Full soon I grew sick of my sanctified sot,
The regiment at large for a husband I got;
From the gilded spontoon to the fife I was ready,
I asked no more but a sodger laddie.

But the peace it reduc'd me to beg in despair,
Till I met old boy in a Cunningham fair,
His rags regimental, they flutter'd so gaudy,
My heart it rejoic'd at a sodger laddie.

And now I have liv'd – I know not how long,
And still I can join in a cup and a song;
But whilst with both hands I can hold the glass steady,
Here's to thee, my hero, my sodger laddie.

RECITATIVO

Poor Merry-Andrew, in the neuk,
Sat guzzling wi a tinkler-hizzie;
They mind't na wha the chorus teuk,
Between themselves they were sae busy:
At length, wi drink an courting dizzy,
He stoiter'd up an made a face;
Then turn'd an laid a smack on Grizzie,
Syne tun'd his pipes wi grave grimace.

AIR
Tune: 'Auld Sir Symon.'

Sir Wisdom's a fool when he's fou;
Sir Knave is a fool in a session;

He's there but a prentice I trow,
But I am a fool by profession.

My grannie she bought me a beuk,
An I held awa to the school;
I fear I my talent misteuk,
But what will ye hae of a fool?

For drink I would venture my neck;
A hizzie's the half of my craft;
But what could ye other expect
Of ane that's avowedly daft?

I ance was tied up like a stirk,
For civilly swearing and quaffin;
I ance was abus'd i' the kirk,
For towsing a lass i' my daffin.

Poor Andrew that tumbles for sport,
Let naebody name wi a jeer;
There's even, I'm tauld, i' the Court
A tumbler ca'd the Premier.

Observ'd ye yon reverend lad
Mak faces to tickle the mob;
He rails at our mountebank squad,
It's rivalship just i' the job!

And now my conclusion I'll tell,
For faith! I'm confoundedly dry;
The chiel that's a fool for himsel,
Guid Lord! he's far dafter than I.

RECITATIVO

Then niest outspak a raucle carlin,
Wha kent fu' weel to cleek the sterlin;
For mony a pursie she had hooked,
An had in mony a well been douked;
Her love had been a Highland laddie,
But weary fa' the waefu' woodie!

Wi sighs an sobs she thus began
To wail her braw John Highlandman.

AIR
Tune: 'O, an ye were dead, Guidman.'

A Highland lad my love was born,
The Lalland laws he held in scorn;
But he still was faithfu' to his clan,
My gallant, braw John Highlandman.

Chorus
Sing hey my braw John Highlandman!
Sing ho my braw John Highlandman!
There's not a lad in a' the lan'
Was match for my John Highlandman.

With his philibeg an tartan plaid,
An guid claymore down by his side,
The ladies' hearts he did trepan,
My gallant, braw John Highlandman.

Sing hey, &c.

We ranged a' from Tweed to Spey,
An liv'd like lords an ladies gay;
For a Lalland face he feared none,
My gallant, braw John Highlandman.

Sing hey, &c.

They banish'd him beyond the sea.
But ere the bud was on the tree,
Adown my cheeks the pearls ran,
Embracing my John Highlandman.

Sing hey, &c.

But, och! they catch'd him at the last,
And bound him in a dungeon fast:
My curse upon them every one,

They've hang'd my braw John Highlandman!

Sing hey, &c.

And now a widow, I must mourn
The pleasures that will ne'er return:
The comfort but a hearty can,
When I think on John Highlandman.

Sing hey, &c.

RECITATIVO

A pigmy scraper on his fiddle,
Wha us'd at trystes an fairs to driddle.
Her strappin limb and gausy middle
(He reach'd nae higher)
Had hol'd his heartie like a riddle,
An blawn't on fire.

Wi hand on hainch, and upward e'e,
He croon'd his gamut, one, two, three,
Then in an *arioso* key,
The wee Apoll
Set off wi *allegretto* glee
His giga solo.

AIR
Tune: 'Whistle owre the lave o't.'

Let me ryke up to dight that tear,
An go wi me an be my dear;
An then your every care an fear
May whistle owre the lave o't.

Chorus
I am a fiddler to my trade,
An a' the tunes that e'er I played,
The sweetest still to wife or maid,
Was whistle owre the lave o't.

At kirns an weddins we'se be there,

An O sae nicely's we will fare!
We'll bowse about till Daddie Care
Sing whistle owre the lave o't.

I am, &c.

Sae merrily's the banes we'll pyke,
An sun oursel's about the dyke;
An at our leisure, when ye like,
We'll whistle owre the lave o't.

I am, &c.

But bless me wi your heav'n o charms,
An while I kittle hair on thairms,
Hunger, cauld, an a' sic harms,
May whistle owre the lave o't.

I am, &c.

RECITATIVO

Her charms had struck a sturdy caird,
As weel as poor gut-scraper;
He taks the fiddler by the beard,
An draws a roosty rapier –
He swoor, by a' was swearing worth,
To speet him like a pliver,
Unless he would from that time forth
Relinquish her for ever.

Wi ghastly e'e poor tweedle-dee
Upon his hunkers bended,
An pray'd for grace wi ruefu' face,
An so the quarrel ended.
But tho his little heart did grieve
When round the tinkler prest her,
He feign'd to snirtle in his sleeve,
When thus the caird address'd her:

AIR
Tune: 'Clout the Cauldron.'

My bonie lass, I work in brass,
A tinkler is my station:
I've travell'd round all Christian ground
In this my occupation;
I've taen the gold, an been enrolled
In many a noble squadron;
But vain they search'd when off I march'd
To go an clout the cauldron.
I've taen the gold, &c.

Despise that shrimp, that wither'd imp,
With a' his noise an cap'rin;
An take a share with those that bear
The budget and the apron!
And by that stowp! my faith an houp,
And by that dear Kilbaigie,
If e'er ye want, or meet wi scant,
May I ne'er weet my craigie.
And by that stowp, &c.

RECITATIVO

The caird prevail'd – th' unblushing fair
In his embraces sunk;
Partly wi love oercome sae sair,
An partly she was drunk:
Sir Violino, with an air
That show'd a man o spunk,
Wish'd unison between the pair,
An made the bottle clunk
To their health that night.

But hurchin Cupid shot a shaft,
That play'd a dame a shavie –
The fiddler rak'd her, fore and aft,

Behint the chicken cavie.
Her lord, a wight of Homer's craft,
Tho limpin wi the spavie,
He hirpl'd up, an lap like daft,
An shor'd them Dainty Davie.
O boot that night.

He was a care-defying blade
As ever Bacchus listed!
Tho Fortune sair upon him laid,
His heart, she ever miss'd it.
He had no wish but – to be glad,
Nor want but – when he thirsted;
He hated nought but – to be sad,
An thus the muse suggested
His sang that night.

AIR
Tune: 'For a' that, an a' that.'

I am a Bard of no regard,
Wi gentle folks an a' that;
But Homer-like, the glowrin byke,
Frae town to town I draw that.

Chorus
For a' that, an a' that,
An twice as muckle's a' that;
I've lost but ane, I've twa behin',
I've wife eneugh for a' that.

I never drank the Muses' stank,
Castalia's burn, an a' that;
But there it streams an richly reams,
My Helicon I ca' that.

For a' that, &c.

Great love I bear to a' the fair,
Their humble slave an a' that;

But lordly will, I hold it still
A mortal sin to thraw that.

For a' that, &c.

In raptures sweet, this hour we meet,
Wi mutual love an a' that;
But for how lang the flie may stang,
Let inclination law that.

For a' that, &c.

Their tricks an craft hae put me daft,
They've taen me in, an a' that;
But clear your decks, and here's – 'The Sex!'
I like the jads for a' that.

Chorus
For a' that, an a' that,
An twice as muckle's a' that;
My dearest bluid, to do them guid,
They're welcome till't for a' that.

RECITATIVO

So sung the bard – and Nansie's wa's
Shook with a thunder of applause,
Re-echod from each mouth!
They toom'd their pocks, they pawn'd their duds,
They scarcely left to coer their fuds,
To quench their lowin drouth:
Then owre again, the jovial thrang
The poet did request
To lowse his pack an wale a sang,
A ballad o the best;
He rising, rejoicing,
Between his twa Deborahs,
Looks round him, an found them
Impatient for the chorus.

AIR
Tune: 'Jolly Mortals, fill your Glasses.'

See the smoking bowl before us,
Mark our jovial ragged ring!
Round and round take up the chorus,
And in raptures let us sing –

Chorus
A fig for those by law protected!
Liberty's a glorious feast!
Courts for cowards were erected,
Churches built to please the priest.

What is title, what is treasure,
What is reputation's care?
If we lead a life of pleasure,
Tis no matter how or where!

A fig for, &c.

With the ready trick and fable,
Round we wander all the day;
And at night in barn or stable,
Hug our doxies on the hay.

A fig for, &c.

Does the train-attended carriage
Thro the country lighter rove?
Does the sober bed of marriage
Witness brighter scenes of love?

A fig for, &c.

Life is al a variorum,
We regard not how it goes;
Let them cant about decorum,
Who have character to lose.

A fig for, &c.

Here's to budgets, bags and wallets!
Here's to all the wandering train.
Here's our ragged brats and callets,
One and all cry out, Amen!

Chorus
A fig for those by law protected!
Liberty's a glorious feast!
Courts for cowards were erected,
Churches built to please the priest.

This work was omitted from the Kilmarnock and both Edinburgh Editions and had to wait for a Glasgow printing by Stewart and Meikle in 1799 along with *The Poet's Welcome* and *Holy Willie's Prayer*, which were considered at the the time similarly doubtful in taste, if not in execution. It still seems an unrealised play with songs.

The Cotter's Saturday Night

Let not Ambition mock their useful toil,
Their homely joys, and destiny obscure;
Nor Grandeur hear, with a disdainful smile,
The short and simple annals of the Poor.

1785/86

The headpiece this time, by Thomas Gray, refers the reader to the 'annals of the poor', and Burns, in this long poem which was composed over the winter of 1785/6, suggests a very different Saturday to the one enjoyed by the Jolly Beggars. Also typically, it was first recited by Burns to Gilbert in the course of a Sunday walk on February afternoon in 1786. It is a Sunday sort of poem. Using a sub-Spenserian stanza which owes more to Beattie and Shenstone, it plods respectably along its measured way much in the manner of the homeward-making cotter of the title. Modelled on the English style, it is the least Scottish of his works. It echoes Gray, and is perhaps the most artificial of the major poems, and for that reason, it is the nearest thing to dull that Burns has ever been. However, its sentimental picture of rural life and family, and the acute observation shown by the poet, lifts it far above the banal, and for a long time, especially in Victorian times, it was the most popular of all his works. After all,

From scenes like these, old Scotia's grandeur springs
That make her lov'd at home, rever'd abroad;
Princes and lords are but the breath of kings
'An honest man's the noblest work of God';

The Burnsian theme in the last line is also a quote, as he indicated. The whole thing seems derivative, but then as he said himself, he took *'the hint of the plan and the title from The Farmer's Ingle by Fergusson'*. If only he had emulated the latter's Scottishness. That being said, it is still worthy of its place in the Burns canon because it offers a portrait, however simplistic, of the kind of family life he would like to have known himself in Ayrshire, and, in the figure

of the cotter, he created a genuine tribute to his beloved father,
even if it is slightly idealised. But then when is love any less than
ideal?

My lov'd, my honour'd, much respected friend!
No mercenary bard his homage pays;
With honest pride, I scorn each selfish end,
My dearest meed, a friend's esteem and praise:
To you I sing, in simple Scottish lays,
The lowly train in life's sequester'd scene,
The native feelings strong, the guileless ways,
What Aiken in a cottage would have been;
Ah! tho his worth unknown, far happier there I ween!

November chill blaws loud wi angry sugh;
The short'ning winter-day is near a close;
The miry beasts retreating frae the pleugh;
The black'ning trains o craws to their repose:
The toil-worn Cotter frae his labour goes, –
This night his weekly moil is at an end,
Collects his spades, his mattocks, and his hoes,
Hoping the morn in ease and rest to spend,
And weary, oer the moor, his course does hameward bend.

At length his lonely cot appears in view,
Beneath the shelter of an aged tree;
Th' expectant wee-things, toddlin, stacher through
To meet their dead, wi flichterin noise and glee.
His wee bit ingle, blinkin bonilie,
His clean hearth-stane, his thrifty wifie's smile,
The lisping infant, prattling on his knee,
Does a' his weary kiaugh and care beguile,
And makes him quite forget his labour and his toil.

Belyve, the elder bairns come drapping in,
At service out, amang the farmers roun;
Some ca' the pleugh, some herd, some tentie rin
A cannie errand to a neibor town:

Their eldest hope, their Jenny, woman-grown,
In youthfu' bloom-love sparkling in her e'e-
Comes hame, perhaps to shew a braw new gown,
Or deposite her sair-won penny-fee,
To help her parents dear, if they in hardship be.

With joy unfeign'd, brothers and sisters meet,
And each for other's weelfare kindly speirs:
The social hours, swift-wing'd, unnotic'd fleet:
Each tells the uncos that he sees or hears.
The parents, partial, eye their hopeful years;
Anticipation forward points the view;
The mother, wi her needle and her shears,
Gars auld claes look amaist as weel's the new;
The father mixes a' wi admonition due.

Their master's and their mistress' command,
The younkers a' are warned to obey;
And mind their labours wi an eydent hand,
And ne'er, tho out o sight, to jauk or play;
'And O! be sure to fear the Lord alway,
And mind your duty, duly, morn and night;
Lest in temptation's path ye gang astray,
Implore His counsel and assisting might:
They never sought in vain that sought the Lord aright.'

But hark! a rap comes gently to the door;
Jenny, wha kens the meaning o the same,
Tells how a neibor lad came oer the moor,
To do some errands, and convoy her hame.
The wily mother sees the conscious flame
Sparkle in Jenny's e'e, and flush her cheek;
With heart-struck anxious care, enquires his name,
While Jenny hafflins is afraid to speak;
Weel-pleased the mother hears, it's nae wild, worthless rake.

Wi kindly welcome, Jenny brings him ben;
A strappin youth, he takes the mother's eye;

Blythe Jenny sees the visit's no ill taen;
The father cracks of horses, pleughs, and kye.
The youngster's artless heart oerflows wi joy,
But blate an laithfu', scarce can weel behave;
The mother, wi a woman's wiles, can spy
What makes the youth sae bashfu' and sae grave,
Weel-pleas'd to think her bairn's respected like the lave.

O happy love! where love like this is found:
O heart-felt raptures! bliss beyond compare!
I've paced much this weary, mortal round,
And sage experience bids me this declare, –
'If Heaven a draught of heavenly pleasure spare –
One cordial in this melancholy vale,
Tis when a youthful, loving, modest pair
In other's arms, breathe out the tender tale,
Beneath the milk-white thorn that scents the evening gale.'

Is there, in human form, that bears a heart,
A wretch! a villain! lost to love and truth!
That can, with studied, sly, ensnaring art,
Betray sweet Jenny's unsuspecting youth?
Curse on his perjur'd arts! dissembling smooth!
Are honour, virtue, conscience, all exil'd?
Is there no pity, no relenting ruth,
Points to the parents fondling oer their child?
Then paints the ruin'd maid, and their distraction wild?

But now the supper crowns their simple board,
The halesome parritch, chief of Scotia's food;
The sowp their only hawkie does afford,
That, 'yont the hallan snugly chows her cood:
The dame brings forth, in complimental mood,
To grace the lad, her weel-hain'd kebbuck, fell;
And aft he's prest, and aft he ca's it guid:
The frugal wifie, garrulous, will tell
How twas a towmond auld, sin lint was i' the bell

The cheerfu' supper done, wi serious face,
They, round the ingle, form a circle wide;
The sire turns oer, with patriarchal grace,
The big ha' bible, ance his father's pride:
His bonnet rev'rently is laid aside,
His lyart haffets wearing thin and bare;
Those strains that once did sweet in Zion glide,
He wales a portion with judicious care;
And 'Let us worship God!' he says with solemn air.

They chant their artless notes in simple guise,
They tune their hearts, by far the noblest aim;
Perhaps Dundee's wild-warbling measures rise;
Or plaintive Martyrs, worthy of the name;
Or noble Elgin beets the heaven-ward flame;
The sweetest far of Scotia's holy lays:
Compar'd with these, Italian trills are tame;
The tickl'd ears no heart-felt raptures raise;
Nae unison hae they with our Creator's praise.

The priest-like father reads the sacred page,
How Abram was the friend of God on high;
Or Moses bade eternal warfare wage
With Amalek's ungracious progeny;
Or how the royal bard did groaning lie
Beneath the stroke of Heaven's avenging ire;
Or Job's pathetic plaint, and wailing cry;
Or rapt Isaiah's wild, seraphic fire;
Or other holy seers that tune the sacred lyre.

Perhaps the Christian volume is the theme,
How guiltless blood for guilty man was shed;
How He, who bore in Heaven the second name,
Had not on earth whereon to lay His head:
How His first followers and servants sped;
The precepts sage they wrote to many a land:
How he, who lone in Patmos banished,
Saw in the sun a mighty angel stand,

And heard great Bab'lon's doom pronounc'd by Heaven's
  command.

Then, kneeling down to Heaven's Eternal King,
The saint, the father, and the husband prays:
Hope 'springs exulting on triumphant wing',
That thus they all shall meet in future days,
There, ever bask in uncreated rays,
No more to sigh, or shed the bitter tear,
Together hymning their Creator's praise,
In such society, yet still more dear;
While circling Time moves round in an eternal sphere.

Compar'd with this, how poor Religion's pride,
In all the pomp of method, and of art;
When men display to congregations wide

Devotion's ev'ry grace, except the heart!
The Power, incens'd, the pageant will desert,
The pompous strain, the sacerdotal stole;
But haply, in some cottage far apart,
May hear, well-pleas'd, the language of the soul;
And in His Book of Life the inmates poor enroll.

Then homeward all take off their sev'ral way;
The youngling cottagers retire to rest:
The parent-pair their secret homage pay,
And proffer up to Heaven the warm request,
That he who stills the raven's clam'rous nest,
And decks the lily fair in flow'ry pride,
Would, in the way His wisdom sees the best,
For them and for their little ones provide;
But chiefly, in their hearts with grace divine preside.

From scenes like these, old Scotia's grandeur springs,
That makes her lov'd at home, rever'd abroad;
Princes and lords are but the breath of kings,
'An honest man's the noblest work of God;'
And certes, in fair virtue's heavenly road,

The cottage leaves the palace far behind;
What is a lordling's pomp? a cumbrous load,
Disguising oft the wretch of human kind,
Studied in arts of hell, in wickedness refin'd!

O Scotia! my dear, my native soil!
For whom my warmest wish to Heaven is sent,
Long may thy hardy sons of rustic toil
Be blest with health, and peace, and sweet content!
And O! may Heaven their simple lives prevent
From luxury's contagion, weak and vile!
Then howe'er crowns and coronets be rent,
A virtuous populace may rise the while,
And stand a wall of fire around their much-lov'd isle.

O Thou! who pour'd the patriotic tide,
That stream'd thro Wallace's undaunted heart,
Who dar'd to nobly stem tyrannic pride,
Or nobly die, the second glorious part:
(The patriot's God peculiarly thou art,
His friend, inspirer, guardian, and reward!)
O never, never Scotia's realm desert;
But still the patriot, and the patriot-bard
In bright succession raise, her ornament and guard!

This poem is dedicated in the first verse to Robert Aiken, the
Mauchline solicitor and Burns's '*chief patron*'. Aiken was a skilled
orator and elocutionist. Burns later said that he was '*read into
fame*' by the lawyer, who encouraged subscriptions to the first
edition by reciting from the manuscript selected excerpts from the
works to intending patrons.

The Auld Farmer's New-Year Morning Salutation to his Auld Mare Maggie

*On giving her the accustomed ripp of corn to hansel
in the New Year*

1786

I must immediately state my interest here, in that I have always considered this one of my favourite Burns pieces. Featured in the Kilmarnock Edition, it allows a young man of 27 (the poet himself) to look ahead to old age, and at the same time look back from it to supposed scenes of his life reflected in the working relationship he had with his horse. It is a real *tour de force*, and a compliment not only to the writer's poetic skill but to the understanding it shows of the farmer's reliance on his beasts. They are partners in his rural enterprise and none is closer than the horse. The parallel between its aging and his getting older is touchingly drawn, and their almost 30 years together is signposted by all that they have survived together. A man could say no more about his wife on their 30th wedding anniversary, and hopefully with the same warm humour and observation that Burns employs here.

A Guid New-year I wish thee, Maggie!
Hae, there's a ripp to thy auld baggie:
Tho thou's howe-backit now, an knaggie,
I've seen the day
Thou could hae gaen like ony staggie,
Out-owre the lay.

Tho now thou's dowie, stiff, an crazy,
An thy auld hide as white's a daisie,
I've seen thee dappl't, sleek an glaizie,
A bonie gray:
He should been tight that daur't to raize thee,
Ance in a day

Thou ance was i' the foremost rank,
A filly buirdly, steeve, an swank;
An set weel down a shapely shank,
As e'er tread yird;
An could hae flown out-owre a stank,
Like ony bird.

It's now some nine-an-twenty year,
Sin thou was my guid-father's mear;
He gied me thee, o tocher clear,
An fifty mark;
Tho it was sma, twas weel-won gear,
An thou was stark.

When first I gaed to woo my Jenny,
Ye then was trotting wi your minnie:
Tho ye was trickie, slee, an funnie,
Ye ne'er was donsie;
But hamely, tawie, quiet, an cannie,
An unco sonsie.

That day, ye pranc'd wi muckle pride,
When ye bure hame my bonie bride:
An sweet an gracefu she did ride,
Wi maiden air!
Kyle-Stewart I could bragged wide
For sic a pair.

Tho now ye dow but hoyte and hobble,
An wintle like a saumont coble,
That day, ye was a jinker noble,
For heels an win'!
An ran them till they a' did wauble,
Far, far, behin'!

When thou an I were young an skeigh,
An stable-meals at fairs were dreigh,
How thou wad prance, and snore, an skreigh

An tak the road!
Town's-bodies ran, an stood abeigh,
An' ca't thee mad.

When thou was corn't, an I was mellow,
We took the road aye like a swallow:
At brooses thou had ne'er a fellow,
For pith an speed;
But ev'ry tail thou pay't them hollowm
Whare'er thou gaed.

The sma, droop-rumpl't, hunter cattle
Might aiblins waur't thee for a brattle;
But sax Scotch mile, thou try't their mettle,
An gart them whaizle:
Nae whip nor spur, but just a wattle
O saugh or hazel.

Thou was a noble fittie-lan',
As e'er in tug or tow was drawn!
Aft thee an I, in aught hours' gaun,
In guid March-weather,
Hae turn'd sax rood beside our han',
For days thegither.

Thou never braing't, an fetch't, an fliskit;
But thy auld tail thou wad hae whiskit,
An spread abreed thy weel-fill'd brisket,
Wi pith an power;
Till sprittie knowes wad rair't an riskit
An slypet owre.

When frosts lay lang, an snaws were deep,
An threaten'd labour back to keep,
I gied thy cog a wee bit heap
Aboon the timmer:
I ken'd my Maggie wad na sleep,
For that, or simmer.

In cart or car thou never reestit;
The steyest brae thou wad hae fac't it;
Thou never lap, an sten't, and breastit,
Then stood to blaw;
But just thy step a wee thing hastit,
Thou snoov't awa.

My pleugh is now thy bairn-time a',
Four gallant brutes as e'er did draw;
Forbye sax mae I've sell't awa,
That thou hast nurst:
They drew me thretteen pund an twa,
The vera warst.

Mony a sair daurk we twa hae wrought,
An wi the weary warl fought!
An mony an anxious day, I thought
We wad be beat!
Yet here to crazy age we're brought,
Wi something yet.

An think na, my auld trusty servan',
That now perhaps thou's less deservin,
An thy auld days may end in starvin;
For my last fow,
A heapit stimpart, I'll reserve ane
Laid by for you.

We've worn to crazy years thegither;
We'll toyte about wi ane anither;
Wi tentie care I'll flit thy tether
To some hain'd rig,
Whare ye may nobly rax your leather,
Wi sma fatigue.

Burns was to become an accomplished horseman, thank to his
Excise duties, but without being 'horsey'. He always had a fine
understanding of his various horses at different times of his life.

While he had to borrow a horse to ride to Edinburgh in 1786, he owned Jenny Geddes, bought for £4 in the Grassmarket, and on her he toured the Border Country. Pegasus was his mount in Dumfries. He had another Maggie, but she was to be tethered within the pages of Tam o Shanter.

The Twa Dogs

A tale

1786

On the night before his father died, Burns's favourite dog, Luath, died, killed by a person, or persons unknown. He thought he would do something in rhyme for the dog, and came up with a fanciful project entitled *Stanzas to the Memory of a Quadruped Friend*, 'but this plan was given up for the Tale as it now stands'. He wrote to John Richmond on 17 February 1786 telling him – '*I have likewise compleated my poem on the Dogs, but have not yet shown it to the world.*' This was the first poem in the Kilmarnock Edition. The octosyllabic couplet used is the one he was also to use in *Tam o Shanter* four years later. This form had a long pedigree in Scottish letters and had been used by Dunbar and other Makars, like Sir David Lindsay of the Mount, and later by Semple, Ramsay and Fergusson. Burns was very much at home in it and this is seen in the easy, conversational style he adopts for the dogs. Once again, it is a 'dialogue-piece' and the total action is their conversation. It ends by each going their separate ways as Hornbook and the Devil did in the previous poem. Meantime, we have enjoyed their contrasting points of view as each speaks for the two sides of Scottish society – those who have and those who have to work for it. It also highlights the two sides of Burns – Luath was who he was thought by many to be, and Caesar, who he might like to have been, but both canine characters speak in a kind of certain Scots tongue, which reveals the man he really was.

Twas in that place o Scotland's Isle
That bears the name of auld King Coil,
Upon a bonie day in June,
When wearin thro the afternoon,
Twa dogs, that were na thrang at hame,
Forgather'd ance upon a time.
The first I'll name, they ca'd him Caesar,

Was keepit for 'His Honor's' pleasure:
His hair, his size, his mouth, his lugs,
Shew'd he was nane o Scotland's dogs;
But whalpit some place far abroad,
Whare sailors gang to fish for cod.
His locked, letter'd, braw brass collar
Shew'd him the gentleman an scholar;
But though he was o high degree,
The fient a pride, nae pride had he;
But wad hae spent an hour caressin,
Ev'n wi a tinkler-gipsy's messin:
At kirk or market, mill or smiddie,
Nae tawted tyke, tho e'er sae duddie,
But he wad stan't, as glad to see him,
An stroan't on stanes an hillocks wi him.
The tither was a ploughman's collie –
A rhyming, ranting, raving billie,
Wha for his friend an comrade had him,
And in freak had Luath ca'd him,
After some dog in Highland Sang,
Was made lang syne, – Lord knows how lang.
He was a gash an faithfu' tyke,
As ever lap a sheugh or dyke.
His honest, sonsie, baws'nt face
Aye gat him friends in ilka place;
His breast was white, his touzie back
Weel clad wi coat o glossy black;
His gawsie tail, wi upward curl,
Hung owre his hurdie's wi a swirl.

Nae doubt but they were fain o ither,
And unco pack an thick thegither;
Wi social nose whiles snuff'd an snowkit;
Whiles mice an moudieworts they howkit;
Whiles scour'd awa in lang excursion,
An worry'd ither in diversion;

Until wi daffin' weary grown
Upon a knowe they set them down.
An there began a lang digression.
About the 'lords o the creation.'

Caesar

I've aften wonder'd, honest Luath,
What sort o life poor dogs like you have;
An' when the gentry's life I saw,
What way poor bodies liv'd ava.
Our laird gets in his racked rents,
His coals, his kane, an a' his stents:
He rises when he likes himsel;
His flunkies answer at the bell;
He ca's his coach; he ca's his horse;
He draws a bonie silken purse,
As lang's my tail, where, thro the steeks,
The yellow letter'd Geordie keeks.
Frae morn to e'en, it's nought but toiling
At baking, roasting, frying, boiling;
An tho the gentry first are stechin,
Yet ev'n the ha' folk fill their pechan
Wi sauce, ragouts, an sic like trashtrie,
That's little short o downright wastrie.
Our whipper-in, wee, blasted wonner,
Poor, worthless elf, it eats a dinner,
Better than ony tenant-man
His Honour has in a the lan':
An what poor cot-folk pit their painch in,
I own it's past my comprehension.

Luath

Trowth, Caesar, whiles they're fash't eneugh:
A cottar howkin in a sheugh,
Wi dirty stanes biggin a dyke,
Baring a quarry, an sic like;

Himsel, a wife, he thus sustains,
A smytrie o wee duddie weans,
An nought but his han-darg, to keep
Them right an tight in thack an rape.
An when they meet wi sair disasters,
Like loss o health or want o masters,
Ye maist wad think, a wee touch langer,
An they maun starve o cauld an hunger:
But how it comes, I never kent yet,
They're maistly wonderfu contented;
An buirdly chiels, an clever hizzies,
Are bred in sic a way as this is.

Caesar

But then to see how ye're negleckit,
How huff'd, an cuff'd, an disrespeckit!
Lord man, our gentry care as little
For delvers, ditchers, an sic cattle;
They gang as saucy by poor folk,
As I wad by a stinkin brock.
I've notic'd, on our laird's court-day, –
An mony a time my heart's been wae, –
Poor tenant bodies, scant o cash,
How they maun thole a factor's snash;
He'll stamp an threaten, curse an swear
He'll apprehend them, poind their gear;
While they maun stan', wi aspect humble,
An hear it a', an fear an tremble!
I see how folk live that hae riches;
But surely poor-folk maun be wretches!

Luath

They're no sae wretched's ane wad think.
Tho constantly on poortith's brink,
They're sae accustom'd wi the sight,
The view ot gives them little fright.

Then chance and fortune are sae guided,
They're aye in less or mair provided:
An tho fatigued wi close employment,
A blink o rest's a sweet enjoyment.
The dearest comfort o their lives,
Their grushie weans an faithfu wives;
The prattling things are just their pride,
That sweetens a' their fire-side.
An whiles twalpennie worth o nappy
Can mak the bodies unco happy:
They lay aside their private cares,
To mind the Kirk and State affairs;
They'll talk o patronage an priests,
Wi kindling fury i' their breasts,
Or tell what new taxation's comin,
An ferlie at the folk in Lon'on.
As bleak-fac'd Hallowmass returns,
They get the jovial, rantin kirns,
When rural life, of ev'ry station,
Unite in common recreation;
Love blinks, Wit slaps, an social Mirth
Forgets there's Care upo the earth.
That merry day the year begins,
They bar the door on frosty win's;
The nappy reeks wi mantling ream,
An sheds a heart-inspiring steam;
The luntin pipe, an sneeshin mill,
Are handed round wi right guid will;
The cantie auld folks crackin crouse,
The young anes rantin thro the house –
My heart has been sae fain to see them,
That I for joy hae barkit wi them.
Still it's owre true that ye hae said,
Sic game is now owre aften play'd;
There's mony a creditable stock
O decent, honest, fawsont folk,

Are riven out baith root an branch,
Some rascal's pridefu greed to quench,
Wha thinks to knit himsel the faster
In favour wi some gentle master,
Wha, aiblins, thrang a parliamentin,
For Britain's guid his saul indentin –

Caesar

Haith, lad, ye little ken about it:
For Britain's guid! guid faith! I doubt it.
Say rather, gaun as Premiers lead him:
An saying ay or nos they bid him:
At operas an plays parading,
Mortgaging, gambling, masquerading:
Or maybe, in a frolic daft,
To Hague or Calais takes a waft,
To mak a tour an' tak a whirl,
To learn *bon ton*, an see the worl.
There, at Vienna, or Versailles,
He rives his father's auld entails;
Or by Madrid he takes the rout,
To thrum guitars an fecht wi nowt;
Or down Italian vista startles,
Whore-hunting amang groves o myrtles:
Then bowses drumlie German-water,
To mak himsel look fair an fatter,
An clear the consequential sorrows,
Love-gifts of Carnival signoras.
For Britain's guid! for her destruction!
Wi dissipation, feud, an faction.

Luath

Hech, man! dear sirs! is that the gate
They waste sae mony a braw estate!
Are we sae foughten an harass'd
For gear to gang that gate at last?

O would they stay aback frae courts,
An please themsels wi country sports,
It wad for ev'ry ane be better,
The laird, the tenant, an the cotter!
For thae frank, rantin, ramblin billies,
Feint haet o them's ill-hearted fellows;
Except for breakin o their timmer,
Or speakin lightly o their limmer,
Or shootin of a hare or moor-cock,
The ne'er-a-bit they're ill to poor folk,
But will ye tell me, Master Caesar,
Sure great folk's life's a life o pleasure?
Nae cauld nor hunger e'er can steer them,
The very thought ot need na fear them.

Caesar

Lord, man, were ye but whiles whare I am,
The gentles, ye wad ne'er envy them!
It's true, they need na starve or sweat,
Thro winter's cauld, or simmer's heat:
They've nae sair wark to craze their banes,
An fill auld age wi grips an granes:
But human bodies are sic fools,
For a' their colleges an schools,
That when nae real ills perplex them,
They mak enow themsel's to vex them;
An aye the less they hae to sturt them,
In like proportion, less will hurt them.
A country fellow at the pleugh,
His acre's till'd, he's right eneugh;
A country girl at her wheel,
Her dizzen's dune, she's unco weel;
But gentlemen, an ladies warst,
Wi ev'n-down want o wark are curst.
They loiter, lounging, lank an lazy;
Tho deil-haet ails them, yet uneasy;

Their days insipid, dull, an tasteless;
Their nights unquiet, lang, an restless.
An ev'n their sports, their balls an races,
Their galloping through public places,
There's sic parade, sic pomp, an art,
The joy can scarcely reach the heart.
The men cast out in party-matches,
Then sowther a' in deep debauches.
Ae night they're mad wi drink an whoring,
Niest day their life is past enduring.
The ladies arm-in-arm in clusters,
As great an gracious a' as sisters;
But hear their absent thoughts o ither,
They're a' run-deils an jads thegither.
Whiles, owre the wee bit cup an platie,
They sip the scandal-potion pretty;
Or lee-lang nights, wi crabbit leuks
Pore owre the devil's pictur'd beuks;
Stake on a chance a farmer's stackyard,
An cheat like ony unhanged blackguard.
There's some exceptions, man an' woman;
But this is gentry's life in common.

By this, the sun was out of sight,
An darker gloamin brought the night;
The bum-clock humm'd wi lazy drone;
The kye stood rowtin i' the loan;
When up they gat an shook their lugs,
Rejoic'd they werena men but dogs;
An each took aff his several way,
Resolv'd to meet some ither day.

It was another Luath – but another dog – who was to jump
between Burns and Jean at a penny-fee wedding during Race Week
in 1785, causing Burns to remark, looking straight at Jean, '*I wish
I could find a lassie would love me as much as my dog did.*' Jean
was not immediately impressed, and was less so next day when

the same dog ran over her washing as she laid it out to dry on Mauchline Green, but she called out to Burns as he pulled the dog away, '*Have ye found your lassie yet?*' He then knew that he had, for within weeks they were lovers and man and wife within a few years. But it all started between them from the incidents with Luath, and Jean Armour loved Burns from then till his death at 37, and for 37 years afterwards till her own death in the very same house.

Address to the Unco Guid

Or the Rigidly Righteous

1786

This was an addition to the Edinburgh Edition and the germ of it lay in a comment made in his Commonplace Book in March 1784, when he noted

> *Every man, even the worst, have [sic] something good about them... I have yet found among (blackguards) some of the noblest Virtues, Magnanimity, Generosity, disinterested friendship, and even modesty, in the highest perfection.*

Burns believed that there was an innate good in every human being, and that every one was innocent until proved guilty. The most guilty, in his eyes, were those who committed harm by pretending to be good. These people were always roused to great indignation by the sexual act, and for triflings acts, which Burns termed 'daffin' but they considered as heinous sin. Quite deliberately, he chose a Biblical quotation, rendered in Scots, from Solomon, to underscore his poetical intention. Taking out his quiver of satirical arrows, he aimed them, one after another, into the soft underbelly of those canting Kirk-folk, whom he knew so well, first with Bess Paton at Tarbolton and then with Jean at Mauchline. His accusers sat in their pews like prim peacocks, but to him, they were sitting ducks. And, as in *Holy Willie's Prayer*, his aim was true – and deadly. He was an advocate for passion. He knew his case was water-tight, and the verdict of posterity has confirmed this.

O ye wha are sae guid yoursel,
Sae pious and sae holy,
Ye've nought to do but mark and tell
Your neibours' fauts and folly!
Whase life is like a weel-gaun mill,
Supplied wi store o water;
The heaped happer's ebbing still,
An still the clap plays clatter.

Hear me, ye venerable core,
As counsel for poor mortals
That frequent pass douce Wisdom's door
For glaikit Folly's portals:
I, for their thoughtless, careless sakes,
Would here propone defences –
Their donsie tricks, their black mistakes,
Their failings and mischances.

Ye see your state wi theirs compared,
And shudder at the niffer;
But cast a moment's fair regard,
What maks the mighty differ;
Discount what scant occasion gave,
That purity ye pride in;
And (what's aft mair than a' the lave),
Your better art o hidin.

Think, when your castigated pulse
Gies now and then a wallop!
What ragings must his veins convulse,
That still eternal gallop!
Wi wind and tide fair i' your tail,
Right on ye scud your sea-way;
But in the teeth o baith to sail,
It maks a unco lee-way.

See Social Life and Glee sit down,
All joyous and unthinking,
Till, quite transmugrified, they're grown
Debauchery and Drinking:
O would they stay to calculate
Th' eternal consequences;
Or your more dreaded hell to state,
Damnation of expenses!

Ye high, exalted, virtuous dames,
Tied up in godly laces,

Before ye gie poor Frailty names,
Suppose a change o cases;
A dear-lov'd lad, convenience snug,
A treach'rous inclination –
But let me whisper i' your lug,
Ye're aiblins nae temptation.

Then gently scan your brother man,
Still gentler sister woman;
Tho they may gang a kennin wrang,
To step aside is human:
One point must still be greatly dark, –
The moving Why they do it;
And just as lamely can ye mark,
How far perhaps they rue it.

Who made the heart, tis He alone
Decidedly can try us;
He knows each chord, its various tone,
Each spring, its various bias:
Then at the balance let's be mute,
We never can adjust it;
What's done we partly may compute,
But know not what's resisted.

The close management of the argument here suggests the fine courtroom lawyer Burns might have made. This would have released all his actor's intincts which were already evident in his oratory at Masonic meetings, which is recorded, and the reports of his impromtu replies at various gatherings in Edinbugh and on his tours in Scotland. He was a formidable debater, and only William Smellie, of the *Encyclopedia Brtitannica*, was reputed to be his equal. This very facility, however, was capable of making him as many enemies as friends. A good tongue, as he was to find, can work both ways.

To a Mountain Daisy

On turning one down with the plough

1786

From Mossgiel, Mauchline. 20 April 1786

*To John Kennedy, Clerk, Dumfries House, near Mauchline.
I have here likewise enclosed a small piece, the very latest
of my productions. I am a good deal pleased with some
sentiments myself, as they are just the native, querulous
feelings of a heart which, as the elegantly melting Gray
says, 'melancholy as marked for her own.'*

No introduction could be better for this almost-perfect little
poem, the very distillation of fine sentiment and tenderness,
which Burns produced when his own affairs were 'in the wind' to
use his own phrase and things looked very black for him on all
counts. He was being pressed by his family, sued by the Armours,
hounded by the Kirk Session and emigration to the Indies seemed
the only way out. Small wonder he was melancholy. Then, on a
spring day on the farm he accidently drives his ploughshare
through the stem of one of the smallest flowers there is, a gowan,
(the original title of the poem) and everything stops while this
hugely-compassionate man considers the terrible thing he has
done, he has broken a flower. It is a vast thought, that he should
feel so concerned about what so many would never notice, still
less ponder. This shows the soul of the man, and the resulting
poem, a twin to the other plough poem (*To a Mouse*), shows the
giant size of the heart in its concern for something so small and
so apparently insignificant. One is reminded of Young's lines,

> *Stars rush, and final ruin fiercely drives
> Her ploughshare oer creation.*

For Burns, the little gowan, or daisy, represents all of creation,
and it makes no matter the size or worth of anything that is life-
worthy, it is the fact that it has life at all. This is what makes the
humanitarian, and how he compresses it into nine verses is what

makes the poet. All the sympathy, understanding, compassion
and love for a fellow-creature is in these lines, and it is no exag-
geration to say that this is, in effect, however seemingly pes-
simistic, one of his finest love-poems, because it indicates a love
of all living things.

> Wee, modest crimson-tipp'd flow'r,
> Thou's met me in an evil hour;
> For I maun crush amang the stoure
> Thy slender stem:
> To spare thee now is past my pow'r,
> Thou bonie gem.
>
> Alas! it's no thy neibor sweet,
> The bonie lark, companion meet,
> Bending thee 'mang the dewy weet,
> Wi spreckl'd breast!
> When upward-springing, blythe, to greet
> The purpling east.
>
> Cauld blew the bitter-biting north
> Upon thy early, humble birth;
> Yet cheerfully thou glinted forth
> Amid the storm,
> Scarce rear'd above the parent-earth
> Thy tender form.
>
> The flaunting flow'rs our gardens yield,
> High shelt'ring woods and wa's maun shield;
> But thou, beneath the random bield
> O clod or stane,
> Adorns the histie stibble field,
> Unseen, alane.
>
> There, in thy scanty mantle clad,
> Thy snawie bosom sun-ward spread,
> Thou lifts thy unassuming head
> In humble guise;

But now the share uptears thy bed,
And low thou lies!

Such is the fate of artless maid,
Sweet flow'ret of the rural shade!
By love's simplicity betray'd,
And guileless trust;
Till she, like thee, all soil'd, is laid
Low i' the dust.

Such is the fate of simple bard,
On life's rough ocean luckless starr'd!
Unskilful he to note the card
Of prudent lore,
Till billows rage, and gales blow hard,
And whelm him oer!

Such fate to suffering worth is giv'n,
Who long with wants and woes has striv'n,
By human pride or cunning driv'n
To mis'ry's brink;
Till wrench'd of ev'ry stay but Heav'n,
He, ruin'd, sink!

Ev'n thou who mourn'st the Daisy's fate,
That fate is thine-no distant date;
Stern Ruin's plough-share drives elate,
Full on thy bloom,
Till crush'd beneath the furrow's weight,
Shall be thy doom!

To a Louse

On seeing one on a lady's bonnet at church

1786

The sub-title sets the picture and also reminds us of how much Burns was a church-goer in his young manhood, and not always to sit on the cutty-stool to take the minister's rebuke for three Sundays running, although it must be admitted that this rite was a generous part of his attendances. However, on this occasion, he was in his place and behind one of the Mauchline belles. It was typical that he should fix his gaze in the nape of the neck, always a highly erogenous area in the young female, specially when a wisp of stray hair plays on a slender neck. To a man of Burns's ready sensuality it would draw a response at once, and a rhyme, when he had time to think about it. In this case, though, seeing lice on such an unlikely head, provoked not only a poem but a telling satire on manners.

From a running commentary on events, it gradually ascends, verse by verse, to the rueful philosophy of the last six-line stanza which gives us the memorable '*to see ourselves as ithers see us*', a salutary thought which draws the reader up sharp from the comedy of the young lady's unwitting indignity to the realisation that we never know how we really look, or sound, to other people. Even if we did, it is no guarantee that we would avoid the 'blunder' or escape the 'foolish notion'. What is certain is that this straight-forward effusion caused people to think, and perhaps even glance behind them next time they were in church.

Ha! whaur ye gaun, ye crowlin ferlie?
Your impudence protects you sairly;
I canna say but ye strunt rarely,
Owre gauze and lace;
Tho, faith! I fear ye dine but sparely
On sic a place.

Ye ugly, creepin, blastit wonner,

Detested, shunn'd by saunt an sinner,
How daur ye set your fit upon her –
Sae fine a lady?
Gae somewhere else and seek your dinner
On some poor body.

Swith! in some beggar's haffet squattle;
There ye may creep, and sprawl, and sprattle,
Wi ither kindred, jumping cattle,
In shoals and nations;
Whaur horn nor bane ne'er daur unsettle
Your thick plantations.

Now haud you there, ye're out o sight,
Below the fatt'rels, snug and tight;
Na, faith ye yet! ye'll no be right,
Till ye've got on it –
The verra tapmost, tow'rin height
O Miss' bonnet.

My sooth! right bauld ye set your nose out,
As plump an grey as ony groset:
O for some rank, mercurial rozet,
Or fell, red smeddum,
I'd gie you sic a hearty dose ot,
Wad dress your droddum.

I wad na been surpris'd to spy
You on an auld wife's flainen toy;
Or aiblins some bit dubbie boy,
On's wyliecoat;
But Miss' fine Lunardi! fye!
How daur ye dot?

O Jeany, dinna toss your head,
An set your beauties a' abread!
Ye little ken what cursed speed
The blastie's makin:

Thae winks an' finger-ends, I dread,
Are notice takin.

O wad some Power the giftie gie us
To see oursels as ithers see us!
It wad frae mony a blunder free us,
An foolish notion:
What airs in dress an gait wad lea'e us,
An ev'n devotion!

The 'Lunardi' referred to is the balloon-shaped bonnet which was very fashionable at the time due to the exploits of Vincenzo Lunardi, an Italian aerial traveller, who, in 1775, made several balloon ascents from Glasgow and Edinburgh, and published details in his *Account of Five Aerial Voyages in Scotland* published in 1786, the same year as the above poem was published in the Kilmarnock Edition. The manuscript of *To a Louse* is now in the Bodleian Library in Oxford.

The Holy Fair

1786

This piece is headed by a quote from Hypocrisy-a-la-Mode, which ends,

And for a mantle large and broad,
He wrapt him in Religion.

This was Burns's favourite *motif* in dealing with religion in his satires, to concentrate on the hypocritical nature of religion itself in some of its practices, and especially in some of its practitioners. In this case, he is dealing with the ministers and their congregations who flocked to a concentration of preaching and prayer-meetings held in tents and booths and open platforms pitched on a field beside the church, but with ready access also to the back door of Nance Tinnock's Tavern. 'The Holy Fair', as it was popularly called, was nonetheless a sacramental occasion, normally held on the second Sunday in August following the annual Communion in the parish, and it was intended as a form of retreat and confirmation, but over the weekend it generally degenerated into a merry occasion for all concerned, except for the ministers and their elders, of course.

As usual, Burns moved among the crowds, keeping his eyes and ears open and the resulting 'report' is full of rich comment, sly observations and a few home truths. There is also an informed *critique* on the various preaching styles. Burns had heard them all. Tradition has it that Burns recited the complete poem in Nance Tinnock's tavern just a few days later – and Jean Armour was in the audience to hear him.

Upon a simmer Sunday morn
When Nature's face is fair,
I walked forth to view the corn,
An snuff the caller air.
The rising sun owre Galston muirs
Wi glorious light was glintin;

The hares were hirplin down the furrs,
The lav'rocks they were chantin
Fu' sweet that day.

As lightsomely I glowr'd abroad,
To see a scene sae gay,
Three hizzies, early at the road,
Cam skelpin up the way.
Twa had manteeles o dolefu' black,
But ane wi lyart lining;
The third, that gaed a wee a-back,
Was in the fashion shining
Fu' gay that day.

The twa appear'd like sisters twin,
In feature, form, an claes;
Their visage wither'd, lang an thin,
An sour as only slaes:
The third cam up, hap-stap-an'-lowp,
As light as ony lambie,
An wi a curchie low did stoop,
As soon as e'er she saw me,
Fu' kind that day.

Wi bonnet aff, quoth I, 'Sweet lass,
I think ye seem to ken me;
I'm sure I've seen that bonie face
But yet I canna name ye.'
Quo she, an laughin as she spak,
An taks me by the han's,
'Ye, for my sake, hae gien the feck
Of a' the ten comman's
A screed some day.'

'My name is Fun-your cronie dear,
The nearest friend ye hae;
An this is Superstition here,
An that's Hypocrisy.

I'm gaun to Mauchline Holy Fair,
To spend an hour in daffin:
Gin ye'll go there, yon runkl'd pair,
We will get famous laughin
At them this day.'

Quoth I, 'Wi a' my heart, I'll dot;
I'll get my Sunday's sark on,
An meet you on the holy spot;
Faith, we'se hae fine remarkin!'
Then I gaed hame at crowdie-time,
An soon I made me ready;
For roads were clad, frae side to side,
Wi mony a weary body
In droves that day.

Here farmers gash, in ridin graith,
Gaed hoddin by their cotters;
There swankies young, in braw braid-claith,
Are springing owre the gutters.
The lasses, skelpin barefit, thrang,
In silks an scarlets glitter;
Wi sweet-milk cheese, in mony a whang,
An farls, bak'd wi butter,
Fu' crump that day.

When by the plate we set our nose,
Weel heaped up wi ha'pence,
A greedy glowr black-bonnet throws,
An we maun draw our tippence.
Then in we go to see the show:
On ev'ry side they're gath'rin;
Some carrying dails, some chairs an stools,
An some are busy bleth'rin
Right loud that day.

Here stands a shed to fend the show'rs,
An screen our countra gentry;

There Racer Jess, an twa-three whores,
Are blinkin at the entry.
Here sits a raw o tittlin jads,
Wi heaving breast an bare neck;
An there a batch o wabster lads,
Blackguarding frae Kilmarnock,
For fun this day.

Here, some are thinkin on their sins,
An some upo' their claes;
Ane curses feet that fyl'd his shins,
Anither sighs an prays:
On this hand sits a chosen swatch,
Wi screwed-up, grace-proud faces;
On that a set o chaps, at watch,
Thrang winkin on the lasses
To chairs that day.

O happy is that man, an blest!
Nae wonder that it pride him!
Whase ain dear lass, that he likes best,
Comes clinkin down beside him!
Wi arms repos'd on the chair back,
He sweetly does compose him;
Which, by degrees, slips round her neck,
An's loof upon her bosom,
Unkend that day.

Now a' the congregation oer
Is silent expectation;
For Moodie speels the holy door,
Wi tidings o damnation:
Should Hornie, as in ancient days,
'Mang sons o God present him,
The vera sight o Moodie's face,
To's ain het hame had sent him
Wi fright that day.

Hear how he clears the point o faith
Wi rattlin and wi thumpin!
Now meekly calm, now wild in wrath,
He's stampin, an he's jumpin!
His lengthen'd chin, his turned-up snout,
His eldritch squeel an gestures,
O how they fire the heart devout,
Like cantharidian plaisters
    On sic a day!

But hark! the tent has chang'd its voice,
There's peace an rest nae langer;
For a' the real judges rise,
They canna sit for anger,
Smith opens out his cauld harangues,
On practice and on morals;
An aff the godly pour in thrangs,
To gie the jars an barrels
    A lift that day.

What signifies his barren shine,
Of moral powers an reason?
His English style, an gesture fine
Are a' clean out o season.
Like Socrates or Antonine,
Or some auld pagan heathen,
The moral man he does define,
But ne'er a word o faith in
    That's right that day.

In guid time comes an antidote
Against sic poison'd nostrum;
For Peebles, frae the water-fit,
Ascends the holy rostrum:
See, up he's got, the word o God,
An meek an mim has view'd it,
While Common-sense has taen the road,

An aff, an up the Cowgate
Fast, fast that day.

Wee Miller neist the guard relieves,
An Orthodoxy raibles,
Tho in his heart he weel believes,
An thinks it auld wives' fables:
But faith! the birkie wants a manse,
So, cannilie he hums them;
Altho his carnal wit an sense
Like hafflins-wise oercomes him
At times that day.

Now, butt an ben, the change-house fills,
Wi yill-caup commentators;
Here's cryin out for bakes and gills,
An there the pint-stowp clatters;
While thick an thrang, an loud an lang,
Wi logic an wi scripture,
They raise a din, that in the end
Is like to breed a rupture
O wrath that day.

Leeze me on drink! it gies us mair
Than either school or college;
It kindles wit, it waukens lear,
It pangs us fou o knowledge:
Be't whisky-gill or penny wheep,
Or ony stronger potion,
It never fails, or drinkin deep,
To kittle up our notion,
By night or day.

The lads an lasses, blythely bent
To mind baith saul an' body,
Sit round the table, weel content,
An steer about the toddy:

On this ane's dress, an that ane's leuk,
They're makin observations;
While some are cozie i' the neuk,
An forming assignations
To meet some day.

But now the Lord's ain trumpet touts,
Till a' the hills are rairin,
And echoes back return the shouts;
Black Russell is na sparin:
His piercin words, like Highlan' swords,
Divide the joints an marrow;
His talk o Hell, whare devils dwell,
Our vera 'sauls does harrow'
Wi fright that day!

A vast, unbottom'd, boundless pit,
Fill'd fou o lowin brunstane,
Whase raging flame, an scorching heat,
Wad melt the hardest whun-stane!
The half-asleep start up wi fear,
An think they hear it roarin;
When presently it does appear,
Twas but some neibor snorin
Asleep that day.

Twad be owre lang a tale to tell,
How mony stories past;
An how they crouded to the yill,
When they were a' dismist;
How drink gaed round, in cogs an caups,
Amang the furms an benches;
An cheese an bread, frae women's laps,
Was dealt about in lunches
An dawds that day.

In comes a gawsie, gash guidwife,
An sits down by the fire,

Syne draws her kebbuck an her knife;
The lasses they are shyer:
The auld guidmen, about the grace
Frae side to side they bother;
Till some ane by his bonnet lays,
An gies them't like a tether,
Fu' lang that day.

Waesucks! for him that gets nae lass,
Or lasses that hae naething!
Sma need has he to say a grace,
Or melvie his braw claithing!
O wives, be mindfu' ance yoursel
How bonie lads ye wanted;
An dinna for a kebbuck-heel
Let lasses be affronted
On sic a day!

Now Clinkumbell, wi rattlin tow,
Begins to jow an croon;
Some swagger hame the best they dow,
Some wait the afternoon.
At slaps the billies halt a blink,
Till lasses strip their shoon:
Wi faith an hope, an love an drink,
They're a' in famous tune
For crack that day.

How mony hearts this day converts
O sinners and o lasses!
Their hearts o stane, gin night, are gane
As saft as ony flesh is:
There's some are fou o love divine;
There's some are fou o brandy;
An mony jobs that day begin,
May end in houghmagandie
Some ither day.

One can't help think how right James Perry was in 1794 to offer Burns a job with the London *Morning Chronicle*. All he had to do was write something like this poem, once a week, and in return, he would receive a guinea a week – more than the fifty pounds per annum he earned with the Excise – but Burns had one of his fits of anxiety, due to political pressures, and regretfully declined the offer.

Address to a Haggis

1786

This inconsequential trifle, given by many Burnsians a much over-rated place in the Burns canon, began, as so many of his verses did, as an improvised verse at a friend's house. Even then, it was never intended as anything more than a humourous extravanganza of a moment at table, but since the Burns Federation set the Burns Suppers in train at the end of the 19th-century, it has been set in stone as a mandatory part of that questionable rite all over the world, and is delivered in a stentorian bellow every 25 January by a perspiring gentlemen in a kilt to a generally uncomprehending audience and with the accompaniment of a slightly bemused chef, bagpipes, pipes, claymores and the inevitable tray of drams.

Fair fa' your honest, sonsie face,
Great chieftain o the pudding-race!
Aboon them a' ye tak your place,
Painch, tripe, or thairm:
Weel are ye wordy o a grace
As lang's my arm.

The groaning trencher there ye fill,
Your hurdies like a distant hill,
Your pin was help to mend a mill
In time o need,
While thro your pores the dews distil
Like amber bead.

His knife see rustic Labour dight,
An cut you up wi ready sleight,
Trenching your gushing entrails bright,
Like ony ditch;
And then, O what a glorious sight,
Warm-reekin, rich!

Then, horn for horn, they stretch an strive:
Deil tak the hindmost! on they drive,
Till a' their weel-swall'd kytes belyve
Are bent like drums;
Then auld Guidman, maist like to rive,
Bethankit! hums.

Is there that owre his French ragout
Or olio that wad staw a sow,
Or fricassee wad make her spew
Wi perfect sconner,
Looks down wi sneering, scornfu' view
On sic a dinner?

Poor devil! see him owre his trash,
As feckles as wither'd rash,
His spindle shank, a guid whip-lash;
His nieve a nit;
Thro blody flood or field to dash,
O how unfit!

But mark the Rustic, haggis-fed,
The trembling earth resounds his tread.
Clap in his walie nieve a blade,
He'll mak it whissle;
An legs an arms, an hands will sned,
Like taps o trissle.

Ye Pow'rs, wha mak mankind your care,
And dish them out their bill o fare,
Auld Scotland wants nae skinking ware
That jaups in luggies;
But, if ye wish her gratefu' prayer
Gie her a haggis!

According to Hogg, Burns was dining with Andrew Bruce and his family on Castlehill, when he gave a spontaneous version of the last verse. According to Chambers, he was eating with the

Morrisons in Mauchline. Whichever it was, this verse, with additional preceding verses, appeared in the *Caledonian Mercury* on 19 December 1786, and was notable as the first-ever printing of anything by Burns in a newspaper. The poem was then further adapted, proof of Burns's constant reworking of pieces, for the *Scots Magazine* of 1787. A misprint in the second 1787 Edinburgh Edition caused *skinking* in the third line of the final verse to be rendered as *stinking* and this has come to be known as the 'stinking edition' ever since.

On Meeting with Lord Daer

1786

It must be admitted that our Robert could be a bit of a snob on occasions, and the evening of Tuesday 23 October 1786 was one of them. On that night, Basil William Douglas Hamilton, the Lord Daer, at 23, four years younger than Burns, was staying at Catrine, the country home of Professor Dugald Stewart, who held the Chair of Philosophy at Edinburgh University. Daer, the second son of the Earl of Selkirk, was a student of his, and since Stewart had received a copy of the Kilmarnock Edition only recently from Dr John McKenzie in Mauchline, and was highly impressed by it, it was only natural that both should be invited to dinner at Catrine. Meeting the young lord among the guests, Burns was just as impressed, if somewhat surprised, by the aristocrat's friendly manner, and flattered by his attention, and the result was this very untypical praise of a '*young birkie ca'd a lord*'. Even a lord who believed, or said he believed, in socialism and the principles of the French Revolution, as Burns did.

It was Burns's first meeting with nobility, but it wasn't to be the last time Burns was taken in by the guile shown by the upper class in putting the lower orders at their ease, and even if the air of the piece resulting from the occasion is mock-serious, it is only a little mock. Burns would gladly have changed places with his fellow-guest. If only to remove himself from the drudge of daily 'darg' and the time it took from his real avocation which was writing verse and making songs. From his position, well below the salt, any position above it seemed better, and therefore desirable. For the rest of his time moving among society in Edinburgh and on his tours he was to evince the same unsettling mixture of awe and disdain that was to mark his behaviour with any class other than his own. He felt himself equal to anyone but he realised that, in the world's eyes, some were more equal than others. It wasn't deep, or fatal, but the chip on the broad shoulders of this supremely gifted man was there, and it only showed in his

occasional resentment of the place that had been given him. And
in works like this.

This wot ye all whom it concerns,
I, Rhymer Robin, *alias* Burns,
October twenty-third,
A ne'er-to-be-forgotten day,
Sae far I sprackl'd up the brae,
I dinner'd wi a Lord.

I've been at drucken writers' feasts,
Nay, been bitch-fou 'mang godly priests –
Wi rev'rence be it spoken! –
I've even join'd the honour'd jorum,
When mighty Squireships of the quorum,
Their hydra drouth did sloken.

But wi a Lord! – stand out my shin,
A Lord-a Peer-an Earl's son!
Up higher yet, my bonnet
An sic a Lord! – lang Scoth ells twa,
Our Peerage he oerlooks them a',
As I look oer my sonnet.

But O for Hogarth's magic pow'r!
To show Sir Bardie's willyart glow'r,
An how he star'd and stammer'd,
When, goavin, as if led wi branks,
An stumpin on his ploughman shanks,
He in the parlour hammer'd.

To meet good Stewart little pain is,
Or Scotia's sacred Demosthenes.
Thinks I: 'They are but men!'
But 'Burns'! – My Lord – Good God I doited
My knees on ane anither knoited
As faltering I gaed ben.

I sidying shelter'd in a nook,
An at his Lordship steal't a look,
Like some portentous omen;
Except good sense and social glee,
An (what surpris'd me) modesty,
I marked nought uncommon.

I watch'd the symptoms o the Great,
The gentle pride, the lordly state,
The arrogant assuming;
The fient a pride, nae pride had he,
Nor sauce, nor state, that I could see,
Mair than an honest ploughman.

Then from his Lordship I shall learn,
Henceforth to meet with unconcern
One rank as weel's another;
Nae honest, worthy man need care
To meet with noble youthful Daer,
For he but meets a brother.

Professor Stewart was to remain a good and understanding friend to Burns in Edinburgh and took steps to see that he met with like minds in the capital. He may even have been behind the failed move to offer Burns the Chair of Agriculture at the the University. There is no record of Burns's ever meeting Lord Daer again.

On Seeing a Wounded Hare

1789

On 21 April 1789, Burns wrote to Mrs Dunlop,

> *Two mornings ago, as I was at a very early hour sewing in the fields, I heard a shot, and presently a poor little hare limped by me very much hurt. You will easily guess this set my humanity in tears and my indignation in arms. The following was the result.*

Writing to Alexander Cunningham on 4 May 1789, he added,

> You will guess my indignation at the inhuman fellow who could shoot a hare at this season, when all of them have young ones; and it gave me no little gloomy satisfaction to see the poor injured creature escape him.

> Inhuman man! curse on thy barb'rous art,
> And blasted be thy murder-aiming eye;
> May never pity soothe thee with a sigh,
> Nor ever pleasure glad thy cruel heart!

> Go live, poor wanderer of the wood and field!
> The bitter little that of life remains:
> No more the thickening brakes and verdant plains
> To thee a home, or food, or pastime yield.

> Seek, mangled wretch, some place of wonted rest,
> No more of rest, but now thy dying bed!
> The sheltering rushes whistling oer thy head,
> The cold earth with thy bloody bosom prest.

> Perhaps a mother's anguish adds its woe;
> The playful pair crowd fondly by thy side;
> Ah! helpless nurslings, who will now provide
> That life a mother only can bestow!

Oft as by winding Nith I, musing, wait
The sober eve, or hail the cheerful dawn,
I'll miss thee sporting oer the dewy lawn,
And curse the ruffian's aim, and mourn thy hapless fate.

Dr Gregory, a doctor, and the inventor of 'Gregory's Mixture', took exception to Burns's handling of the metre in this poem and, in a letter dated 2 June 1789, offered suggestions, some of which Burns accepted, but Dr Gregory persisted in further supercillious comments until Burns, exasperated, exclaimed,

Dr Gregory is a good man, but he crucifies me.

To Collector Mitchell

1795

John Mitchell had trained first for the ministry but changed to the
Excise just before Burns came to Dumfries. The two became good
friends and Burns often sent drafts of his work for Mitchell's com-
ments. When Burns first became seriously ill at the end of 1795,
Mitchell did all he could to help him. Burns wrote to him on
Hogmanay of that year asking, in verse form, for a guinea
advance on his salary, till he got back to work. Mitchell obliged
him at once.

Friend of the Poet, tried and leal,
Wha, wanting thee, might beg or steal;
Alake! alake! the meikle deil
Wi a' his witches
Are at it, skelpin jig and reel,
In my poor pouches!

I modestly fu' fain wad hint it,
That one-pound-one, I sairly want it;
If wi the hizzie down ye sent it,
It would be kind;
And while my heart wi life-blood dunted,
I'd bear't in mind.

So may the auld year gang out moaning
To see the new come laden, groaning,
Wi double plenty oer the loanin
To thee and thine:
Domestic peace and comforts crowning
The hale design

Postscript

Ye've heard this while how I've been licket,
And by fell death was nearly nicket;
Grim loon! he got me by the fecket,

And sair me sheuk;
But by gude luck I lap a wicket,
And turned a neuk.

But by that health – I've got a share ot.
And by that life – I'm promised mair ot,
My hale and weel I'll tak' a care ot,
A tentier way;
Then farewell folly, hide and hair ot,
For ance and aye!

Unusually for Burns, he added a postscript, remarking on the gravity of his illness but being optimistic about his return to health and work in 1796. He did get back to work in the February, but he had to take time off again in April and by mid-July he had to take to his bed again. During all his time off, his shifts were covered by his workmates, Lewars and Stobie, prompted by Collector Mitchell, and with approval of the highest authorities, so that Burns was paid, albeit on a diminishing scale, until the last.

On the late Captain Grose's peregrinations through Scotland

(Collecting the antiquities of that kingdom)

1789

Captain Francis Grose, a sometime soldier, Richmond Herald in the College of Arms and now antiquarian, was described by Burns in the summer of 1789, as *'a cheerful-looking grig of an old, fat fellow, wheeling about in his own carriage with a pencil and paper in his hand'* in search of subjects to draw for his next book, *The Antiquities of Scotland*. Burns, meeting the colourful Englishman at a dinner given by Captain Riddel at Friar's Carse, recommended that he look at the ruins of Old Alloway Kirk and also sent him details of stories associated with that place. Grose was interested but not caught until, at the end of the year, Burns sent him a version of the stories which he had done in Scots verse, saying – *'Should you think it worthy a place in your Scots Antiquities, it will lengthen not a little the altitude of my Muse's pride.'* Burns called his poem, *Tam o Shanter – A Tale*. Needless to say, Grose was only too happy to print it, but he was beaten to it by the *Edinburgh Magazine* which printed it in March 1791, a month before its first publication. In this, Grose himself publicly acknowledged his debt to the bard:

> *To my ingenious friend, Robert Burns, I have been seriously obligated: he was not only at the pains of making out what was worthy of most notice in Ayrshire, the county hon-oured by his birth, but he also wrote, expressly for this work, the pretty tale annexed to Alloway Church.*

Burns greatly enjoyed the company of the jovial, little man. *'I have never seen a man of more original observation, anecdote and remark,'* he wrote to Mrs Dunlop. He also recommended him to Professor Stewart in Edinburgh. Burns penned several little, light-hearted pieces about Grose, but this poem, printed in the

Edinburgh Evening Courant of 27 August 1789, is by far his best
tribute to him.

Hear, Land o Cakes, and brither Scots,
Frae Maidenkirk to Johnie Groat's;
If there's a hole in a' your coats,
I rede you tent it:
A chield's amang you takin notes,
And, faith, he'll prent it:

If in your bounds ye chance to light
Upon a fine, fat fodgel wight,
O stature short, but genius bright,
That's he, mark weel;
And wow! he has an unco sleight
O cauk and keel.

By some auld, houlet-haunted biggin,
Or kirk deserted by its riggin,
It's ten to ane ye'll find him snug in
Some eldritch part,
Wi deils, they say, Lord save's! colleaguin
At some black art.

Ilk ghaist that haunts auld ha' or chaumer,
Ye gipsy-gang that deal in glamour,
And you, deep-read in hell's black grammar,
Warlocks and witches,
Ye'll quake at his conjuring hammer,
Ye midnight bitches.

It's tauld he was a sodger bred,
And ane wad rather fa'n than fled;
But now he's quat the spurtle-blade,
And dog-skin wallet,
And taen the – Antiquarian trade,
I think they call it.

He has a fouth o auld nick-nackets:
Rusty airn caps and jinglin jackets,
Wad haud the Lothians three in tackets,
A towmont gude;
And parritch-pats and auld saut-backets,
Before the Flood.

Of Eve's first fire he has a cinder;
Auld Tubalcain's fire-shool and fender;
That which distinguished the gender
O Balaam's ass:
A broomstick o the witch of Endor,
Weel shod wi brass.

Forbye, he'll shape you aff fu' gleg
The cut of Adam's philibeg;
The knife that nickit Abel's craig
He'll prove you fully,
It was a faulding jocteleg,
Or lang-kail gullie.

But wad ye see him in his glee,
For meikle glee and fun has he,
Then set him down, and twa or three
Gude fellows wi him:
And port, O port! shine thou a wee,
And Then ye'll see him!

Now, by the Pow'rs o verse and prose!
Thou art a dainty chield, O Grose!
Whae'er o thee shall ill suppose,
They sair misca' thee;
I'd take the rascal by the nose,
Wad say, 'Shame fa' thee!'

In 1791, Grose left for Ireland to investigate its antiquities but died there soon afterwards in an apoplectic fit and was buried in Dublin.

Tam o Shanter

A tale

1790

This is a work that has in it all that is best in Burns; his wit and wisdom, humour and humanity, warmth of personality, and, above all, the searing observation of character that makes everyone and everything in the opus, even the Devil himself, so real and utterly believable. The whole things goes at a gallop, literally at a gallop, but even as we are carried along its careering way, we are aware that we are in the presence of poetic genius. *Tam o Shanter* not only leaps the Brig o Doon successfully but makes that greater leap of the imagination which carries us into high art. It emerges from the crucible of the poet's imagination, white-hot and true. It needed little hammering or smelting to give it its final polish. It comes from the furnace of his mind, ready-made and right. It was a good job of work, and he knew it.

More than two centuries later, it still stands as the high-point of his poetic output, an epic as immortal as its author. He himself thought it his masterwork. '*I look on Tam o Shanter*,' he said, '*to be my standard performance in the poetical line.*' Written mostly in the Scottish vernacular but with English insertions, it is still, despite its uncompromising use of the Ayrshire dialect of the time, accessible to audiences all over the world as one of the great works of Scottish literature. The tale of Tam o Shanter belongs to Scottish legend, and to Ayrshire legend in particular, but its telling in this instance by a poet inspired, makes it the property of posterity.

Its events are centred on reputed happenings in Alloway Kirk, a ruined church a little over half a mile from the clay cottage where Burns himself was born. As a boy he would have grown up familiar with the many tales that surrounded the ancient building which was supposed to be haunted by the devil. When Captain Grose asked Burns, at the home of a mutual friend, Captain Robert Riddell, if he had any ideas about interesting sites in the south-west of Scotland, it was natural that the young farmer-poet should think at once about Alloway Kirk – where, by the way, his own father was buried.

Burns supplied Grose with three stories in prose, each of which supplied something of the genesis of what was to become Tam o Shanter. He wrote:

Among the many witch-stories I have heard relating to Alloway Kirk, I distinctly remember only two or three. The first concerned a farmer, or farmer's servant, who was 'plodding and plashing homeward with his plough-irons on his shoulder, having been getting repairs of them at a neighbouring smithy' when he was 'struck aghast by discovering through the horrors of (a) storm, a light, which... plainly shewed itself to proceed from the haunted edifice.' Whether fortified by prayer or drink, or impelled by mere curiosity, he ventured nearer. He saw a 'kind of kettle or cauldron, depending from the roof over a fire, simmering some heads of unchristened children, limbs of executed malefactors, etc...' Without ceremony, the honest ploughman, unhooked the cauldron from the fire, and pouring out the damnable ingredients, inverted on his head, and carried it fairly home, where it remained long in his family, a living evidence of the truth of the story.

The second anecdote dealt with a farmer from Carrick who, on a market-day in the town of Ayr, returned home by way of Alloway Kirk at the 'wizard hour between night and morning.' He was 'surprised and entertained' to see 'a dance of witches merrily footing it round their old sooty black-guard master, who was keeping them all alive by the sound of his bagpipe.' The farmer, stopping his horse to observe them closer could 'plainly descry the faces of many old women of his acquaintance... all in their smocks: and one of them happening unluckily to have a smock which was considerably too short to answer the purpose of that dress...' Our farmer was so tickled by this sight that he involuntarily burst out 'Weel luppen, Maggie, wi' the short sark!' Then, recollecting himself he instantly spurred his horse to the top of his speed. Luckily the bridge of the River Doon was near, and it is 'universally known that no diabolical power can pursue you beyond the middle of a running stream... When he reached the arch of the bridge, one of the vengeful hags actually sprang to seize him – but it was too late; nothing was on her side of the stream but the horse's tail, which immediately gave way at her infernal grip, as if blasted by a stroke of lightning; the farmer was beyond her reach... but the tail-less condition of that vigorous steed remained to the last hour of his life an awful warning to Carrick farmers not to stay too late in Ayr markets.'

Burns insisted that the third, and final tale was *'equally true'* and he had it from the *'best authorities in Ayrshire.'* This was the story of a shepherd boy *'who fell in with a crew of man and women busily pulling stems of ragwort... and when they got astride of (them), they called out 'Up horsie!' and flew up like Pegasus through the air. The foolish boy cried 'Up horsie!' with the rest, and, strange to tell, away he flew with the company. The cavalcade stopt at Bordeaux, where... they quaffed away at the merchant's best cellar until the morning. The poor shepherd boy, being equally a stranger to the scene and to liquor, got himself hopelessly drunk; and when the rest took to horse, he fell asleep and was found next day by the merchant and by somebody who understood Scotch. By some means or other he got home and lived long enough to tell the world this wondrous tale.'*

These then were the disparate strands which Burns took to weave his own particular narrative. He also added the real-life figure of Robert Graham, a tenant of the farm of Shanter on Carrick shore, who owned a boat called the *Tam o Shanter* and had a wife, Kate, who was famous for her temper. Tradition has it that Graham's horse, a long-tailed grey mare, had waited longer than usual for her master at the tavern door, and *'certain humourists plucked her tail to such an extent so as to leave it little better than a stump.'*

It is not known what turned Burns from prose to poetry with these tales, but the gregarious Grose had first met Burns at the dinner-table and no doubt he wanted the same sparkle and wit that marked the Scot's convivial conversation, and he might well have suggested that he work the material 'to his own voice' as it were. Or it may have been just another Burns whim to work in rhyme. After all, that's what he knew best. Whatever the motive, he took his time in getting down to it. He had started on the project during 1789 but it was not till a year later that he finished it. The final poetic mix was given the motto from the medieval poet, Gavin Douglas – '*Of brownies and bogillis full is this book*' – then Tam was ready to ride his faithful Maggie into legend.

Lockhart, on Cromek's authority accepts Jean Armour's opinion that Tam o Shanter was the work of a single day but as Burns himself said – '*All my poetry is the effect of easy composition, but of laborious correction.*' There speaks the professional. One cannot blame Mrs Burns for believing that her husband's work arrived 'finished' so to speak. His own verdict on *Tam o Shanter* was given in a letter to Mrs Dunlop in April 1791, when he said that it '*showed a finishing polish... which I despair of ever excelling*'.

It was first composed on Ellisland Farm one autumn day when Burns was seen by his chief labourer, William Clark, '*striding up and doon the broo o the Scaur, recitin' to himsel' like one dementit.*' Clark ran to tell Mrs Burns, but she advised everyone to leave him alone –'*He's best on his lane when the mood is on him.*' When later, it started to rain, it was Jean who had to go out to him. When he came indoors again, he came in with *Tam o Shanter*.

He recited the first completed draft to Robert Ainslie when that old friend visited the family from Edinburgh. It must have been quite an occasion. A poet is not always the best reader of his own work, but Robert Burns had the looks and voice of an actor, and his powers of conversation are well documented. To have seen him then, at 32 years of age, at the height of his powers, recite his own best work in front of his own fireside, to his family and closest friends, must have been as theatrically telling as any play.

When chapman billies leave the street,
And drouthy neebors neebors meet;
When market days are wearing late,
An folk begin to tak the gate;
While we sit bousing at the nappy,
An getting fou and unco happy,
We think na on the lang, Scots miles,
The mosses, waters, slaps and styles,
That lie between us and our hame,
Whare sits our sulky, sullen dame,
Gathering her brows like gathering storm,
Nursing her wrath to keep her warm.

This truth fand honest Tam o Shanter,
As he frae Ayr ae night did canter;
(Auld Ayr, wham ne'er a town surpasses
For honest men and bonie lasses.)
O Tam, hads't thou been sae wise
As taen thine ain wife Kate's advice!
She tauld thee weel thou was a skellum,
A blethering, blustering, drunken blellum;
That frae November till October
Ae market-day thou was na sober;
That ilka melder, wi the miller
Thou sat as lang as thou had siller;
That every naig was ca'd a shoe on,
The smith and thee gat roaring fou on;
That at the L-d's house, even on Sunday,
Thou drank wi Kirkton Jean till Monday.
She prophesied that late or soon
Thou would be found deep-drown'd in Doon;
Or catch'd wi warlocks in the mirk
By Alloway's auld haunted kirk.

Ah, gentle dames, it gars me greet,
To think how many counsels sweet
How many lengthen'd, sage advices,

The husband frae the wife despises!
But to our tale:

Ae market-night,
Tam had got planted unco right;
Fast by an ingle, bleezing finely,
Wi reaming swats that drank divinely;
And at his elbow, Souter Johnny,
His ancient, trusty, drouthy crony;
Tam loed him like a very brother;
They'd been fou for weeks thegither.
The night drave on wi sangs and clatter;
And ay the ale was growing better;
The Landlady and Tam grew gracious,
Wi favours, secret, sweet, and precious:
The Souter tauld his queerest stories;
The Landlord's laugh was ready chorus;
The storm without might rair and rustle,
Tam did na mind the storm a whistle.
Care, mad to see a man sae happy,
E'en drown'd himsel amang the nappy:
As bees flee hame wi lades o treasure,
The minutes winged their way wi pleasure:
Kings may be blest, but Tam was glorious,
O'er a' the ills o life victorious!
But pleasures are like poppies spread,
You seize the flower, its bloom is shed;
Or like the snow falls on the river,
A moment white – then melts for ever;
Or like the borealis race,
That flit ere you can point their place;
Or like the rainbow's lovely form
Evanishing amid the storm.
Nae man can tether time nor tide;
The hour approaches Tam maun ride;

That hour, o night's black arch the key-stane,
That dreary hour he mounts his beast in;
And sic a night he taks the road in,
As ne'er poor sinner was abroad in.
The wind blew as twad blawn its last;
The rattling showers rose on the the blast;
The speedy gleams the darkness swallow'd;
Loud, deep, and lang, the thunder bellow'd:
That night a child might understand,
The Deil had business on his hand.

Weel mounted on his gray mare, Meg,
A better never lifted leg,
Tam skelpit on thro dub and mire,
Despising, wind, and rain, and fire;
Whiles holding fast his gude blue bonnet;
Whiles crooning oer some auld Scots sonnet;
Whiles glow'ring round wi prudent cares,
Lest bogles catch him unawares:

Kirk Alloway was drawing nigh,
Whare ghaists and houlets nightly cry.
By this time he was cross the foord,
Whare, in the snaw, the chapman smoor'd;
And past the birks and meikle stane
Whare drunken Charlie brak's neck-bane;
And thro the whins and by the cairn,
Whare hunters fand the murder'd bairn;
And near the thorn, abune the well,
Whare Mungos mither hang'd hersel.
Before him Doon pours all his floods;
The doubling-storm roars through the woods;
The lightnings flash frae pole to pole;
Near and more near the thunders roll:
When, glimmering thro the groaning trees,
Kirk-Alloway seem'd in a bleeze;
Thro ilka bore the beams were glancing;

And loud resounded mirth and dancing.
Inspiring bold John Barleycorn!
What dangers thou canst make us scorn!
Wi tippenny, we fear nae evil;
Wi usquabae, we'll face the devil!
The swats sae ream'd in Tammy's noddle,
Fair play, he car'd na deils a boddle.
But Maggie stood right sair astonish'd,
Till, by the heel and hand admonish'd,
She ventured forward on the light;
And vow! Tam saw an unco sight!
Warlocks and witches in a dance;
Nae cotillion brent new frae France,
But hornpipes, jigs, strathspeys and reels,
Put life and mettle in their heels.
A winnock-bunker in the east,
There sat auld Nick, in shape o beast;
A towzie tyke, black, grim and large,
To gie them music was his charge:
He screw'd the pipes and gart them skirl,
Till roof and rafters a' did dirl.

Coffins stood round, like open presses,
That shaw'd the dead in their last dresses;
And by some devilish cantraip slight
Each in his cauld hand held a light.
By which heroic Tam was able
To note upon the haly table:
A murderer's banes in gibbet airns;
Twa-span lang, wee unchristen'd bairns;
A thief, new-cutted frae a rape,
Wi his last gasp his gab did gape;
Five tomahawks wi blood red-rusted;
Five scymitars, wi murder crusted;
A garter, which a babe had strangled;
A knife, a father's throat had mangled,

Whom his ain son o life bereft,
The grey hairs yet stack to the heft;
Wi mair o horrible and awefu'
Which even to name wad be unlawfu'.

Three Lawyers' tongues, turn'd inside out,
Wi lies seam'd like a beggar's clout;
Three priests' tongues, rotten, black as muck,
Lay stinking, vile, in every neuk –

As Tammie glow'red amaz'd, and curious,
The mirth and fun grew fast and furious:
The piper loud and louder blew;
The dancers quick and quicker flew;
They reel'd, they set, they cross'd, they cleekit,
Til ilka carlin swat and reekit,
And coost her duddies to the work,
And linket at it in her sark!

Now Tam, O Tam! had they been queans,
A' plump and strappin in their teens,
Their sarks, instead o creeshy flannen,
Been snaw-white seventeen hunder linnen!
Thir breeks o mine, my only pair,
That once were plush, o gude blue hair,
I wad hae gien them off my hurdies,
For ae blink o the bonie burdies!
But wither'd beldames, auld and droll,
Rigwoodie hags was spean a foal,
Lowping and flinging on a crummock,
I wonder didna turn thy stomach.
But Tam kend what was what fu' brawlie;
There was ae winsome wench and wawlie,
That night enlisted in the core,
(Lafter kend on Carrick shore;
For mony a beast to dead she shot,
And perish'ed mony a boat,

And shook baith meikle corn and bear,
And kept the countryside in fear;
Her cutty sark, o Paisley harn,
That while a lassie she had worn,
In longitude tho sorely scanty,
It was her best, and she was vaunty.
Ah! little kend thy reverend grannie,
That sark she coft for her wee Nannie,
Wi twa pund Scots, (twas a' her riches),
Wad ever grac'd a dance of witches!
But here my Muse her wing maun cour;
Sic flights are far beyond her pow'r;
To sing how Nannie lap and flang,
(A souple jade she was, and strang),
And how Tam stood, like ane bewitch'd,
And thought his very e'en enrich'd;
Even Satan glowr'd, and fidg'd fu' fain,
And hotch'd and blew wi' might and main:
Till first ae caper, syne anither,
Tam tint his reason a'thegither'
And roars out, 'Weel done, Cutty-sark!'

And in an instant, all was dark:
And scarcely had he Maggie rallied,
When out the hellish legion sallied.

As bees bizz out wi angry fyke,
When plundering herds assail thie byke,
As open pussie's mortal foes,
When pop! she starts before their nose;
As eager runs the market-crowd,
When 'Catch the thief!' resounds aloud;
So Maggie rins, the witches follow,
Wi mony an eldritch skreech and hollow.

Ah, Tam! Ah, Tam! thou'll get thy fairin!
In holl they'll roast thee like a herrin!

In vain thy Kate awaits thy comin!
Kate soon will be a woefu woman!
Now, do thy speedy utmost, Meg,
And win the key-stane of the brig;
There at them thou thy tail may toss,
A running stream they dare na cross.

But ere the key-stane she could make,
The fient a tail she had to shake!
For Nannie, far before the rest,
Hard upon noble Maggie prest,
And flew at Tam wi furious ettle;
But little wist she Maggie's mettle-
Ae spring brought off her master hale,
But left behind her ain gray tale.
The carlin claught her by the rump
And left poor Maggie scarce a stump.

Now, what this tale o truth shall read,
Ilk man and mother's son take heed:
Whene'er to drink you are inclin'd,
Or cutty-sarks run in your mind,
Think, ye may buy the joys oer dear,
Remember Tam o Shanter's mare.

Since it first appeared in print, *Tam o Shanter* has lent itself to interpretation and illustration by many famous artists. Its incidents lend themselves naturally to painting and animation and there have been many visual versions, but only one composer of world status has found inspiration in the tale, and that is the English-born trumpeter, conductor and composer, Sir Malcolm Arnold. He had read Lockhart's biography of the poet and was immediately attracted to the musical potential of *Tam o Shanter*. Sir Malcolm says –

> *I reached the conclusion that the dramatic poem presented*
> *a tremendous opportunity for a momentous musical work*
> *with possiblities of moments of good-humoured pantomime*

with whooping horns and off-beat accents; and I hope my
work reflects my thoughts on Tam o Shanter.'

He also added,

It was no Burnsian flash-in-the-pan.

The Arnold work ends with what one musicologist described as
'*a glorious apotheosis of a hymn tune returning in glory with
descending scales in the strings, and bells pealing.*' Written in 1955,
it was first heard at a Henry Wood Promenade on 16 August of
that year with the Royal Philharmonic Orchestra under Sir
Malcolm's own baton. Its first Scottish performance was by the
Scottish National Orchestra under Sir Alexander Gibson at the
Usher Hall on 23 March 1956. Since that time, it has been per-
formed frequently all over the world.

In September 1996, the present writer was privileged to make
a vocal recording, with Sir Malcolm's kind permission, of the
Burns text against the music and the resulting *Tam o Shanter* CD
was mastered by John oLeary of Word Pictures Ltd in Auckland,
New Zealand. What was astonishing was how well the words fit-
ted the music. Yet it ought not to have been a surprise. So attuned
was Burns to the tempo and rhythm of the lines and to its mighty
overall sweep that it was already a virtual libretto-in-waiting.

It is fitting that this consideration of his poetic work should
end on the high note of this unconventional epic, but there was a
lesser versifier who still had a verse for every occasion. This was
the Burns who rhymed for fun.

PART TWO

The Rhymer

EPISTLES, ADDRESSES, EPIGRAMS, EPITHETS, ELEGIES AND EPITAPHS

Epistle to John Rankine
Epistle to Davie
Second Epistle to Davie
Epistle to J. Lapraik
Second Epistle to J. Lapraik
Epistle to William Simpson
Epitle to John Goldie
Third Epistle to J. Lapraik
Epistle to Rev John McMath
Epistle to James Smith
Epistle to Major Logan
Epistle to A Young Friend
Epistle to Hugh Parker
Epistle to James Tennant of Glenconnor
Epistle to Robert Graham Esq of Fintry
Epistle to Dr Blacklock
Epistle to Maxwell of Terraughty
The Rights of Women
Epigrams and Epithets
Elegies and Epitaphs

A Rhyme for all Reasons

All Burns's writing began as a private act of observation in the pages of his first Commonplace Book in 1783 when he was 24 years of age. Before that, however, he had flirted with songwriting much as he had flirted with the subjects that inspired them, but it is worth noting that these songs came annually for the first three years. He was a slow starter in what was to become, by the end, half his short life's work. His first writing was as a hired quill. From the time of the dancing classes at Dalrymple, around 1777, after the move to Lochlea, he began to act more and more as a 'blackfoot' to his companions, like Jamie Smith and James Candlish, in their wooing of their respective sweethearts. Not only would he speak to the girls on his friends' behalf, he would write their letters for them.

His first published letter (to William Niven, from 'Lochlee') is dated from the end of 1780, but you can be sure that by that time he was already scribbling away at any excuse. His penmanship is another indication of his love of writing. He wrote a good hand, and his management of what must have been an unsubtle goose-feather is nearly as remarkable as the precocious quality he already showed in the content of his various missives. This wide-spread, miscellaneous writing was all part of his self-imposed training programme in the same way that his constant reading was. Everything was grist to the mill of churning out anything that fed his unceasing appetite for words.

This need to speak for others gave him a rare insight into char-acter and the working of heart and mind in his 'compears' and this understanding of relationships was never to leave. For one who had hardly moved off the farm until he came to Lochlea, and never out of Ayrshire until he went to Edinburgh, and never out of Scotland, apart from a couple of days each in Newcastle and Carlisle, he had an extraordinary worldliness and sophistication. It was this that was to so astonish the Edinburgh gentry. This was no agricultural oaf, not by a wide acre. Part of this *savoir faire* was imbibed from reading of course, but much more from merely keeping his eyes and ears open as he grew up.

The human condition, in its basic definition, varies only in quality. Whether rich or poor, the same instincts apply and this knowledge was at the root of his egalitarianism. Even if his creed of universal brotherhood was ideal, even Utopian, it was exactly according to the thinking of his day. Later circumstances meant that he had to play the gentry at their own game, but at this time he was as free as he was ever to be, and, unfettered as he was, he could let himself go. This he did, in his verses, and as he grew more assured, they got better and better.

The poems and songs are already evidence of this in his Ayrshire years, but just as telling is the range of his miscellaneous writing, even in the smaller pieces. His aim in the satire was always to be good and he also excelled in the verse-portrait. It might only be in a couplet, but we can see the person on the page. The Epistles, the Epigrams, the Elegies and the Epitaphs were all only formal extensions of the original letters, but they were the sign-posts on the road he took to make himself into a writer of the first rank.

Epistle John Rankine

(Enclosing some poems)

1784

John Rankine was a tenant-farmer at Adamhill near Tarbolton
and befriended Burns after the Burns family had come to Lochlea.
Rankine had a rough and ready humour, but a good heart. His
practical jokes were accepted in good part in the community and
he was noted for the telling of his dreams. Burns found him a like
mind in his dealings with the Kirk Session and a ready listener for
any sexual exploits. Burns, in this epistle, couches the seduction
of Bess Paton, for instance, in terms of the hunting field, similes
which the farmer Rankine would readily understand. Burns wrote
this letter-epistle in this way in response to Rankine's guess that
Bess was pregnant, and to tell him that he had already settled
matters with the Tarbolton Kirk Session on account of Bess and
paid his guinea for the poor as required. Now he was saying he
would therefore make sure he got his money's worth before the
baby was due. It was hardly gentlemanly but these were country
matters being discussed by two countrymen.

> O Rough, rude, ready-witted Rankine,
> The wale o cocks for fun an drinkin!
> There's mony godly folks are thinkin,
> Your dreams and tricks
> Will send you, Korah-like, a-sinkin
> Straught to auld Nick's.
>
> Ye hae saw mony cracks an cants,
> And in your wicked, drucken rants,
> Ye mak a devil o the saunts,
> An fill them fou;
> And then their failings, flaws, an wants,
> Are a' seen thro.
>
> Hypocrisy, in mercy spare it!
> That holy robe, O dinna tear it!

Spare't for their sakes, wha aften wear it –
The lads in black;
But your curst wit, when it comes near it,
Rives't aff their back.

Think, wicked Sinner, wha ye're skaithing:
It's just the Blue-gown badge an claithing
O saunts; tak that, ye lea'e them naething
To ken them by
Frae ony unregenerate heathen,
Like you or I.

I've sent you here some rhyming ware,
A' that I bargain'd for, an mair;
Sae, when ye hae an hour to spare,
I will expect,
Yon sang ye'll sen't, wi cannie care,
And no neglect.

Tho faith, sma heart hae I to sing!
My muse dow scarcely spread her wing;
I've play'd mysel a bonie spring,
An danc'd my fill!
I'd better gaen an sair't the king,
At Bunkjer's Hill.

Twas ae night lately, in my fun,
I gaed a rovin wi the gun,
An brought a paitrick to the grun –
A bonie hen;
And, as the twilight was begun,
Thought nane wad ken.

The poor, wee thing was little hurt;
I straikit it a wee for sport,
Ne'er thinkin they wad fash me for't;
But, Deil-ma-care!
Somebody tells the poacher-court
The hale affair.

Some auld, us'd hands had taen a note,
That sic a hen had got a shot;
I was suspected for the plot;
I scorn'd to lie;
So gat the whissle o my groat,
An pay't the fee.

But by my gun, o guns the wale,
An by my pouther an my hail,
An by my hen, an by her tail,
I vow an swear!
The game shall pay, oer muir an dale,
For this, niest year.

As soon's the clockin-time is by,
An the wee pouts begun to cry,
Lord, I'se hae sporting by an by
For my gowd guinea,
Tho I should herd the buckskin kye
For't in Virginia.

Trowth, they had muckle for to blame!
Twas neither broken wing nor limb,
But twa-three draps about the wame,
Scarce thro the feathers;
An baith a yellow George to claim,
An thole their blethers!

It pits me aye as mad's a hare;
So I can rhyme nor write nae mair;
But pennyworths again is fair,
When time's expedient:
Meanwhile I am, respected Sir,
Your most obedient.

Burns later sent Rankine a silver snuff box and a mock epitaph.

He who of Rankine sang lies stiff and deid
And a green, grassy hillock hides his heid;
Alas! Alas! A devilish change indeed.

Epistle to Davie

(A brother poet)

1784

Davie Sillar was a year younger than Burns, and like him was a farmer's son and was similarly largely self-taught. They also shared a love of verse-making, playing the fiddle and courting girls. Sillar painted a likely picture of the emerging Burns in a memoir he wrote of that time when they were young men together in the Tarbolton Bachelors Club.

Mr Robert Burns was some time in the parish of Tarbolton prior to my acquaintance with him. His social disposition easily procured him acquaintance; but a certain satirical seasoning, with which he and all poetic geniuses are to some degree influenced, while it set the rustic circle in a roar, was not unaccompanied by its kindred attendant – suspicious fear. I recollect his neighbour saying he had a great deal to say for himself, and that they suspected his principles. He wore the only tied hair in the parish; and in the church, his plaid, which was of a particular colour, I think fillemot, he wrapped in a particular manner round his shoulder...

We frequently met on Sundays at church, when, between sermons, instead of going with our friends to the inn, we often took a walk in the field. In these walks I have been frequently struck by his facility in addressing the fair sex; and how many times, when I have been bashfully anxious how to express myself, he would have entered into conversation with them with the greatest ease and freedom; and it was generally a death-blow to our conversation, however agreeable, to meet a female acquaintance.

While winds frae aff Ben-Lomond blaw,
An bar the doors wi driving snaw,

An hing us owre the ingle,
I set me down to pass the time,
An spin a verse or twa o rhyme,
In hamely, westlin jingle.
While frosty winds blaw in the drift,
Ben to the chimla lug,
I grudge a wee the great-folk's gift,
That live sae bien an snug:
I tent less, and want less
Their roomy fire-side;
But hanker, and canker,
To see their cursed pride.

It's hardly in a body's pow'r
To keep, at times, frae being sour,
To see how things are shar'd;
How best o chiels are whiles in want,
While coofs on countless thousands rant,
And ken na how to wair't;
But, Davie, lad, ne'er fash your head,
Tho we hae little gear;
We're fit to win our daily bread,
As lang's we're hale and fier:
'Mair spier na, nor fear na,'
Auld age ne'er mind a feg;
The last ot, the warst ot
Is only but to beg.

To lie in kilns and barns at e'en,
When banes are craz'd, and bluid is thin,
Is doubtless, great distress!

Yet then content could make us blest;
Ev'n then, sometimes, we'd snatch a taste
Of truest happiness.
The honest heart that's free frae a'
Intended fraud or guile,

However Fortune kick the ba',
Has aye some cause to smile;
An mind still, you'll find still,
A comfort this nae sma;
Nae mair then we'll care then,
Nae farther can we fa'.

What tho, like commoners of air,
We wander out, we know not where,
But either house or hal',
Yet nature's charms, the hills and woods,
The sweeping vales, and foaming floods,
Are free alike to all.
In days when daisies deck the ground,
And blackbirds whistle clear,
With honest joy our hearts will bound,
To see the coming year:
On braes when we please, then,
We'll sit an sowth a tune;
Syne rhyme till't we'll time till't,
An sing't when we hae done.

It's no in titles nor in rank;
It's no in wealth like Lon'on bank,
To purchase peace and rest:
It's no in makin muckle, mair;
It's no in books, it's no in lear,
To make us truly blest:
If happiness hae not her seat
An centre in the breast,
We may be wise, or rich, or great,
But never can be blest;
Nae treasures, nor pleasures
Could make us happy lang;
The heart ay's the part ay
That makes us right or wrang.

Think ye, that sic as you and I,
Wha drudge an drive thro wet and dry,
Wi never-ceasing toil;
Think ye, are we less blest than they,
Wha scarcely tent us in their way,
As hardly worth their while?
Alas! how aft in haughty mood,
God's creatures they oppress!
Or else, neglecting a' that's guid,
They riot in excess!
Baith careless and fearless
Of either heaven or hell;
Esteeming and deeming
It's a' an idle tale!

Then let us cheerfu' acquiesce,
Nor make our scanty pleasures less,
By pining at our state:
And, even should misfortunes come,
I, here wha sit, hae met wi some –
An's thankfu' for them yet.
They gie the wit of age to youth;
They let us ken oursel;
They make us see the naked truth,
The real guid and ill:
Tho losses an crosses
Be lessons right severe,
There's wit there, ye'll get there,
Ye'll find nae other where.

But tent me, Davie, ace o hearts!
(To say aught less wad wrang the cartes,
And flatt'ry I detest)
This life has joys for you and I;
An joys that riches ne'er could buy,
An joys the very best.
There's a' the pleasures o the heart,

The lover an the frien';
Ye hae your Meg, your dearest part,
And I my darling Jean!
It warms me, it charms me,
To mention but her name:
It heats me, it beets me,
An sets me a' on flame!

O all ye Pow'rs who rule above!
O Thou whose very self art love!
Thou know'st my words sincere!
The life-blood streaming thro my heart,
Or my more dear immortal part,
Is not more fondly dear!
When heart-corroding care and grief
Deprive my soul of rest,
Her dear idea brings relief,
And solace to my breast.
Thou Being, All-seeing,
O hear my fervent pray'r;
Still take her, and make her
Thy most peculiar care!

All hail! ye tender feelings dear!
The smile of love, the friendly tear,
The sympathetic glow!
Long since, this world's thorny ways
Had number'd out my weary days,
Had it not been for you!
Fate still has blest me with a friend,
In ev'ry care and ill;
And oft a more endearing band –
A tie more tender still.
It lightens, it brightens
The tenebrific scene,
To meet with, and greet with
My Davie, or my Jean!

O, how that name inspires my style!
The words come skelpin, rank an file,
Amaist before I ken!
The ready measure rins as fine,
As Phoebus an the famous Nine
Were glowrin owre my pen.
My spaviet Pegasus will limp,
Till ance he's fairly het;
And then he'll hilch, and stilt, an jimp,
And rin an unco fit:
But least then the beast then
Should rue this hasty ride,
I'll light now, and dight now
His sweaty, wizen'd hide.

Burns played 'blackfoot' for Sillar in his courtship of Peggy Orr, but Peggy later jilted Davie and married a shoemaker. Sillar married someone else not long after. Gilbert remembers weeding the garden with Robert as he recited this Epistle, and he thought it was in the summer of 1784. The reference to Jean Armour would indicate that Burns had already met her in the previous April, and not, as thought, in the April of 1785.

Second Epistle to Davie

1785

In these epistles, Burns uses the Scottish Metre of Alexander Montgomerie, the 16th-century Makar who invented it. It is known to scholars as the quartozain, or 'The Cherry and The Slae' from the poem in which Montgomerie first used it, influenced by other Makars like Dunbar and Alexander Scott who had preceded him. It can be seen then that Burns knew these old sources through his reading Watson's collections of Scots poetry, and he helped to preserve them by using them as his stanza form for much of his rhyming work at this time. Montgomerie's metrical scheme remains a very Scottish stanza form. At the time of writing, Burns was still smarting from having Jean repudiate him on her father's order, but was engrossed in preparing material for the Kilmarnock Edition. He did not include either of his epistles to Davie in that famous first book.

Auld Neibour,
I'm three times doubly oer your debtor,
For your auld-farrant, frien'ly letter;
Tho I maun say't I doubt ye flatter,
Ye speak sae fair;
For my puir, silly, rhymin clatter
Some less maun sair.

Hale be your heart, hale be your fiddle,
Lang may your elbuck jink diddle,
To cheer you thro the weary widdle
O war'ly cares;
Till barins' barins kindly cuddle
Your auld grey hairs.

But Davie, lad, I'm red ye're glaikit;
I'm tauld the muse ye hae negleckit;
An, gif it's sae, ye sud by lickit
Until ye fyke;

Sic haun's as you sud ne'er be faikit,
Be hain't wha like.

For me, I'm on Parnassus' brink,
Rivin the words to gar them clink;
Whiles dazed wi love, whiles dazed wi drink,
Wi jads or masons;
An whiles, but aye owre late, I think
Braw sober lessons.

Of a' the thoughtless sons o man,
Commen' to me the bardie clan;
Except it be some idle plan
o rhymin clink,
The devil haet, – that I sud ban –
They ever think.

Nae thought, nae view, nae scheme o livin,
Nae cares to gie us joy or grievin,
But just the pouchie put the neive in,
An while ought's there,
Then, hiltie, skiltie, we gae scrievin,
An fash nae mair.

Leeze me on rhyme! it's aye a treasure,
My chief, amaist my only pleasure;
At hame, a-fiel', at wark, or leisure,
The Muse, poor hizzie!
Tho rough an raploch be her measure,
She's seldom lazy.

Haud to the Muse, my daintie Davie:
The warl' may play you mony a shavie;
But for the Muse, she'll never leave ye,
Tho e'er sae puir,
Na, even tho limpin wi the spavie
Frae door tae door.

The second epistle was published as a Preface to Sillar's own book of poems which came out in Kilmarnock in 1789, in the wake of Burns's volume, but it failed as did most of Sillar's enterprises. He failed as a poet, as a composer, as a schoolmaster and as a grocer, but then, when he was finally made bankrupt, a wealthy brother died and left Davie all his money. Sillar then joined the Irvine Town Council and lived out his last prosperous years until his death in 1830, three years after helping to form the Irvine Burns Club.

Epistle to J. Lapraik

(An old Scottish Bard – 1 April 1785)

John Lapraik was a farmer near Muirkirk. He married John Rankine's sister, Margaret, but then was imprisoned for debt when the failure of the Ayr Bank in 1773 ruined him. While in prison, he turned his hand to rhyming, and on his release, he published a book in 1778, which had a small success and allowed him to set up as an inn-keeper and postmaster at Muirsmill. Burns greatly admired John's work, and recommended him to Johnson at the Scottish Musical Museum, but the real importance of their relationship was that it stimulated Burns to write some of his best work in no less than three epistles to Lapraik.

While briers an woodbines budding green,
An paitricks scraichin loud at e'en,
An morning poussie whiddin seen,
Inspire my muse,
This freedom, in an unknown frien',
I pray excuse.

On Fasten-e'en we had a rockin,
To ca' the crack and weave our stockin;
And there was muckle fun and jokin,
Ye need na doubt;
At length we had a hearty yokin
At sang about.

There was ae sang, amang the rest,
Aboon them a' it pleas'd me best,
That some kind husband had addrest
To some sweet wife;
It thirl'd the heart-strings thro the breast,
A' to the life.

I've scarce heard ought describ'd sae weel,
What gen'rous, manly bosoms feel;
Thought I 'Can this be Pope, or Steele,

Or Beattie's wark?'
They tauld me twas an odd kind chiel
About Muirkirk.

It pat me fidgin-fain to hear't,
An sae about him there I speir't;
Then a' that kent him round declar'd
He had ingine;
That nane excell'd it, few cam near't,
It was sae fine:

That, set him to a pint of ale,
An either douce or merry tale,
Or rhymes an sangs he'd made himsel,
Or witty catches –
Tween Inverness an Teviotdale,
He had few matches.

Then up I gat, an swoor an aith,
Tho I should pawn my pleugh an graith,
Or die a cadger pownie's death,
At some dyke-back,
A pint an gill I'd gie them baith,
To hear your crack.

But, first an foremost, I should tell,
Amaist as soon as I could spell,
I to the crambo-jingle fell;
Tho rude an rough –
Yet crooning to a body's sel
Does weel eneugh.

I am nae poet, in a sense;
But just a rhymer like by chance,
An hae to learning nae pretence;
Yet, what the matter?
Whene'er my muse does on me glance,
I jingle at her.

Your critic-folk may cock their nose,
And say, 'How can you e'er propose,
You wha ken hardly verse frae prose,
To mak a sang?'
But, by your leaves, my learned foes,
Ye're maybe wrang.

What's a' your jargon o your schools –
Your Latin names for horns an stools?
If honest Nature made you fools,
What sairs your grammars?
Ye'd better taen up spades and shools,
Or knappin-hammers.

A set o dull, conceited hashes
Confuse their brains in college classes!
They gang in stirks, and come out asses,
Plain truth to speak;
An syne they think to climb Parnassus
By dint o Greek!

Gie me ae spark o nature's fire,
That's a' the learning I desire;
Then tho I drudge thro dub an mire
At pleugh or cart,
My muse, tho hamely in attire,
May touch the heart.

O for a spunk o Allan's glee,
Or Fergusson's the bauld an slee,
Or bright Lapraik's, my friend to be,
If I can hit it!
That would be lear eneugh for me,
If I could get it.

Now, sir, if ye hae friends enow,
Tho real friends, I b'lieve, are few;
Yet, if your catalogue be fu',

I'se no insist:
But, gif ye want ae friend that's true,
I'm on your list.

I winna blaw about mysel,
As ill I like my fauts to tell;
But friends, an folk that wish me well,
They sometimes roose me;
Tho I maun own, as mony still
As far abuse me.

There's ae wee faut they whiles lay to me,
I like the lasses – Gude forgie me!
For mony a plack they wheedle frae me
At dance or fair;
Maybe some ither thing they gie me,
They weel can spare.

But Mauchline Race, or Mauchline Fair,
I should be proud to meet you there;
We'se gie ae night's discharge to care,
If we forgather;
An hae a swap o rhymin-ware
Wi ane anither.

The four-gill chap, we'se gar him clatter,
An kirsen him wi reekin water;
Syne we'll sit down an tak our whitter,
To cheer our heart;
An faith, we'se be acquainted better
Before we part.

Awa ye selfish, warly race,
Wha think that havins, sense, an grace,
Ev'n love an friendship should give place
To catch-the-plack!
I dinna like to see your face,
Nor hear your crack.

But ye whom social pleasure charms
Whose hearts the tide of kindness warms,
Who hold your being on the terms,
    'Each aid the others,'
Come to my bowl, come to my arms,
    My friends, my brothers!

But, to conclude my lang epistle,
As my auld pen's worn to the gristle,
Twa lines frae you wad gar me fissle,
    Who am, most fervent,
While I can either sing or whistle,
    Your friend and servant.

Lapraik replied with a similar epistle to Burns, sending his son to
deliver it to Burns by hand. The boy found Burns sowing in a field
at Mossgiel. Burns immediately went indoors and replied at once.
It is not known if young Lapraik waited for the answer.

Second Epistle to J. Lapraik
(21 April 1785)

The epistles follow the usual form of the 18th-century verse-letter
– the scene is set, compliments are given to the recipient, then fol-
lows the main matter of the epistle, concluding with an expres-
sion of friendship. In this one, which is mainly autobiographical,
Burns considers that life might just be a matter of luck and he's
had nothing but bad luck of late, but contentment might just be
the fact of accepting one's lot.

> While new-ca'd kye rowte at the stake
> An pownies reek in pleugh or braik,
> This hour on e'enin's edge I take,
> To own I'm debtor
> To honest-hearted, auld Lapraik,
> For his kind letter.
>
> Forjesket sair, with weary legs,
> Rattlin the corn out-owre the rigs,
> Or dealing thro amang the naigs
> Their ten-hours' bite,
> My awkart Muse sair pleads and begs
> I would na write.
>
> The tapetless, ramfeezl'd hizzie,
> She's saft at best an something lazy:
> Quo she, 'Ye ken we've been sae busy
> This month an mair,
> That trowth, my head is grown right dizzie,
> An something sair.'
>
> Her dowff excuses pat me mad;
> 'Conscience,' says I, 'ye thowless jade!
> I'll write, an that a hearty blaud,
> This vera night;
> So dinna ye affront your trade,
> But rhyme it right.'

'Shall bauld Lapraik, the king o hearts,
Tho mankind were a pack o cartes,
Roose you sae weel for your deserts,
In terms sae friendly;
Yet ye'll neglect to shaw your parts
An thank him kindly?'

Sae I gat paper in a blink,
An down gaed stumpie in the ink:
Quoth I, 'Before I sleep a wink,
I vow I'll close it;
An if ye winna mak it clink,
By Jove, I'll prose it!'

Sae I've begun to scrawl, but whether
In rhyme, or prose, or baith thegither;
Or some hotch-potch that's rightly neither,
Let time mak proof;
But I shall scribble down some blether
Just clean aff-loof.

My worthy friend, ne'er grudge an carp,
Tho fortune use you hard an sharp;
Come, kittle up your moorland harp
Wi gleesome touch!
Ne'er mind how Fortune waft and warp;
She's but a bitch.

She's gien me mony a jirt an fleg,
Sin I could striddle owre a rig;
But, by the Lord, tho I should beg
Wi lyart pow,
I'll laugh an sing, an shake my leg,
As lang's I dow!

Now comes the sax-an-twentieth simmer
I've seen the bud upon the timmer,
Still persecuted by the limmer

Frae year to year;
But yet, despite the kittle kimmer,
I, Rob, am here.

Do ye envy the city gent,
Behint a kist to lie an sklent;
Or pursue-proud, big wi cent per cent,
An muckle wame,
In some bit brugh to represent
A bailie's name?

Or is't the paughty, feudal thane,
Wi ruffl'd sark an glancing cane,
Wha thinks himsel nae sheep-shank bane,
But lordly stalks;
While caps and bonnets aff are taen,
As by he walks?

'O Thou wha gies us each guid gift!
Gie me o wit an sense a lift,
Then turn me, if thou please, adrift,
Thro Scotland wide;
Wi cits nor lairds I wadna shift,
In a' their pride!'

Were this the charter of our state,
'On pain o hell be rich an great,'
Damnation then would be our fate,
Beyond remead;
But, thanks to heaven, that's no the gate
We learn our creed.

For thus the royal mandate ran,
When first the human race began;
'The social, friendly, honest man,
Whate'er he be –
Tis he fulfils great Nature's plan,
And none but he.'

O mandate glorious and divine!
The ragged followers o the Nine,
Poor, thoughtless devils! yet may shine
In glorious light,
While sordid sons o Mammon's line
Are dark as night!

Tho here they scrape, an squeeze, an growl,
Their worthless nievefu' of a soul
May in some future carcase howl,
The forest's fright;
Or in some day-detesting owl
May shun the light.

Then may Lapraik and Burns arise,
To reach their native, kindred skies,
And sing their pleasures, hopes an joys,
In some mild sphere;
Still closer knit in friendship's ties,
Each passing year!

When his wife died, Lapraik married Janet Anderson, but he kept
up his verse correspondence with Burns, which prompted the lat-
ter's third epistle to Lapraik.

Epistle to William Simpson

(Schoolmaster, Ochiltree – May 1785)

William Simpson of Ochiltree was trained at Glasgow University to be a minsister but became a teacher instead. He also had pretensions to be a poetaster himself, like Lapraik, and wrote a flattering verse-letter to Burns which elicited this reply in the same vein. Burns had just become a father for the first time via Bess Paton and was watching Jean Armour's condition *'arising more and more to view'*. It was no surprise that he had his first *'irregularities of the heart combined with headaches and fainting fits'* around this time..

I gat your letter, winsome Willie;
Wi gratefu heart I thank you brawlie;
Tho I maun say't, I wad be silly,
And unco vain,
Should I believe, my coaxin billie
Your flatterin strain.

But I'se believe ye kindly meant it:
I sud be laith to think ye hinted
Ironic satire, sidelins sklented
On my poor Musie;
Tho in sic phraisin terms ye've penn'd it,
I scarce excuse ye.

My senses wad be in a creel,
Should I but dare a hope to speel
Wi Allan, or wi Gilbertfield,
The braes o fame;
Or Fergusson, the writer-chiel,
A deathless name.

(O Fergusson! thy glorious parts
Ill suited law's dry, musty arts!
My curse upon your whunstane hearts,

Ye E'nbrugh gentry!
The tithe o what ye waste at cartes
Wad stow'd his pantry!)

Yet when a tale comes i' my head,
Or lassies gie my heart a screed –
As whiles they're like to be my dead,
(O sad disease!)
I kittle up my rustic reed;
It gies me ease.

Auld Coila now may fidge fu' fain,
She's gotten poets o her ain;
Chiels wha their chanters winna hain,
But tune their lays,
Till echoes a' resound again
Her weel-sung praise.

Nae poet thought her worth his while,
To set her name in measur'd style;
She lay like some unkenn'd-of-isle
Beside New Holland,
Or whare wild-meeting oceans boil
Besouth Magellan.

Ramsay an famous Fergusson gied
Forth an Tay a lift aboon;
Yarrow an Tweed, to monie a tune,
Owre Scotland rings;
While Irwin, Lugar, Ayr, an Doon
Naebody sings.

Th' Illissus, Tiber, Thames, an Seine,
Glide sweet in monie a tunefu' line:
But Willie, set your fit to mine,
An cock your crest;
We'll gar our streams an burnies shine
Up wi the best!

We'll sing auld Coila's plains an fells,
Her moors red-brown wi heather bells,
Her banks an braes, her dens and dells,
Whare glorious Wallace
Aft bure the gree, as story tells,
Frae Suthron billies.

At Wallace' name, what Scottish blood
But boils up in a spring-tide flood!
Oft have our fearless fathers strode
By Wallace' side,
Still pressing onward, red-wat-shod,
Or glorious died!

O, sweet are Coila's haughs an woods,
When lintwhites chant amang the buds,
And jinkin hares, in amorous whids,
Their loves enjoy;
While thro the braes the cushat croods
With wailfu' cry!

Ev'n winter bleak has charms to me,
When winds rave thro the naked tree;
Or frosts on hills of Ochiltree
Are hoary gray;
Or blinding drifts wild-furious flee,
Dark'ning the day!

O Nature! a' thy shews an forms
To feeling, pensive hearts hae charms!
Whether the summer kindly warms,
Wi life an light;
Or winter howls, in gusty storms,
The lang, dark night!

The muse, nae poet ever fand her,
Till by himsel he learn'd to wander,
Adown some trottin burn's meander,

An no think lang:
O sweet to stray, an pensive ponder
A heart-felt sang!

The warly race may drudge an drive,
Hog-shouther, jundie, stretch, an strive;
Let me fair Nature's face descrive,
And I, wi pleasure,
Shall let the busy, grumbling hive
Bum owre their treasure.

Fareweel, 'my rhyme-composing' brither!
We've been owre lang unkenn'd to ither:
Now let us lay our heads thegither,
In love fraternal:
May envy wallop in a tether,
Black fiend, infernal!

While Highlandmen hate tools an taxes;
While moorlan's herds like guid, fat braxies;
While terra firma, on her axis,
Diurnal turns;
Count on a friend, in faith an practice,
In Robert Burns.

It was in the final stanza of this epistle that Burns used the name 'Burns' for the first time in print, and only so that it might rhyme with 'turns'. He and Gilbert decided to adopt this spelling of their surname on their removal to Mossgiel and to disassociate themselves from their father's litigatious affairs concluded the previous year in his favour at the High Court in Edinburgh. This name-change was formally adopted in March 1786.

Epistle to John Goldie

(August 1785)

John Goldie was the typical Augustan man of all parts – cabinet-maker, wine merchant, mathematician, astronomer and speculator in coal-mines and canals – but who, more than anything, was addicted to theology. In 1779 he published an *Essay on Various Important Subjects Moral and Divine – being an attempt to distinguish True from False Religion*. Popularly known as 'Goudie's Bible', it was re-printed in 1785, and prompted Burns to write this epistle. Other works by Goldie included *The Gospel recovered from its Captive State and restored to its Original Purity* – in six volumes – London 1784, and also *A Treatise on the Evidence of a Deity* in 1809. Goldie admired Burns's religious views as much as his poetry, and was one of the nine guarantors to the Kilmarnock Edition.

O Gowdie, terror o the whigs,
Dread o blackcoats and rev'rend wigs!
Sour Bigotry, on her last legs,
Girns an looks back,
Wishing the ten Egyptian plagues
May seize you quick.

Poor gapin, glowrin Superstition!
Wae's me, she's in a sad condition:
Fye: bring Black Jock, her state physician,
To see her water;
Alas, there's ground for great suspicion
She'll ne'er get better.

Enthusiasm's past redemption,
Gane in a gallopin consumption:
Not a' her quacks, wi a' their gumption,
Can ever mend her;
Her feeble pulse gies strong presumption,
She'll soon surrender.

Auld Orthodoxy lang did grapple,
For every hole to get a stapple;
But now she fetches at the thrapple,
An fights for breath;
Haste, gie her name up in the chapel,
Near unto death.

It's you an Taylor are the chief
To blame for a' this black mischief;
But, could the Lord's ain folk get leave,
A toom tar barrel
An twa red peats wad bring relief,
And end the quarrel.

For me, my skill's but very sma,
An skill in prose I've nane ava;
But quietlins-wise, between us twa,
Weel may you speed!
And tho they sud your sair misca',
Ne'er fash your head.

E'en swinge the dogs, and thresh them sicker!
The mair they squeel aye chap the thicker;
And still 'mang hands a hearty bicker
O something stout;
It gars an owthor's pulse beat quicker,
And helps his wit.

There's naething like the honest nappy;
Whare'll ye e'er see men sae happy,
Or women sonsie, saft an sappy,
Tween morn and morn,
As them wha like to taste the drappie,
In glass or horn?

I've seen me daez't upon a time,
I scarce could wink or see a styme;
Just ae half-mutchkin does me prime, –

Ought less is little –
Then back I rattle on the rhyme,
As gleg's a whittle.

The other Goldie known to Burns later in his life could not have
been more different. Colonel Tam Goldie of Goldilea, near Dumfries,
was president of the Loyal Natives, a right-wing political group
formed in 1793 to 'support the laws of the country'. They spread
verses attacking Burns and his 'revolutionary' friend and Burns
replied,

Ye true 'Loyal Natives' attend to my songs;
In uproar and riot rejoice the night long!
From Envy and Hatred your core is exempt,
But where is your shield from the darts of Contempt?

Thomas Goldie was not noted for his brains, although he served
as Commissary for the Sheriff Court in Dumfries. This appoint-
ment prompted Burns to the epigram,

Lord, to account who does Thee call,
Or e'er dispute Thy pleasure?
Else why within so thick a wall,
Enclose so poor a treasure?

Third Epistle to J. Lapraik

(13 September 1785)

Burns at this time was in his creative high wave. As well as all the poems of this glorious year, he had written an Attestation of Marriage with Jean to mollify the Armours in view of her discovered pregnancy, and completed *The Jolly Beggars* after a night out with the boys in Poosie Nansie's Tavern, and then, despite having a harvest to get in, he wrote this last epistle to Lapraik.

Guid speed and furder to you, Johnie,
Guid health, hale han's, an weather bonie;
Now, when ye're nickin down fu cannie
The staff o bread,
May ye ne'er want a stoup o bran'y
To clear your head!

May Boreas never thresh your rigs,
Nor kick your rickles aff their legs,
Sendin the stuff oer muirs an haggs
Like drivin wrack!
But may the tapmost grain that wags
Come to the sack!

I'm bizzie, too, an skelpin at it,
But bitter, daudin showers hae wat it;
Sae my auld stumpie pen I gat it
Wi muckle wark,
An took my jocteleg an whatt it,
Like onie clark.

It's now twa month that I'm your debtor,
For your braw, nameless, dateless letter,
Abusin me for harsh ill-nature
On holy men,
While deil a hair yoursel ye're better,
But mair profane.

But let the kirk-folk ring their bells,
Let's sing about our noble sels:
We'll cry nae jads frae heathen hills
To help, or roose us;
But browster wives an whisky stills,
They are the muses.

Your friendship, Sir, I winna quat it,
An if ye mak objections at it,
Then hand in neive some day we'll knot it,
An witness take,
An when wi usquabae we've wat it
It winna break.

But if the beast an branks be spar'd
Till kye be gaun without the herd,
An a' the vittel in the yard,
An theekit right,
I mean your ingle-side to guard
Ae winter night.

Then muse-inspirin' aqua-vitae
Shall make us baith sae blythe and witty,
Till ye forget ye're auld an gatty,
An be as canty
As ye were nine years less than thretty-
Sweet ane an twenty!

But stooks are cowpit wi the blast,
And now the sinn keeks in the west,
Then I maun rin amang the rest,
An quat my chanter;
Sae I subscribe myself in haste,
Yours, Rab the Ranter.

John Lapraik died in 1807 and the Third Epistle was published by
Cromek in his *Reliques* in the following year.

Epistle to Rev John McMath

(Inclosing a copy of 'Holy Willie's Prayer' which he had
requested – Sept.17, 1785)

This epistle comes only a matter of days after his last to Lapraik
and gives yet another indication of what a poetic surge he was on
at this time. He could have written to anyone in any style on any
subject at any length and without strain on either his eyes, his
hand or his imagination. Despite repeating bouts of small dis-
comforts, as long as he had the goosefeather in his hand and
paper before him, he was alive to his very finger-tips. This epistle
also gives a fair idea of Burns's attitude to religion, particularly to
sectarianism and bigotry, and allows him to attack again his *bête-
noir*, hypocrisy.

> While at the stook the shearers cow'r
> To shun the bitter blaudin show'r,
> Or in gulravage rinnin scowr
> To pass the time,
> To you I dedicate the hour
> In idle rhyme.
>
> My Musie, tir'd wi mony a sonnet
> On gown, an ban', an douse black bonnet,
> Is grown right eerie now she's done it,
> Lest they should blame her,
> An rouse their holy thunder on it
> An anathem her.
>
> I own twas rash, an rather hardy,
> That I, a simple, country bardie,
> Should meddle wi a pack sae sturdy,
> Wha, if they ken me,
> Can easy, wi a single wordie,
> Lowse hell upon me.

But I gae mad at their grimaces,
Their sighin, cantin, grace-proud faces,
Their three-mile prayers, an half-mile graces,
Their raxin conscience,
Whase greed, revenge, an pride disgraces
Waur nor their nonsense.

There's Gaw'n, misca'd waur than a beast,
Wha has mair honour in his breast
Than mony scores as guid's the priest
Wha sae abus'd him:
And may a bard no crack his jest
What way they've us'd him?

See him, the poor man's friend in need,
The gentleman in word an deed –
An shall his fame an' honour bleed
By worthless, skellums,
An not a muse erect her head
To cowe the blellums?

O Pope, had I thy satire's darts
To gie the rascals their deserts,
I'd rip their rotten, hollow hearts,
An tell aloud
Their jugglin hocus-pocus arts
To cheat the crowd.

God knows, I'm no the thing I should be,
Nor am I even the thing I could be,
But twenty times I rather would be
An atheist clean,
Than under gospel colours hid be
Just for a screen.

An honest man may like a glass,
An honest man may like a lass,
But mean revenge, an malice fause

He'll still disdain,
An then cry zeal for gospel laws,
Like some we ken.

They take religion in their mouth;
They talk o mercy, grace, an truth,
For what? – to gie their malice skouth
On some puir wight,
An hunt him down, owre right and ruth,
To ruin straight.

All hail, Religion! maid divine!
Pardon a muse sae mean as mine,
Who in her rough imperfect line
Thus daurs to name thee;
To stigmatise false friends of thine
Can ne'er defame thee.

Tho blotch't and foul wi mony a stain,
An far unworthy of thy train,
With trembling voice I tune my strain,
To join with those
Who boldly dare thy cause maintain
In spite of foes:

In spite o crowds, in spite o mobs,
In spite o undermining jobs,
In spite o dark banditti stabs
At worth an merit,
By scoundrels, even wi holy robes,
But hellish spirit.

O Ayr! my dear, my native ground,
Within thy presbyterial bound
A candid liberal band is found
Of public teachers,
As men, as Christians too, renown'd,
An manly preachers.

Sir, in that circle you are nam'd;
Sir, in that circle you are fam'd;
An some, by whom your doctrine's blam'd
(Which gies you honour)
Even, sir, by them your heart's esteem'd,
An winning manner.

Pardon this freedom I have taen,
An if impertinent I've been,
Impute it not, good Sir, in ane
Whase heart ne'er wrang'd ye,
But to his utmost would befriend
Ought that belang'd ye.

'Guid McMath' succeeded Dr Woodrow as minister at Tarbolton, but, unfortunately, took to drink and resigned to join the army as a private soldier. He retired at length to the Isle of Mull where he died in 1825.

Epistle to James Smith

1786

Jamie Smith was Burns's *confidante* and co-conspirator in many of the village wooings indulged in by Burns and his friends around Mauchline from 1785. Smith was in receipt of some of Burns's frankest letters on this subject, as he too had become the father of a love-child, and was in some sympathy with his friend's pre-marital complications. Smith was a member of the convivial 'Court of Equity' at the Whitefoord and his loyalty to Burns, his wit and his amorous propensities were much appreciated by the fledgling poet. Burns headed the epistle with a quote from Blair:

> *Friendship, mysterious cement of the soul!*
> *Sweet'ner of Life, and soldier of Society!*
> *I owe thee much.*

In the seventh stanza, Burns gives the first notice of his putting his verses into a book, and he can't hide his excitement in the lines that follow.

Dear Smith, the slee'st, pawkie thief,
That e'er attempted stealth or rief!
Ye surely hae some warlock-brief
Owre human hearts;
For ne'er a bosom yet was prief
Against your arts.

For me, I swear by sun an moon,
An ev'ry star that blinks aboon,
Ye've cost me twenty pair o shoon,
Just gaun to see you;
An ev'ry ither pair that's done,
Mair taen I'm wi you.

That auld, capricious carlin, Nature,
To mak amends for scrimpit stature,

She's turn'd you off, a human creature
On her first plan,
And in her freaks, on ev'ry feature
She's wrote the Man.

Just now I've taen the fit o rhyme,
My barmie noddle's working prime.
My fancy yerkit up sublime,
Wi hasty summon;
Hae ye a leisure-moment's time
To hear what's comin?

Some rhyme a neibor's name to lash;
Some rhyme (vain thought!) for needfu' cash;
Some rhyme to court the countra clash,
An raise a din;
For me, an aim I never fash;
I rhyme for fun.

The star that rules my luckless lot,
Has fated me the russet coat,
An damn'd my fortune to the groat;
But, in requit,
Has blest me with a random-shot
O countra wit.

This while my notion's taen a sklent,
To try my fate in guid, black prent;
But still the mair I'm that way bent,
Something cries 'Hooklie!'
I red you, honest man, tak tent?
Ye'll shaw your folly;

'There's ither poets, much your betters,
Far seen in Greek, deep men o letters,
Hae thought they had ensur'd their debtors,
A' future ages;
Now moths deform, in shapeless tatters,
Their unknown pages.'

Then farewell hopes o laurel-boughs,
To garland my poetic brows!
Henceforth I'll rove where busy ploughs
Are whistlin thrang,
An teach the lanely heights an howes
My rustic sang.

I'll wander on, wi tentless heed
How never-halting moments speed,
Till fate shall snap the brittle thread;
Then, all unknown,
I'll lay me with th inglorious dead
Forgot and gone!

But why o death being a tale?
Just now we're living sound and hale;
Then top and maintop crowd the sail,
Heave Care oer-side!
And large, before Enjoyment's gale,
Let's tak the tide.

This life, sae far's I understand,
Is a' enchanted fairy-land,
Where Pleasure is the magic-wand,
That, wielded right,
Maks hours like minutes, hand in hand,
Dance by fu' light.

The magic-wand then let us wield;
For ance that five-an-forty's speel'd,
See, crazy, weary, joyless eild,
Wi wrinkl'd face,
Comes hostin, hirplin owre the field,
Wi creepin pace.

When ance life's day draws near the gloamin,
Then fareweel vacant, careless roamin;

An fareweel cheerfu' tankards foamin,
An social noise:
An fareweel dear, deluding woman,
The joy of joys!

O Life! how pleasant, in thy morning,
Young Fancy's rays the hills adorning!
Cold-pausing Caution's lesson scorning,
We frisk away,
Like school-boys, at th' expected warning,
To joy an play.

We wander there, we wander here,
We eye the rose upon the brier,
Unmindful that the thorn is near,
Among the leaves;
And tho the puny wound appear,
Short while it grieves.

Some, lucky, find a flow'ry spot,
For which they never toil'd nor swat;
They drink the sweet and eat the fat,
But care or pain;
And haply eye the barren hut
With high disdain.

With steady aim, some Fortune chase;
Keen hope does ev'ry sinew brace;
Thro fair, thro foul, they urge the race,
An seize the prey:
Then cannie, in some cozie place,
They close the day.

And others, like your humble servan',
Poor wights! nae rules nor roads observin,
To right or left eternal swervin,
They zig-zag on;

Till, curst with age, obscure an starvin,
They aften groan.

Alas! what bitter toil an straining –
But truce with peevish, poor complaining!
Is fortune's fickle Luna waning?
E'n let her gang!
Beneath what light she has remaining,
Let's sing our sang.

My pen I here fling to the door,
And kneel, ye Pow'rs! and warm implore,
'Tho I should wander Terra o'er,
In all her climes,
Grant me but this, I ask no more,
Aye rowth o rhymes.'

'Gie dreepin roasts to countra lairds,
Till icicles hing frae their beards;
Gie fine braw claes to fine life-guards,
And maids of honour;
An yill an whisky gie to cairds,
Until they sconner.'

'A title, Dempster merits it;
A garter gie to Willie Pitt;
Gie wealth to some be-ledger'd cit,
In cent per cent;
But give me real, sterling wit,
And I'm content.'

'While ye are pleas'd to keep me hale,
I'll sit down oer my scanty meal,
Be't water-brose or muslin-kail,
Wi cheerfu' face,
As lang's the Muses dinna fail
To say the grace,'

An anxious ee I never throws
Behint my lug, or by my nose;
I jouk beneath Misfortune's blows
As weel's I may;
Sworn foe to sorrow, care, and prose,
I rhyme away.

O ye douce folk that live by rule,
Grave, tideless-blooded, calm an cool,
Compar'd wi you – O fool! fool! fool!
How much unlike!
Your hearts are just a standing pool,
Your lives, a dyke!

Nae hair-brain'd, sentimental traces
In your unletter'd, nameless faces!
In *arioso* trills and graces
Ye never stray;
But *gravissimo*, solemn basses
Ye hum away.

Ye are sae grave, nae doubt ye're wise;
Nae ferly tho ye do despise
The hairum-scairum, ram-stam boys,
The rattling squad:
I see ye upward cast your eyes –
Ye ken the road!

Whilst I – but I shall haud me there,
Wi you I'll scarce gang ony where –
Then, Jamie, I shall say nae mair,
But quat my sang,
Content wi you to mak a pair.
Whare'er I gang.

Smith was in the drapery trade with a shop in Mauchline but after
a bad investment with calico-printing in Linlithgow in 1787, he

emigrated in the following year to St Louis, Jamaica, and died there, still a young man. His may have been a disappointing life but he inspired one of Burns's best efforts in this epistle.

Epistle to Major Logan

(Mossgiel, 30 October 1786)

Burns really enjoyed meeting this cheerful, convivial professional soldier who once described his incarceration as a prisoner in the American War as *'plenty to eat and drink and no parades'*. The ex-officer was an accomplished fiddler, and he and Burns often had sessions at Park House in Ayr where the major lived with his mother and unmarried sister in some comfort and not a little indulgence. The sister was also an attraction for Burns, but it was her brother, William, who got the Epistle.

Hail, thairm-inspirin, rattlin Willie!
Tho fortune's road be rough an hilly
To every fiddling, rhyming billie,
We never heed,
But take it like the unback'd filly,
Proud o her speed.

May still your life from day to day
Nae lente largo in the play,
But allegretto forte gay,
Harmonious flow,
A sweeping, kindling, bauld strathspey –
Encore! Bravo!

A' blessings on the cheery gang
Wha dearly like a jig or sang,
An never think o right an wrang
But square an rule,
But as the clegs o feeling stang,
Are wise or fool.

My hand-wal'd curse keep hard in chase
The harpy, hoodock, purse-proud race,
Wha count on poortith as disgrace!
Their tuneless hearts,

May fireside discords jar a bass
To a' their parts!

But come, your hand, my careless brither!
I' th' ither warl, if ther's anither –
An that there is, I've little swither
About the matter –
We, cheek for chow, shall jog thegither –
I'se ne'er bid better!

We've faults and failins – granted clearly!
We're frail, backsliding mortals merely;
Eve's bonie squad, priests wyte them sheerly
For our grand fa';
But still, but still, I like them dearly –
God bless them a'!

Ochon for poor Castilian drinkers,
When they fa' foul o earthly jinkers!
The witching, curs'd, delicious blinkers
Hae put me hyte,
An gart me weet my waukrife winkers,
Wi girnin spite.

But by yon moon – and that's high swearin!
An every star within my hearin,
An by her een wha was a dear ane
I'll ne'er forget,
I hope to gie the jads a clearin,
In fair play yet!

My loss I mourn, but not repent it;
I'll seek my pursie whare I tint it;
Ance to the Indies I were wonted,
Some cantraip hour
By some sweet elf I'll yet be dinted;
Then vive l'amour

Faites mes baisemains respectueuse
To sentimental sister Susie,

And honest Lucky: no to roose you,
Ye may be proud
That sic a couple Fate allows ye,
To grace your blood.

Nae mair at present can I measure,
An trowth! my rhymin ware's nae treasure;
But when in Ayr, some half-hour's leisure,
Be't light, be't dark
Sir Bard will do himself the pleasure
To call at Park.

His eating and drinking excesses eventually led to Major Logan's seeking medical help. The minister called to sympathise with his parishioner's suffering and to warn him that he will require fortitude, to which the gallant major replied, '*You mean fifty-tude, I think.*'

Epistle to A Young Friend

(15 May 1786)

The young friend concerned here was Andrew Hunter Aiken, the first son of Robert Aiken, 'Orator Bob', the Ayr lawyer and Burns's keenest promoter in the bid for subscriptions for the Kilmarnock Edition. It seems that young Andrew was going off to Liverpool to start his commercial career in shipping, and the father asked Burns for a few lines to mark the occasion. He got more than he knew, and it is to be hoped that young Andrew appreciated the basic wisdom of these words of a man who was only 27 himself and had never set foot outside of Ayrshire. At any rate, the advice seemed to have had its effect, as young Andrew went on to become a very successful merchant, eventually settling in Riga, on the Baltic, where he became the British Consul, and where he subsequently died in 1831.

I lang hae thought, my youthfu' friend,
A' something to have sent you,
Tho it should serve nae ither end
Than just a kind memento:
But how the subject-theme may gang,
Let time and chance determine;
Perhaps it may turn out a sang:
Perhaps turn out a sermon.

Ye'll try the world soon, my lad;
And, Andrew dear, believe me,
Ye'll find mankind an unco squad,
And muckle they may grieve ye:
For care and trouble set your thought,
Ev'n when your end's attained;
And a' your views may come to nought,
Where ev'ry nerve is strained.

I'll no say, men are villains a';
The real, harden'd wicked,
Wha hae nae check but human law,
Are to a few restricked;
But, Och! mankind are unco weak,
An little to be trusted;
If self the wavering balance shake,
It's rarely right adjusted!

Yet they wha fa' in fortune's strife,
Their fate we shouldna censure;
For still, th' important end of life
They equally may answer;
A man may hae an honest heart,
Tho poortith hourly stare him;
A man may tak a neibor's part,
Yet hae nae cash to spare him.

Aye free, aff-han', your story tell,
When wi a bosom crony;
But still keep something to yoursel,
Ye scarcely tell to ony:
Conceal yoursel as weel's ye can
Frae critical dissection;
But keek thro ev'ry other man,
Wi sharpen'd, sly inspection.

The sacred lowe o weel-plac'd love,
Luxuriantly indulge it;
But never tempt th' illicit rove,
Tho naething should divulge it:
I waive the quantum o the sin,
The hazard of concealing;
But, Och! it hardens a' within,
And petrifies the feeling!

To catch dame Fortune's golden smile,
Assiduous wait upon her;

And gather gear by ev'ry wile
That's justified by honour;
Not for to hide it in a hedge,
Nor for a train attendant;
But for the glorious privilege
Of being independent.

The fear o hell's a hangman's whip,
To haud the wretch in order;
But where ye feel your honour grip,
Let that aye be your border;
Its slightest touches, instant pause –
Debar a' side-pretences;
And resolutely keep its laws,
Uncaring consequences.

The great Creator to revere,
Must sure become the creature;
But still the preaching cant forbear,
And ev'n the rigid feature:
Yet ne'er with wits profane to range,
Be complaisance extended;
An atheist-laugh's a poor exchange
For Deity offended!

When ranting round in pleasure's ring,
Religion may be blinded;
Or if she gie a random sting,
It may be little minded;
But when on life we're tempest driv'n –
A conscience but a canker –
A correspondence fix'd wi Heav'n,
Is sure a noble anchor!

Adieu, dear, amiable youth!
Your heart can ne'er be wanting!
May prudence, fortitude, and truth,
Erect your brow undaunting!

In ploughman phrase, 'God send you speed,'
Still daily to grow wiser;
And may ye better reck the rede,
Then ever did th' adviser!

When the epistle appeared as one of the six in the Kilmarnock
Edition, it caused a little controversy, in that William Niven of
Kirkoswald, a schooldays friend of Burns and his first correspon-
dent, claimed that the epistle had first been addressed to him. In
this, he was supported by the Reverend Hamilton Paul, who had
known them both, but when challenged to produce the original
manuscript, Niven could not do so. Niven, who became Deputy-
Lieutenant for Ayrshire in 1810, never made his claim known to
Burns as far as is known, but he insisted to the end of his life that
he was the original dedicatee.

Epistle to Hugh Parker

(12 June 1788)

Hugh was brother to Major William and both were friends from
the time of the first Kilmarnock printing. The major was the
Right Worshipful Master of the Lodge and Hugh was a banker, of
whom Burns wrote – '*I hope Hughoc is going on and prospering
with God and Miss McCauslin.*' Burns, at this time, had taken
over at Ellisland but, as yet, hadn't a house to live in. While it was
being built, he squatted in a hut on the property, and here accu-
rately described his circumstances to Mrs Dunlop.

> *Here I am, a solitary inmate of an old smoky spence; far
> from every object I love, or by whom I am beloved; nor any
> acquaintance older than yesterday except Jenny Geddes,
> the old mare I ride on.*

Jenny Geddes was the horse he had bought in the Grassmarket of
Edinburgh the year before for his Border tour and she was still
with him. Yet, despite the conditions, he could still take time to
write an epistle, even if he said on the end line that it wasn't.

In this strange land, this uncouth clime,
A land unknown to prose or rhyme;
Where words ne'er cross't the Muse's heckles,
Nor limpit in poetic shackles:
A land that Prose did never view it,
Except when drunk he stacher't thro it;
Here, ambush'd by the chimla cheek,
Hid in an atmosphere of reek,
I hear a wheel thrum i' the neuk,
I hear it – for in vain I leuk.
The red peat gleams, a fiery kernel,
Enhusked by a fog infernal:
Here, for my wonted rhyming raptures,
I sit and count my sins by chapters;

For life and spunk like ither Christians,
I'm dwindled down to mere existence,
Wi nae converse but Gallowa bodies,
Wi nae kenn'd face but Jenny Geddes,
Jenny, my Pegasean pride!
Dowie she saunters down Nithside,
And aye a westlin leuk she throws,
While tears hap oer her auld brown nose!
Was it for this, wi cannie care,
Thou bure the Bard through many a shire?
At howes, or hillocks never stumbled,
And late or early never grumbled?
O had I power like inclination,
I'd heeze thee up a constellation,
To canter with the Sagitarre,
Or loup the ecliptic like a bar;
Or turn the pole like any arrow;
Or, when auld Phoebus bids good-morrow,
Down the zodiac urge the race,
And cast dirt on his godship's face;
For I could lay my bread and kail
He'd ne'er cast saut upo thy tail.
Wi a' this care and a' this grief,
And sma, sma prospect of relief,
And nought but peat reek i' my head,
How can I write what ye can read?
Tarbolton, twenty-fourth o June,
Ye'll find me in a better tune;
But till we meet and weet our whistle,
Tak this excuse for nae epistle.

It is good to acknowledge the place of the Parker brothers in the
Burns Story, and how Willie had drummed up support for the
poet in Kilmarnock, enough to set the printer's presses rolling and
set the embryo poet on his way. Of course, the masonic contacts
were invaluable all round, and it was not the first time Burns was

to be helped by fellow-members of the craft. From Lodge St David No 174 at Tarbolton, where he was raised to the degree of Master in 1784, to St Johns Lodge at Kilmarnock in 1786, which referred to him as 'Poet Burns' for the first time, to his investiture as Masonic Bard of the Canongate Lodge of Kilwinning No 2 on 1 March 1787 he knew nothing but helping hands and handshakes all the way through, till, at St Andrew's Lodge, in the presence of all the lodges of Scotland, and visitors from England, the Right Worshipful Grand Master installed him as Poet Laureate of the Scottish Craft Freemasonry, a position he still holds to this day.

It was in another St Andrew's Lodge (in Irvine) that he wrote his *Stanza Added in a Mason Lodge*, with an aside made regarding the drink taken by him at masonic meetings: '*Do not upbraid me... If I do not drink with them, they won't thank me for my company.*'

> *Then fill up a bumper, and make it oerflow,*
> *And honours Masonic prepare for to throw,*
> *May every true brother of the Compass and Square*
> *Have a big-bellied bottle when harrassed with care!*

And honours masonic were certainly thrown at him. Lodge St Ebbe No 70 made him a Royal Arch Mason on 19 May 1787, and it was thanks to these events, and other rites and ceremonies, that this ertswhile ploughman was able to move with such ease and poise through the then hierarchy of Augustan Scotland. Everyone involved in the Edinburgh second edition was masonic, as were most of his Edinburgh friends and temporary landlords. There are lodges named after him all over the world, and even the ubiquitous Burns Supper has its basis in masonic 'harmony boards'. His work is littered with masonic allusions. In the *Address to the Deil* –

> *When mason's mystic word an grip*
> *In storms and tempest raise you up...*

And in 'On the Late Captain Grose's peregrinations through Scotland' –

> Of Eve's first fire he has a cinder;
> Auld Tubalcain's fire-shool and fender...

Tubal Cain, the first artificer in metals, is the password for the raising of a mason to the degree of Master Mason. Many of the characters in his poems were fraternally recognised. 'Dr Hornbook', for instance, was fellow-mason John Wilson. So was Tam Samson, of the Elegy for Tam Samson and many 'brethren of the mystic level may hing their head in wofu' bevel...' including the Parker brothers.

Burns referred to himself in one letter to George Thomson as the Priest of the Nine, in which he meant the Nine Muses, but he might easily have meant the Nine Masonic Gentlemen of Kilmarnock who made the First Edition possible, and therefore allowed Burns's poetic legacy in verse and song to be made available to posterity.

When he thought he was emigrating in 1786, it was to his fellow-masons he said his official goodbye to Scotland in The Farewell to the Brethren of St James's Lodge, Tarbolton.

> Adieu! a heart-warm, fond adieu;
> Dear Brothers of the Mystic Tie!
> Ye favoured, ye enlighten'd few
> Companions of my social joy!
> Tho I to foreign lands must hie,
> Pursuing Fortune's slidd'ry ba';
> With melting heart and brinful eye,
> I'll mind you still, tho far awa.
>
> Oft have I met your social band,
> And spent the cheerful festive night:
> Oft, honour's with supreme command,
> Presided oer the Sons of Light;
> And by that Hieroglyphic bright,
> Which none but Craftsmen ever saw!

Strong Mem'ry on my heart shall write
Those happy scenes, when far awa.

May freedom, Harmony, and Love,
Unite you in the Grand Design,
Beneath th' Omnicient Eye above –
The glorious Architect Divine,
That you may keep th' Unerring Line,
Still rising by the Plummet's Law,
Till Order bright completely shine,
Shall be my pray'r when far awa.

And you, farewell! whose merits claim
Justly that Highest Badge to wear:
Heav'n bless your honour'd noble name,
To Masonry and Scotia dear!
A last request permit me here
When yearly ye assemble a',
One round, I ask it with a tear,
To him, the bard that's far awa.

Fortunately, he was only to be as far away as Edinburgh.

Epistle to James Tennant of Glenconnor

1788

James Tennant was the miller at Ochiltree and the eldest son of John Tennant of Glenconnor (*guid auld Glen*), the friend and neighbour to William Burness at Alloway, and the man to whom Burns turned to for what turned out to be unfortunate advice regarding the lease of Ellisland Farm in 1788. He had also been a witness at Robert's baptism, and Burns always held him and his large family in high esteem. Burns went to John Murdoch's English School in Ayr in the summer of 1773 with John, the second son, and the first son by old Tennant's second wife, William. These, and other sons like David, Charles, and Robert Tennant are all mentioned in this epistle as '*Auchenbay*', '*the manly tar, my mason-billie,*' '*Wabster Charlie*', '*Preacher Willie*' and '*Singing Sannock*'.

Auld comrade dear, and brither sinner,
How's a' the folk about Glenconner?
How do you this blae eastlin wind,
Tha'ts like to blaw a body blind?
For me, my faculties are frozen,
My dearest member nearly dozen'd.
I've sent you here, by Johnie Simpson
Twa sage philosophers to glimpse on:
Smith, wi his sympathetic feeling,
An Reid, to common sense appealing.
Philosophers have fought and wrangled,
An meikle Greek an Latin mangled,
Till, wi their logic-jargon tir'd
An in the depth of science mir'd,
To common sense they now appeal –
What wives and wabsters see and feel!

But, hark ye friend! I charge you strictly,
Peruse them, an return them quickly:

For now I'm grown sae cursed douse
I pray and ponder butt the house;
My shins, my lane, I there sit roastin,
Perusing Bunyan, Brown an Boston,
Till, by and by, if I haud on,
I'll grunt a real gospel groan.
Already I begin to try it,
To cast my e'en up like a pyet
When by the gun she tumbles o'er,
Flutt'ring an gasping in her gore:
Sae shortly you shall see me bright,
A burning an a shining light.

My heart-warm love to guid auld Glen,
The ace an wale of honest men:
When bending down wi auld grey hairs
Beneath the load of years and cares,
May He who made him still support him,
An views beyond the grave comfort him!
His worthy fam'ly far and near,
God bless them a' wi grace and gear!

My auld schoolfellow, preacher Willie,
The manly tar, my Mason-billie,
And Auchenbay. I wish him joy;
If he's a parent, lass or boy,
May he be dad, and Meg the mither,
Just five-and-forty years thegither!
And no forgetting wabster Charlie,
I'm tauld he offers very fairly.
An, Lord, remember singing Sannock,
Wi hale breeks, saxpence, an a bannock!
And next, my auld acquaintance, Nancy,
Since she is fitted to her fancy,
An her kind stars hae airted till her;
A guid chiel wi a pickle siller!
My kindest, best respects, I sen' It,

To cousin Kate, and sister Janet:
Tell them, frae me wi chiels be cautious,
For, faith! they'll aiblins fin' them fashious;
To grant a heart is fairly civil,
But to grant a maidenhead's the devil!

An lastly, Jamie, for yoursel,
May guardian angels tak a spell
An steer you seven miles south o Hell!
But first, before you see Heaven's glory,
May ye get monie a merrie story,
Monie a laugh, and monie a drink,
And ay enugh o needfu' clink!

Now fare ye weel, an joy be wi you!
For my sake, this I beg it o you:
Assist poor Simpson a' ye can;
Ye'll fin' him just an honest man,
Sae I conclude, and quat my chanter,
Yours, saint or sinner,

Old John Tennant founded something of a dynasty. All the sons made their mark one way or another. James was Burns's '*auld comrade dear and brither sinner*' and according to a neighbour, '*a dungoen of wit*'. John was a skilled farmer and gave evidence before a Committee of the House of Commons on the state of Scottish Agriculture. David became a merchant sailor, losing his hand in naval battle. He refused a knighthood. Charles invented a bleaching process which laid the basis of the family fortune through his factory in Glasgow. William was a Chaplain to the Forces in India and on his retiral was given a Doctorate by Glasgow University. From this enterprisng family tree came Sir Charles Tennant of the the Glen and in the present day, the Hon Colin Tennant, a good friend to Her Royal Highness, the Princess Margaret Rose.

Epistle to Robert Graham Esq of Fintry

(Requesting a favour – 10 September 1788)

Robert Graham of Fintry, near Dundee, became Commissioner of
the Scottish Board of Excise in 1787, and in the same year met
Burns, who was on his Highland tour with William Nicol, at
Athole House, home of the Duke of Athole. The two men got on
well enough for Burns to write to him in the following year,
'requesting the favour' of his help in the matter of Burns's appli-
cation to be admitted as an Officer in the Excise. This idea had
been put into Burns's head by his doctor while in Edinburgh,
'Lang Sandy' Wood, who had the idea that a kind of sinecure
could be found for Burns which might keep him while he contin-
ued to write. It was along these lines that Dr Wood made the ini-
tial approach to Graham. That Burns should follow this up with
his own letter proved his own enthusiasm for the idea, and also
illustrated the wisdom in any new enterprise, which was always
to start at the top. Needless to say, his application was approved,
but it did not turn out to be the sinecure that Burns had hoped
for. All the same, whenever Burns got into any trouble while on
Excise service, it was always to Graham of Fintry that he would
turn, and Robert Graham was never to fail him. And it all started
from this epistle.

When Nature her great master-piece design'd,
And fram'd her last, best work, the human mind,
Her eye intent on all the mazy plan,
She form'd of various parts the various Man.
Then first she calls the useful many forth;
Plain plodding Industry, and sober Worth:
Thence peasants, farmers, native sons of earth,
And merchandise' whole genus take their birth:
Each prudent cit a warm existence finds,
And all mechanics' many-apron'd kinds.
Some other rarer sorts are wanted yet,
The lead and buoy are needful to the net:

The caput mortuum of gross desires
Makes a material for mere knights and squires;
The martial phosphorus is taught to flow,
She kneads the lumpish philosophic dough,
Then marks th' unyielding mass with grave designs,
Law, physic, politics, and deep divines;
Last, she sublimes th' Aurora of the poles,
The flashing elements of female souls.

The order'd system fair before her stood,
Nature, well pleas'd, pronounc'd it very good;
But ere she gave creating labour oer,
Half-jest, she tried one curious labour more.
Some spumy, fiery, ignis fatuus matter,
Such as the slightest breath of air might scatter;
With arch-alacrity and conscious glee,
(Nature may have her whim as well as we,
Her Hogarth-art perhaps she meant to show it),
She forms the thing and christens it – a Poet:
Creature, tho oft the prey of care and sorrow,
When blest to-day, unmindful of to-morrow;
A being form'd t' amuse his graver friends,
Admir'd and prais'd-and there the homage ends;
A mortal quite unfit for Fortune's strife,
Yet oft the sport of all the ills of life;
Prone to enjoy each pleasure riches give,
Yet haply wanting wherewithal to live;
Longing to wipe each tear, to heal each groan,
Yet frequent all unheeded in his own.

But honest Nature is not quite a Turk,
She laugh'd at first, then felt for her poor work:
Pitying the propless climber of mankind,
She cast about a standard tree to find;
And, to support his helpless woodbine state,
Attach'd him to the generous, truly great:
A title, and the only one I claim,
To lay strong hold for help on bounteous Graham.

Pity the tuneful Muses' hapless train,
Weak, timid landsmen on life's stormy main!
Their hearts no selfish stern absorbent stuff,
That never gives-tho humbly takes enough;
The little fate allows, they share as soon,
Unlike sage proverb'd Wisdom's hard-wrung boon:
The world were blest did bliss on them depend,
Ah, that 'the friendly e'er should want a friend!'
Let Prudence number oer each sturdy son,
Who life and wisdom at one race begun,
Who feel by reason and who give by rule,
(Instinct's a brute, and sentiment a fool!)
Who make poor 'will do wait upon 'I should' –
We own they're prudent, but who feels they're good?
Ye wise ones hence! ye hurt the social eye!
God's image rudely etch'd on base alloy!
But come ye who the godlike pleasure know,
Heaven's attribute distinguished – to bestow!
Whose arms of love would grasp the human race:
Come thou who giv'st with all a courtier's grace;
Friend of my life, true patron of my rhymes!
Prop of my dearest hopes for future times.
Why shrinks my soul half blushing, half afraid,
Backward, abash'd to ask thy friendly aid?
I know my need, I know thy giving hand,
I crave thy friendship at thy kind command;
But there are such who court the tuneful Nine –
Heavens! should the branded character be mine!
Whose verse in manhood's pride sublimely flows,
Yet vilest reptiles in their begging prose.
Mark, how their lofty independent spirit
Soars on the spurning wing of injured merit!
Seek not the proofs in private life to find
Pity the best of words should be but wind!
So, to heaven's gates the lark's shrill song ascends,
But grovelling on the earth the carol ends.

In all the clam'rous cry of starving want,
They dun Benevolence with shameless front;
Oblige them, patronise their tinsel lays –
They persecute you all your future days!
Ere my poor soul such deep damnation stain,
My horny fist assume the plough again,
The pie-bald jacket let me patch once more,
On eighteenpence a week I've liv'd before.
Tho, thanks to Heaven, I dare even that last shift,
I trust, meantime, my boon is in thy gift:
That, plac'd by thee upon the wish'd-for height,
Where, man and nature fairer in her sight,
My Muse may imp her wing for some sublimer flight.

Lang Sandy Wood, who, incidentally, was the first man in Edinburgh to own an umbrella, attended Burns when the poet dislocated his knee in a fall from a carriage in which he was returning from the theatre with William Wood, the actor. He had received his Excise Commission on 14 July 1789 and he addressed Fintry again 'on receiving a favour' on 10 August. It was in the the form of a sonnet, and was one of few exercises Burns made in fine writing.

I call no Goddess to inspire my strains:
A fabled Muse may suit a Bard that feigns.
Friend of my life! my ardent spirit burns,
And all the tribute of my heart returns,
For boons accorded, goodness ever new,
The gift still dearer as the giver you.
Thou orb of day! thou other paler light!
And all ye many sparkling stars of night!
If aught that giver from my mind efface,
If I that giver's bounty e'er disgrace,
Then roll to me along your wand'ring spheres
Only to number out a villain's years!
I lay my hand upon my swelling breast,
And grateful would, but cannot, speak the rest.

NOTE:

On 31 January 1794, Burns also sent an '*Epistle to Miss Graham of Fintry*', whose lines, addressed to Anne Graham, were written in studied imitation of Shenstone and the 'elegantly melting Gray'.

Epistle to Dr Blacklock

(Ellisland, 21 October 1789)

Dr Blacklock had been blind from infancy. He was supported at the University of Edinburgh by friends like David Hume and became, for a time, minister at Kirkudbright, but his blindness made it impractical and he was retired to Edinburgh to pursue his literary interests, take pupils and boarders, and write poor verses which were published to no great acclaim. Nevertheless, he was one of Edinburgh's most respected literary figures and a good judge of letters. It was a message from him, dated 4 September 1786, and delivered through the Rev George Lowrie of Loudon, that diverted Burns from his Jamaica project and encouraged him to try for a second edition in Edinburgh. Blacklock had said to Lowrie,

> *It were therefore much to be wished, for the sake of the young man, that a second edition, more numerous than the former, could immediately be printed... a more universal circulation than anything of the kind which has been published within my memory.*

Burns's response was immediate. He said that it *'fired me so much that I posted to Edinburgh without a single acquaintance in* [the] *town.'* When he did finally call on Dr Blacklock, he found that gentleman to have a – *'clear head and an excellent heart'*.

Wow, but your letter made me vauntie!
And are ye hale, and weel and cantie?
I ken'd it still, your wee bit jauntie
Wad bring ye to:
Lord send you aye as weel's I want ye!
And then ye'll do.

The ill-thief blaw the Heron south!
And never drink be near his drouth!
He tauld myself by word o mouth,
He'd tak my letter;

I lippen'd to the chiel in trouth,
And bade nae better.

But aiblins, honest Master Heron
Had, at the time, some dainty fair one
To ware this theologic care on,
And holy study;
And tired o sauls to waste his lear on,
E'en tried the body.

But what d'ye think, my trusty fere,
I'm turned a gauger – Peace be here!
Parnassian queans, I fear, I fear,
Ye'll now disdain me!
And then my fifty pounds a year
Will little gain me.

Ye glaikit, gleesome, dainty damies,
Wha, by Castalia's wimplin streamies,
Lowp, sing, and lave your pretty limbies,
Ye ken, ye ken,
That strang necessity supreme is
'Mang sons o men.

I hae a wife and twa wee laddies;
They maun hae brose and brats o duddies;
Ye ken yoursels my heart right proud is –
I need na vaunt
But I'll sned besoms, thraw saugh woodies,
Before they want.

Lord help me thro this warld o care!
I'm weary sick ot late and air!
Not but I hae a richer share
Than mony ithers;
But why should ae man better fare,
And a' men brithers?

Come, Firm Resolve, take thou the van,

Thou stalk o carl-hemp in man!
And let us mind, faint heart ne'er wan
A lady fair:
Wha does the utmost that he can,
Will whiles do mair.

But to conclude my silly rhyme
(I'm scant o verse and scant o time),
To make a happy fireside clime
To weans and wife,
That's the true pathos and sublime
Of human life.

My compliments to sister Beckie,
And eke the same to honest Lucky;
I wat she is a daintie chuckie,
As e'er tread clay;
And gratefully, my gude auld cockie,
I'm yours for aye.

The Heron mentioned in the second stanza was Galloway-born, Robert Heron, Burns's first biographer, and the source most responsible, together with Dr James Currie, Burns's first editor, for the widely-held belief that Burns died a wastrel and a drunkard. The fact was that Heron, although professing to admire Burns, was not an objective man of letters. He was an opportunist who saw a chance to get in quick with Burns. A former student of Divinity and assistant to Dr Hugh Blair in Edinburgh, he lost that post and took to hack writing, drink, and womanising but not necessarily in that order, and eventually ended his life in Newgate Gaol, in London, imprisoned for debt. There was no blacker kettle to call the Burns pot black, although he showed a shrewd assessment of Burns's worth as a poet. When Heron had visited Burns at Ellisland he was given a letter to take to Dr Blacklock, at whose house the two had first met, in the company of Mr Grierson. Heron, however, failed to deliver the letter, hence Burns's epistolatry explanation to Dr Blacklock above.

Epistle to Maxwell of Terraughty

1790

John Maxwell was a Dumfries joiner who did well enough to buy back the family estate at Terraughty, and by a second marriage, gained an even better one at Munches, near Dalbeattie. By his 71st birthday, on 7 February 1791, he had become one of the leading gentlemen of Dumfriesshire, and Burns acknowledged this with an epistle.

Health to the Maxwell's veteran Chief!
Health, aye unsour'd by care or grief:
Inspir'd, I turn'd Fate's sibyl leaf,
This natal morn,
I see thy life is stuff o prief,
Scarce quite half-worn.

This day thou metes threescore eleven,
And I can tell that bounteous Heaven
(The second-sight, ye ken, is given
To ilka Poet)
On thee a tack o seven times seven
Will yet bestow it.

If envious buckies view wi sorrow
Thy lengthen'd days on this blest morrow,
May Desolation's lang-teeth'd harrow,
Nine miles an hour,
Rake them, like Sodom and Gomorrah,
In brunstane stoure.

But for thy friends, and they are mony,
Baith honest men, and lassies bonie,
May couthie Fortune, kind and cannie,
In social glee,
Wi mornings blythe, and e'enings funny,
Bless them and thee!

Fareweel, auld birkie! Lord be near ye,
And then the deil, he daurna steer ye:
Your friends aye love, your faes aye fear ye;
For me, shame fa' me,
If neist my heart I dinna wear ye,
While Burns they ca' me.

Burns's prediction in the second stanza was proved to be pretty near the mark as John Maxwell died on 25 January (Burns's birth-date) 1814, in his 94th year.

The Rights of Women

An occasional Address spoken by Miss Fontenelle on her Benefit Night

26 November 1792

This was sent to Louisa Fontenelle at the Theatre Royal, Dumfries, with the following comment from the author,

> *In such a bad world as ours, those who add to the scanty sum of our pleasures, are positively our benefactors. To you, Madam, on our humble Dumfries boards, I have been more indebted for entertainment than ever I was in prouder Theatres. Your charms as a woman would secure applause to the most indifferent actress, and your theatrical talents would secure admiration to the plainest figure.*

Burns went to the theatre as often as he could after Edinburgh, and seriously considered writing a play in his last years. He was reading plays to that end, but as his body gave out, he had only stamina enough for the songs. However, before that, he was a regular at the Theatre Royal, only recently built in Dumfries, and he was given a free pass by the management as a compliment to his status in the town.

He had reasons other than a wish to thank a good actress for her performances. The idea was also to reflect Anglo-American Thomas Paine's *Rights of Man*, a political tract which was circulating covertly with great success throughout Britain proclaiming the new Republicanism following the French Revolution of 1791–92. Burns had his own copy, which he had to keep at a neighbour's house in order to avoid a suspicion of sedition. He kept his own revolutionary views just as hidden, but not with complete success. Burns's politics were as prismatic as he was, he had a face for all seasons. Paine, incidentally, was also an Exciseman. Burns used his own *Rights of Women* to implicitly underscore the political themes in the *Rights of Man*.

While Europe's eye is fix'd on mighty things,
The fate of Empires and the fall of Kings;
While quacks of State must each produce his plan,
And even children lisp the Rights of Man;
Amid this mighty fuss just let me mention,
The Rights of Woman merit some attention.

First, in the Sexes' intermix'd connection,
One sacred Right of Woman is, protection.
The tender flower that lifts its head, elate,
Helpless, must fall before the blasts of Fate,
Sunk on the earth, defac'd its lovely form,
Unless your shelter ward th' impending storm.

Our second Right – but needless here is caution,
To keep that right inviolate's the fashion;
Each man of sense has it so full before him,
He'd die before he'd wrong it – tis decorum.
There was, indeed, in far less polish'd days,
A time, when rough rude man had naughty ways,
Would swagger, swear, get drunk, kick up a riot,
Nay even thus invade a Lady's quiet.
Now, thank our stars! those Gothic times are fled;
Now, well-bred men-and you are all well-bred –
Most justly think (and we are much the gainers)
Such conduct neither spirit, wit, nor manners.

For Right the third, our last, our best, our dearest,
That right to fluttering female hearts the nearest;
Which even the Rights of Kings, in low prostration,
Most humbly own – tis dear, dear admiration!
In that blest sphere alone we live and move;
There taste that life of life-immortal love.
Smiles, glances, sighs, tears, fits, flirtations, airs;
Gainst such an host what flinty savage dares,
When awful Beauty joins with all her charms –
Who is so rash as rise in rebel arms?
But truce with kings, and truce with constitutions,

> With bloody armaments and revolutions;
> Let Majesty your first attention summon,
> Ah! ca ira! The Majesty Of Woman!

Burns also wrote an Address for Louisa Fontenelle on her Benefit Night in the following year, and also a delightful verse – '*To Miss Fontenelle, on seeing her in a Favourite Character.*'

> Sweet Naivete of feature,
> Simple, wild, enchanting elf,
> Not to three, but thanks to Nature
> Thou art acting but thyself
>
> Wert thou awkward, stiff, affected,
> Spurning Nature, torturing art,
> Loves and Graces all rejected
> Then indeed thou'dst act a part

Fontenelle married the actor-manager, James Williamson, and later they went to America where she died of the yellow fever in Charleston, North Carolina in 1800.

Epigrams and Epithets

To an Artist

When visiting the studio of an unnamed artist in Edinburgh, Burns penned these lines on the back of a small sketch while watching the actor work on a picture of Jacob's dream.

Dear _____, I'll gie ye some advice,
You'll tak it no uncivil:
You shouldna paint at angels mair,
But try and paint the devil.

To paint an Angel's kittle wark,
Wi Nick, there's little danger:
You'll easy draw a lang-kent face,
But no sae weel a stranger.

At Roslin Inn

After a night's carousing with the painter, Alexander Naysmith, Burns walked with him to Roslin to clear their heads, and when he received the bill, Burns wrote this epigram on the back of the bill. A fair tip, one would think.

My blessings on ye, honest wife!
I ne'er was here before;
Ye've wealth o gear for spoon and knife:
Heart could not wish for more.
Heav'n keep you clear o sturt amd strife,
Till far ayont fourscore,
And by the Lord o death and life,
I'll ne'er gae by your door!

On Rough Roads

Burns, despite a trace of Campbell blood on his father's side, did not enjoy much of his West Highland tour to Inveraray in 1787, disliking the Highlands and all Highlanders.

I'm now arrived-thanks to the gods! –

Thro pathways rough and muddy,
A certain sign that makin roads
Is no this people's study:
Altho I'm not wi Scripture cram'd,
I'm sure the Bible says
That heedless sinners shall be damn'd,
Unless they mend their ways.

On a Country Laird
(Not quite so wise as Solomon)

David Maxwell of Cardoness was a '*stupid, money-loving, dunderpate of a Galloway laird*' who tried to impress Burns with his wealth and the beauty of his estate.

Bless Jesus Christ, O Cardoness,
With grateful, lifted eyes,
Who taught that not the soul alone,
But body too shall rise;
For had He said 'the soul alone
From death I will deliver,'
Alas, alas! O Cardoness,
Then hadst thou lain for ever.

At Brownhill Inn

Burns had the company at breakfast of an English commercial traveller called Ladyman, who kept the scrap on which Burns had scribbled these lines. The landlord's name was Bacon.

At Brownhill we always get dainty good cheer,
And plenty of bacon each day in the year;
We've a' thing that's nice, and mostly in season,
But why always Bacon – come, tell me a reason?

On Francis Grose the Antiquary

The little Englishman was noted for his accumulation of antiquities and effects as well as his generosity of figure. Burns thought the combination was all too much for the Devil.

> The Devil got notice that Grose was a-dying
> So whip! at the summons, old Satan came flying;
> But when he approached where poor Francis lay moaning,
> And saw each bed-post with its burthen a-groaning,
> Astonish'd, confounded, cries Satan – 'By God,
> I'll want him, ere I take such a damnable load!'

On Chloris
(requesting me to give her a sprig of blossomed thorn)

Charles Dibdin, the English singer/composer, 'borrowed' this Burns epigram for a song of his own. Burns had originally written it for Jean Lorimer.

> From the white-blossom'd sloe my dear Chloris requested
> A sprig, her fair breast to adorn:
> No, by Heavens! I exclaim'd,
> let me perish, if ever I plant in that bosom a thorn!

The Keekin Glass

A drunken judge on the Dumfries bench squinted short-sightedly at one of Patrick Miller's beautiful daughters, sitting with her father among the spectators, and reputedly asked one of his fellow-magistrates – '*Wha's yon howlet-faced thing in the corner?*'

> How daur ye ca me howlet-face,
> Ye blear-e'ed, withered spectre?
> Ye only spied the keekin'-glass,
> An there ye saw your picture.

On Maria Riddel

Maria Riddel was the daughter of the Governor of the Leeward
Islands, William Woodley. She married Walter Riddel in 1790 and
settled at Goldilea where she wrote a book about her travels
which Burns persuaded Smellie to publish in Edinburgh. Maria
and Burns had an up and down relationship but when he died,
she wrote a friendly memoir about him.

'Praise Woman still,' his lordship roars,
'Deserv'd or not, no matter?'
But thee, whom all my soul adores,
Ev'n Flattery cannot flatter:
Maria, all my thought and dream,
Inspires my vocal shell;
The more I praise my lovely theme,
The more the truth I tell.

Elegies and Epitaphs

Epitaph on my Honoured Father

William Burnes died at Lochlea on 13 February 1784. His last
words were for his first son – 'It's only you I fret for'. The quote
in the last line is from Alexander Pope.

O ye whose cheek the tear of pity stains,
Draw near with pious rev'rence, and attend!
Here lie the loving husband's dear remains,
The tender father, and the gen'rous friend.
The pitying heart that felt for human woe,
The dauntless heart that fear'd no human pride,
The friend of man – to vice alone a foe;
For 'ev'n his failings lean'd to virtue's side'.

Epitaph for a Wag in Mauchline

This could be any of the Tarbolton Bachelors except Gilbert
Burns. Burns himself and Jamie Smith were to prove early fathers,
but John Richmond followed suit soon after and John 'Clockie'
Brown was quick to follow their example, as witness his appear-
ance in the 'Court of Equity'.

Lament him, Mauline husbands a',
He aften did assist ye;
For had ye staid hale weeks awa,
Your wives they ne'er had missed ye!

Ye Mauchline bairns, as on ye pass
To school in bands thegither,
O, tread ye lightly on his grass –
Perhaps he was your father!

Broom Besoms

These old verses speak for themselves. Some are very old, some
Burns-new, some he has 'borrowed', but all are blue!

Chorus
Buy broom besoms! wha will buy them now;
Fine heather ringers, better never grew.

I maun hae a wife, whatsoe'er she be;
An she be a woman, that's eneugh for me.

If that she be bony, I shall think her right:
If that she be ugly, where's the odds at night!

O, an she be young, how happy shall I be!
If that she be auld, the sooner she will die.

If that she be fruitfu', O! what joy is there!
If she should be barren, less will be my care.

If she like a drappie; she and I'll agree;
If she dinna like it, there's the mair for me.

Be she green or gray; be she black or fair;
Let her be a woman, I shall seek nae mair.

Epitaph
No comment.

Lo worms enjoy the seat of bliss
Where Lords and Lairds afore did kiss.

Epitaph for Gavin Hamilton

Gavin Hamilton was the solicitor in Mauchline who came up with
the scheme to move the Burnes brothers and sisters 'over the hill'
from Lochlea to Mauchline on the death of their father. Hamilton
was a Liberal in Church affairs and supported the 'New Lights',
that is for reform, against the 'Old Lights' who were for the estab-
lished order and the appointment of clergy by the local laird
instead of by the congregation. This little epigram made Burns, in
effect, the Laureate of the New Lights.

The poor man weeps – here Gavin sleeps,
Whom canting wretches blam'd;
But with such as he, where'er he be,
May I be sav'd or damn'd!

In the Kirk of Lamington

The beadle of the kirk found this on one of the windows near where Burns was sitting during the service one Sunday in February 1789. He wasn't too pleased. The minister, Rev Thomas Mitchell, wasn't too happy either.

> As cauld a wind as ever blew,
> A cauld kirk, an in't but few:
> As cauld a minister's e'er spak;
> Ye'se a' be het e'er I come back.

At Whigham's Inn, Sanquhar

Burns often stayed over at Edward Whigham's Queensbury Arms in Sanquhar when travelling by horseback between Mauchline and Ellisland. He put it on a window-pane as a testimonial, and no doubt, this was reflected in his bill next morning.

> Envy, if thy jaundiced eye
> Through this window chance to spy,
> To thy sorrow thou shalt find,
> All that's generous, all that's kind
> Friendship, virtue, every grace,
> Dwelling in this happy place.

On Andrew Turner

A patronising English traveller interrupted Burns's party at the King's Arms, Dumfries, and challenged Burns to write an impromptu verse for a bottle of wine. Asking the Englishman his name and year of birth, Burns retorted with the following – and won the wine for his party.

> In se'enteen hunder'n forty-nine,
> The deil gat stuff to mak a swine,
> An coost it in a corner;
> But wilily he chang'd his plan,
> An shap'd it something like a man,
> An ca'd it Andrew Turner.

On the Death of Robert Ruisseaux

This mock-elegy, dating from around 1787, is a play by Burns on
his own name, the French word 'Ruisseaux', meaning 'streams' or
'burns'.

Now Robin lies in his last lair,
He'll gabble rhyme, nor sing nae mair;
Cauld poverty, wi hungry stare,
Nae mair shall fear him;
Nor anxious fear, nor cankert care,
E'er mair come near him.

To tell the truth, they seldom fash'd him,
Except the moment that they crush'd him;
For sune as chance or fate had hush'd 'em
Tho e'er sae short.
Then wi a rhyme or sang he lash'd 'em,
And thought it sport.

Tho he was bred to kintra-wark,
And counted was baith wight and stark,
Yet that was never Robin's mark
To mak a man;
But tell him, he was learn'd and clark,
Ye roos'd him then!

A Bard's Epitaph

This was the last poem in the Kilmarnock Edition, and is also the
last in this section.

Is there a whim-inspired fool,
Owre fast for thought, owre hot for rule,
Owre blate to seek, owre proud to snool,
Let him draw near;
And owre this grassy heap sing dool,
And drap a tear.

Is there a bard of rustic song,
Who, noteless, steals the crowds among,
That weekly this area throng,
O, pass not by!
But, with a frater-feeling strong,
Here, heave a sigh.

Is there a man, whose judgment clear
Can others teach the course to steer,
Yet runs, himself, life's mad career,
Wild as the wave,
Here pause – and, thro the starting tear,
Survey this grave.

The poor inhabitant below
Was quick to learn the wise to know,
And keenly felt the friendly glow,
And softer flame;
But thoughtless follies laid him low,
And stain'd his name!

Reader, attend! whether thy soul
Soars fancy's flights beyond the pole,
Or darkling grubs this earthly hole,
In low pursuit:
Know, prudent, cautious, self-control
Is wisdom's root.

But now the time for caution and control had passed and, as life gradually ebbed away, he returned to what had started it all when he was little more than a boy – the making of a song:

That I, for poor old Scotland's sake,
Some usefu' plan or book could make,
Or sing a song at least...

PART THREE

The Songwriter

TWENTY SELECTED SONGS

Mary Morison

The Rigs o Barley

Green Grow the Rashes-O

A Rosebud by my Early Walk

Sweet Afton

Of A' the Airts the Wind Can Blaw

John Anderson, my Jo

Ca' the Yowes to the Knowes

To Mary in Heaven

Comin Thro the Rye

The Banks o Doon

Bonie Wee Thing

Ae Fond Kiss

The Deil's Awa wi th' Exciseman

Whistle and I'll Come to Ye, My Lad

Scots Wha Hae

My Love is Like a Red, Red Rose

A Man's A Man

O, Wert Thou in the Cauld Blast

Auld Lang Syne

The Fiddler and the Folk Singer

*When I meet with an old Scots Air that has any facetious
idea in its Name, I have a peculiar pleasure in following out
that idea for a verse or two.*
[Letter to William Dunbar 1788]

The world knows Robert Burns as a poet, scholars recognise in
him a prose stylist and belle-lettrist of the highest order, yet he is
perhaps best known because of his songs. That being said, it must
be added that, while he could notate music and 'take down a
tune', he was not, in the strictest sense, a musician. He was a col-
lecter of old songs, that is, of almost-forgotten tunes or airs, often
with scurrilous words, which he mended judiciously by adding
new words, making them into acceptable songs, or at least, songs
that could be sung again in polite company.

His formal musical education was as occasional as his formal
literary education, and he was a similarly auto-didact. Apart from
a spell at the 'singing school' at Lochlea when a teacher got the
use of a barn, and again at Mauchline when he went to classes to
learn about hymn tunes and 'sacred music', he was entirely self-
taught. His first tentative efforts at composition were all songs
and as self-conscious and stilted as he was himself at fifteen, but
they got better as he got older and more assured, and at the end,
only a little over 20 years later, his lyrics were little works of art
that almost sang themselves. Consonants and vowels chinked easily
together in a mellifluous, almost Italianate, manner that made them
immediately singable, which is why so many of them have lasted
till today. Singers *like* singing them. Always a good test of any lyric.
As Professor Shairp said,

*His songs are not words set to music, [the words] are music
themselves, conceived in an atmosphere of music, rising out
of it, and with music instinct to their last syllable.*

Not every song was such a gem of course. Having written more than half the number of songs attributed to Schubert, who wrote more than 600 in a similar life-span (Schubert died at 31, Burns at 37), it is inevitable that there is plenty of dross among the gold, but having sifted them out, the twenty offered here are among the best of Burns. He had a good ear for a tune and rarely missed a chance of adding a lyric to a melody he thought worthy of words. It was his way of song-saving, putting a lyric lifejacket around the tune so that it can at least stay afloat for a little while longer. In some cases, his 'rescue' was so complete it was virtually the kiss of life.

As he wrote to Charles Sharp of Hoodham in 1790,

I am a fiddler, and a poet, and you, I am told, play an excellent violin and have a standard taste in the Belles Lettres. The other day a brother cat-gut gave me a charming Scottish air of your composition. If I was pleased with the tune, I was enraptured by the title you have given it, and taking up the idea, I have spun it into [the] three stanzas enclosed.

Similarly, he heard a carter whistling a tune in Glasgow and the result was a new song called *Duncan Gray*. When he was in Edinburgh, Signor Urbani gave him an old meoldy which Burns refashioned as *Scots Wha Hae*. In Dumfries, he listened to Thomas Fraser playing skilfully on the hautboy (oboe) and from it came *Blythe Hae I been on Yonder Hill*. He wrote most of his songs in this way. Burns was really more lyricist than composer, but a lyricist of genius as any one of his hundreds of songs can testify. Even if it is only a couplet, there is always a flash of his class somewhere.

He had the capacity for making hard work appear on the page as if it were artless and spontaneous. However, when he tried to compose an original tune, as he did for *Raging Fortune* in 1783, it was genuinely hard work.

I am not musical scholar enough to prick down my tune properly, so it can never see the light, [but] these were the verses I composed to suit... The tune consisted of three parts so that the verses went through the whole air.

He explained it better later, when he said that he

> *needed to sowthe [croon] the melody over and over again*
> *to himself till he kindled the right emotion, and at the same*
> *time, regulated the right rhythm for the words.*

He realised that in song as well as in poetry, it was all a matter of rhythm, as everything in the natural world was. Rhythm, cycles and seasons show the regular beat of life in everything, especially the heartbeat. It all starts from that, and when that stops, so does life itself.

During his tours of Scotland in 1787, he took every opportunity to hear an old song sung, or played on the fiddle by a 'brother cat-gut' as he called any fiddler he met. He had to be prised away from the company of Niel Gow, the famous Highland fiddler, when they met at Gow's house for a day of song talk and playing. He was always on the look-out for musical antiquities. He was a tireless searcher after these timeless fragments, no matter how obscure, and it is largely thanks to his personal efforts that a whole body of Scots minstrelsy was saved for posterity. He explained exactly how he worked in another letter to Thomson.

> *Until I am compleat master of a tune, in my own singing,*
> *(such as it is) I never can compose for it. My way is: I con-*
> *sider the poetic sentiment, correspondent to my idea of the*
> *musical expression; then chuse my theme; begin one*
> *Stanza; when that is composed, which is generally the most*
> *difficult part of the business, I walk out, sit down now &*
> *then, look out for objects in Nature around me that are in*
> *unison or harmony with the cogitations of my fancy &*
> *workings of my bosom; humming every now & then the air*
> *with the verses I have framed: when I feel my Muse begin-*
> *ning to jade, I retire to the solitary fireside of my study, and*
> *there commit my effusions to paper; swinging, at intervals,*
> *on the hind-legs of my elbow-chair, by way of calling forth*
> *my own critical strictures, as my pen goes on...*

It is a pretty picture of the poet at work, although it is hard to reconcile the stilted prose of the letter style and its arch vocabulary with the simple directness and unerring lyric truth in the songs that resulted. If he had no great singing voice, he had an unerring ear for music, although he confessed he had no taste for counterpoint and complicated harmonies.

> *However they may transport and ravish the ears of your connoisseurs, (they) affect my simple lug no otherwise than merely as melodious din. On the other hand, by way of amends, I am delighted with many little melodies which the learned musician despises as silly and insipid.*

Thus we were given songs like *Ye Banks and Braes, Bonny Wee Thing, Flow Gently Sweet Afton*, and so many more.

He had taught himself to play the fiddle just enough to capture a tune from the air, and he sang just enough to make sure his words matched what he could hear. What else did he need? His musical priority was to confirm lyrics rather than to initiate original tunes or delight listeners in performance. His own sister, Mrs Begg, thought him '*no great efficient in music*', although he could read music in manuscript, and that his singing was just like his fiddle-playing,

> *rude and rough, but croonin tae a body's sel does weel enough.*

Well enough at any rate to know a good tune when he heard it. Mrs Begg remembers that he used to play the fiddle in the summer when they sheltered from the rain and

> *in the winter he used to rise early and chop up the gathering coal, then play for the amusement of thae that were in bed. It could not be borne for ever and speedily came to an end.*

In conclusion, one can consider the words of that most-English of poets, Alfred, Lord Tennyson, who advised those interested in the best in poetry to

> *read the exquisite songs of Burns. In shape, each of them has the perfection of a berry; in light the radiance of a dewdrop.*

Mary Morison

1780

Hugh MacDiarmid (Dr Christopher Grieve) was a particular admirer of this lyric. He told the present writer in conversation that he would have given anything to have written that one line – '*Ye are na Mary Morison*'. In the great Scottish writer's opinion that said it all for young love. The English critic, William Hazlitt, wrote of it,

> *Of all the productions of Burns, the pathetic and serious love-songs... are perhaps which take the deepest and most lasting hold of the mind. Such are the lines to Mary Morison.*

W. E. Henley called the lyric 'this little masterpiece of feeling and expression' yet Burns himself had no great opinion of it. In the letter to George Thomson, of 20 March 1793, he wrote.

> *The song prefixed is one of my juvenile works. I leave it among your hands. I do not think it very remarkable either for its merits or demerits.*

For once, Burns's better judgement seemed to have deserted him, but Thomson took him at his word and did not include the song in his Collection until 1818. Since when, it has been acknowledged as one of the sweetest songs in the Burns minstrelsy.

O Mary, at thy window be,
It is the wish'd, the trysted hour!
Those smiles and glances let me see,
That make the miser's treasure poor:
How blythely was I bide the stour,
A weary slave frae sun to sun,
Could I the rich reward secure,
The lovely Mary Morison.

Yestreen, when to the trembling string
The dance gaed thro the lighted ha',

To thee my fancy took its wing,
I sat, but neither heard nor saw:
Tho this was fair, and that was braw,
And yon the toast of a' the town,
I sigh'd, and said among them a',
'Ye are na Mary Morison.'

Oh, Mary, canst thou wreck his peace,
Wha for thy sake wad gladly die?
Or canst thou break that heart of his,
Whase only faut is loving thee?
If love for love thou wilt na gie,
At least be pity to me shown;
A thought ungentle canna be
The thought o Mary Morison.

There was a Mary Morison, who lived in Mauchline from 1784. She was the daughter of the adjutant of 104th Regiment and in 1791, after the amputation of her foot, she died at the age of 20. Some scholars, however, including Mackay, believe the name may be a pseudonym for Alison Begbie (to whom Burns formally proposed by letter in 1780 and was turned down) or Elizabeth Gebbie, neither of whom, it must be said, had very singable surnames. Hence the substitution of 'Mary Morison', but as Professor Kinsey points out, 'Morison is not an uncommon name in Ayrshire and many Morisons are Marys'.

The Rigs o Barley

1783

Burns wrote this fresh evocation of youthful high spirits in the
field to a very old air, *Corn Rigs*, and sent it to Thomson with a
further self-deprecating comment,

> *My song, Rigs o Barley does not altogether please me, but*
> *if I can mend it, I will submit it to your consideration.*

Thomson, fortunately, saw nothing wrong with it and it was pub-
lished as first printed in the Kilmarnock Edition.

It was upon a Lammas night,
When corn rigs are bonie,
Beneath the moon's unclouded light,
I held awa to Annie;
The time flew by, wi tentless heed,
Till, tween the late and early,
Wi sma persuasion she agreed
To see me thro the barley.

Chorus
Corn rigs, an barley rigs,
An corn rigs are bonie:
I'll ne'er forget that happy night,
Amang the rigs wi Annie.

The sky was blue, the wind was still,
The moon was shining clearly;
I set her down, wi right good will,
Amang the rigs o barley:
I ken't her heart was a' my ain;
I lov'd her most sincerely;
I kiss'd her owre and owre again,
Amang the rigs o barley.

Corn rigs, an barley rigs, &c.

I lock'd her in my fond embrace;
Her heart was beating rarely:
My blessings on that happy place,
Amang the rigs o barley!
But by the moon and stars so bright,
That shone that hour so clearly!
She aye shall bless that happy night
Amang the rigs o barley.

Corn rigs, an barley rigs, &c.

I hae been blythe wi comrades dear;
I hae been merry drinking;
I hae been joyfu' gath'rin gear;
I hae been happy thinking:
But a' the pleasures e'er I saw,
Tho three times doubl'd fairly,
That happy night was worth them a',
Amang the rigs o barley.

Corn rigs, an barley rigs, &c.

Annie Rankine, the youngest daughter of Burns's old friend, John
Rankine of Adamahill, always insisted she was the heroine of this
youthful song. She told Chambers, '*I remember it well, when I
was a fair young lassie amang the barley*'. Meeting Burns in
Mauchline after the publication of the poem in 1786, she told him
that she had little expected ever to see her name in print, and was
she the 'Annie' in it? '*Oh ay*,' answered Burns, '*I was just wanting
to give you a cast amang the lave*'. Burns always remained fond
of her and later gave her a lock of his hair in a framed miniature
of himself. She treasured both throughout her long life as Mrs
John Merry, the inn-keeper at Cumnock.

Green Grow the Rashes-O

1783

The original ballad was first published in 1549, with other versions in 1627 and 1740 and each (including one by Alan Ramsay in 1725) was as grossly explicit as the other. Burns's version was no less cheerfully bawdy but is lifted above the scurrilous by its wit and *joi de vivre*. He made a note about in his first Commonplace Book under August 1786,

> *This song is the genuine language of my heart, and will enable anybody to determine which of the classes – the grave or the merry – I belong to.*

As if one had any doubts.

Chorus
Green grow the rashes, O;
Green grow the rashes, O;
The sweetest hours that e'er I spend,
Are spent amang the lasses, O.

There's nought but care on ev'ry han',
In ev'ry hour that passes, O;
What signifies the life o man,
An twere na for the lasses, O.

Green grow, &c.

The warly race may riches chase,
An riches still may fly them, O;
An tho at last they catch them fast,
Their hearts can ne'er enjoy them, O.

Green grow, &c.

But gie me a cannie hour at e'en,
My arms about my dearie, O;
An warly cares, an warly men,
May a' gae tapsalteerie, O!

Green grow, &c.

For you sae douce, ye sneer at this;
Ye're nought but senseless asses, O:
The wisest man the warl e'er saw,
He dearly lov'd the lasses, O.

Green grow, &c.

Auld Nature swears, the lovely dears
Her noblest work she classes, O:
Her prentice han' she try'd on man,
An then she made the lasses, O.

Green grow, &c.

This short excerpt from the long autobiographical letter to Dr
Moore dated 2 February 1787, shows something of the young
Burns of the 'early days' who wrote the first love songs.

*My heart was complete tinder, and was eternally lighted up
by some goddess or another... At plough, scythe, or reap-
hook I feared no competitor, and thus I set absolute want at
defiance; and as I never cared further for my labours than
while I was in actual exercise, I spent the evenings in the way
after my own heart. A country lad seldom carries on a love
adventure without an assistant confidant. I possessed a
curiosity, zeal, and intrepid dexterity that recommended me
as a proper second on these occasions; and I daresay I felt as
much pleasure in being in the secret of half the loves of the
parish of Tarbolton, as ever did statesman in knowing the
intrigues of half the courts of Europe. The grave sons of
science, ambition, or avarice, baptize these things by the
name of follies; but to the sons and daughters of labour and
poverty, they are matters of the most serious nature. To them
the ardent hope, the stolen interview, the tender farewell, are
the greatest and most delicous part of their enjoyments.*

A Rosebud by my Early Walk
1787

Josiah Walker, latterly Professor of Humanity at Glasgow University, first met Burns in Edinburgh in 1787, and it was there he had the opportunity to observe the poet in the act of making a song. He recalled the incident.

> *About the end of October, I called for him at the house of a friend, whose daughter, though not more than twelve, was a considerable proficient in music. I found him seated at the harpsichord of this young lady, listening with keenest interest to his own verse, which she sung and accompanied, and adjusting them to the music by repeated trials of the effect. In this occupation he was so totally absorbed, that it was difficult to draw his attention from it for a moment.*

The air used is given variously as *Rosebud* and by Mackay as *The Shepherd's Wife* but Burns himself said, '*The air of the song is by David Sillar, quondam merchant and now schoolmaster in Irvine*'. He was also one of Burns's closest friends in the Tarbolton times of their youth. It would be a nice touch if this song were indeed their collaboration. Whether it is or not, it remains a delightful effort.

A Rose-bud by my early walk,
Adown a corn-enclosed bawk,
Sae gently bent its thorny stalk,
All on a dewy morning.
Ere twice the shades o dawn are fled,
In a' its crimson glory spread,
And drooping rich the dewy head,
It scents the early morning.

Within the bush her covert nest
A little linnet fondly prest;
The dew sat chilly on her breast,
Sae early in the morning.

She soon shall see her tender brood,
The pride, the pleasure o the wood,
Amang the fresh green leaves bedew'd,
Awake the early morning.

So thou, dear bird, young Jeany fair,
On trembling string or vocal air,
Shall sweetly pay the tender care
That tents thy early morning.
So thou, sweet Rose-bud, young and gay,
Shalt beauteous blaze upon the day,
And bless the parent's evening ray
That watch'd thy early morning.

The 12-year old concerned in the making of the song was Jean,
the daughter of William Cruikshank, a teacher at the Edinburgh
High School, who was also Burns's landlord for a time in 1787 at
St James's Square. When Burns left the city in 1788, he gave Jean
a copy of his Edinburgh Edition, inscribed to – '*Miss Cruikshank,
a very young lady*' and he added the lines beginning,

> *Beauteous rosebud, young and gay*
> *Blooming in thy early May.*

Jean married a Jedburgh solicitor when she grew up and lived as
Mrs James Henderson until 1835.

Sweet Afton

1788

There was almost a conspiracy to link this song with Mary Campbell. Gilbert Burns was adamant on this point, but Burns himself, in enclosing the lyric to Mrs Dunlop on 5 February 1789, says simply,

> *There is a small river, Afton, that falls into Nith, near New Cumnock; which has some charming, wild, romantic scenery on its banks...*

The 'Mary' who is asleep on those banks could be Mary Campbell, the dairy-maid at Coilsfield, whom Gilbert mentions. But was she merely a part of the scenery?

Flow gently, sweet Afton! amang thy green braes,
Flow gently, I'll sing thee a song in thy praise;
My Mary's asleep by thy murmuring stream,
Flow gently, sweet Afton, disturb not her dream.

Thou stockdove whose echo resounds thro the glen,
Ye wild whistling blackbirds in yon thorny den,
Thou green-crested lapwing thy screaming forbear,
I charge you, disturb not my slumbering Fair.

How lofty, sweet Afton, thy neighbouring hills,
Far mark'd with the courses of clear, winding rills;
There daily I wander as noon rises high,
My flocks and my Mary's sweet cot in my eye.

How pleasant thy banks and green valleys below,
Where, wild in the woodlands, the primroses blow;
There oft, as mild Ev'ning weeps over the lea,
The sweet-scented birk shades my Mary and me.

Thy crystal stream, Afton, how lovely it glides,
And winds by the cot where my Mary resides;
How wanton thy waters her snowy feet lave,
As, gathering sweet flowerets, she stems thy clear wave.

Flow gently, sweet Afton, amang thy green braes,
Flow gently, sweet river, the theme of my lays;
My Mary's asleep by thy murmuring stream,
Flow gently, sweet Afton, disturb not her dream.

On the afternoon of the second Sunday in May, 1786, Burns, having received his Certificate of Bachelorhood from the Kirk Session after three Sundays on the Cutty Stool on account of Jean Armour's twins, felt himself a free man again, albeit a reluctant one. Having a scheme to emigrate to the Indies, and having need of a companion, he met, by arrangement, Mary Campbell, where the Faile burn runs into the River Ayr. Holding their hands over the running water, they exchanged Bibles, duly signed, and they solemnly pledged their troth. In his own hand, he had written on one – '*And ye shall not swear by my name falsely. I am the Lord*' (Leviticus ch19 v12) and on the other, '*Thou shalt not foreswear thyself, but shall perform unto the Lord thine oaths*' (Matthew ch5 v33). Beside his signature, '*Robert Burns, Mossgiel*', he put his masonic sign.

What happened after that is not recounted, but they went their separate ways, she to the port of Greenock to stay with relatives and wait for the ship, and he to Kilmarnock to see about printing a book of Scotch poems before joining her. But they never saw each other again. She died of the fever contracted from her sick brother and he let the ship sail, choosing to emigrate to Edinburgh instead.

Of A' the Airts the Wind Can Blaw

(Miss Admiral Gordon's Strathspey)

1788

This song, sometimes entitled *I love my Jean*, was published in Johnson's *Musical Museum* in 1790. Burns noted – '*This air is by Marshall.*' William Marshall was butler to the Duke of Gordon. Burns wrote the song while he was preparing a place for her at Ellisland. She was then staying with the Burns family in Mauchline, which lay in the west, the direction of the sunset as seen from Ellisland. Burns added –

> *The song I composed out of compliment to Mrs Burns.*
> *N.B. It was during the honeymoon.*

Of a' the airts the wind can blaw,
I dearly like the west,
For there the bonie lassie lives,
The lassie I loe best:
There's wild-woods grow, and rivers row,
And mony a hill between:
But day and night my fancy's flight
Is ever wi my Jean.

I see her in the dewy flowers,
I see her sweet and fair:
I hear her in the tunefu' birds,
I hear her charm the air:
There's not a bonie flower that springs,
By fountain, shaw, or green;
There's not a bonie bird that sings,
But minds me o my Jean.

Burns wrote to Peggy Chalmers in August 1788 tell her –

> *I have married my Jean. This was not in consequence of the*
> *attachment of romance, perhaps; but I had a long and*

much-loved fellow-creature's happiness in my determina-
tion, and I durst not trifle with so important a deposit. Nor
have I any cause to repent it. If I have not got polite tattle,
modish manners, and fashionable dress, I am not sickened
and disgusted with the multiform curse of boarding-school
affectation; And I have got the hansomest figure, the sweet-
est temper, the soundest constitution and the kindest heart
in the country... [and] she has (O, the partial lover! you will
cry) the finest 'wood-note wild' I ever heard.

He brought Jean to Ellisland in November 1788 to enjoy what he
later said was the happiest winter of his life with his wife and chil-
dren together for the first time under their own roof.

To make a happy, fire-side clime to weans and wife,
That's the true pathos and sublime of human life.

John Anderson, my Jo

1789

By a splendid irony, this most moving evocation of proved matri-
monial content is derived from a set of verses so lewd that they
were considered unfit for print. An 'improved' version was pub-
lished in the *London Masque* of 1768, a slightly-altered version
of which is preserved in *The Merry Muses*. That Burns should be
able to take this and further 'improve' on it into two meaningful
verses so that it becomes a genuine poetic work, tender and com-
passionate, is not only proof of his writing skills but also of his
deep understanding of the evolving man-woman relationship in a
marriage over time.

The further irony is that the song represents the kind of long
and happy marriage he was never to know himself. This makes
the work all the more poignant.

John Anderson, my jo, John,
When we were first acquent;
Your locks were like the raven,
Your bonie brow was brent;
But now your brow is beld, John,
Your locks are like the snaw;
But blessings on your frosty pow,
John Anderson, my jo.

John Anderson, my jo, John,
We clamb the hill thegither;
And mony a cantie day, John,
We've had wi ane anither:
Now we maun totter down, John,
And hand in hand we'll go,
And sleep thegither at the foot,
John Anderson, my jo.

The fact that Burns did marry his Jean *officially* is still not proved.
His supposed 'marriage' in a civil ceremony in Mauchline, with

Jamie Smith as witness is not documented, and an 'irregular'
arrangement made by Gavin Hamilton, whereby Burns posted a
notice of his intent to take Jean as his spouse is also suspect. What
we do know is that the only 'bit of paper' confirming the legal sta-
tus of Mr and Mrs Robert Burns is an extract from the Mauchline
Parish Register of Marriages following the couple's appearance
before the Kirk Session in the summer of 1788:

> *Burns, Robert, in Mossgiel and Jean Armour in Machlin came
> before the Kirk Session upon 5 Augt, and Acknowledged
> that they were irregularly married some Years ago. The
> Session rebuked both parties for their irregularity and took
> them solemnly bound to adhere to one another as Husband
> and Wife all the days of their life.*

This bawdy version of the song is probably by Burns himself.
It is nothing more than a piece of fun establishing the frustrations
of married sex at a senior level. Even so, it shows the poet's
rollicking command of form and in no way detracts from the
sweet and true poignancy of the first version.

John Anderson, my jo, John,
I wonder what ye mean,
To lie sae lang i' the mornin',
And stir sae late at e'en?
Ye'll bleer a' your een, John,
And why do ye so?
Come sooner to your bed at e'en,
John Anderson, my jo.

John Anderson, my jo, John,
When first that ye began,
Ye had as good a tail-tree,
As ony ither man;
But now its waxen wan, John,
And wrinkles to and fro;
I've twa gae-ups for ae gae-down,
John Anderson, my jo.

I'm backit like a salmon,
I'm breastit like a swan;
My wame it is a down-cod,
My middle ye may span:
Fraw my tap-knoe to my tae, John,
I'm like the new-fa'n snow;
And it's a' for your convenience,
John Anderson, my jo.

O it is a fine thing
To keep out oer the dyke;
But it's a meikle finer thing,
To see your hurdies fyke;
To see your hurdies fyke; John
And hit the rising blow;
It's then I like your chanter-pipe,
John Anderson, my jo.

When ye come on before, John,
See that ye do your best;
When ye begin to haud me,
See that ye grip me fast;
See that ye grip me fast, John,
Until that I cry 'Oh!'
Your back shall crack or I do that,
John Anderson, my jo.

John Anderson, my jo, John,
Ye're welcome when ye please;
It's either in the warm bed
Or else aboon the claes:
Or ye shall hae the horns, John,
Upon your head to grow;
An' that's the cuckold's mallison,
John Anderson, my jo.

Ca' the Yowes to the Knowes

1789 (revised 1794)

Writing to Johnson in 1789 with the first version, Burns said,

*This beautiful song is in the true old Scottish taste, yet I do
not know that either the air or the words were in print
before.*

Chorus
Ca' the yowes to the knowes,
Ca' them where the heather grows,
Ca' them where the burnie rowes,
My bonie dearie.

As I gaed down the water-side,
There I met my shepherd lad:
He row'd me sweetly in his plaid,
And he ca'd me his dearie.

Ca' the yowes, &c.

Will ye gang down the water-side,
And see the waves sae sweetly glide
Beneath the hazels spreading wide,
The moon it shines fu' clearly.

Ca' the yowes, &c.

Ye sall get gowns and ribbons meet,
Cauf-leather shoon upon your feet,
And in my arms ye'se lie and sleep,
An' ye sall be my dearie.

Ca' the yowes, &c.

If ye'll but stand to what ye've said
I'se gang wi thee, my shepherd lad,
And ye may row me in your plaid,
And I sall be your dearie.

Ca' the yowes, &c.

While waters wimple to the sea,
While day blinks in the lift sae hie,
Till clay-cauld death sall blin' my e'e,
Ye sall be my dearie.

Ca' the yowes, &c.

When sending the revised version to Thomson in 1794, he wrote:

*I am flattered that you are adopting Ca' the Yowes to the
Knowes, as it was owing to me that it ever saw the light.
About seven years ago, I was well-acquainted with a worthy
little fellow, a Mr Clunie, who sang it charmingly; and, at my
request, Mr Clarke took it down from his singing, When I
gave it to Johnson I added some stanzas to the song and
added others; but still, it will not do for you... In a solitary
stroll which I took today, I tried my hand at a few, pastoral
lines... Here it is, with all its crudities and imperfections on
its head.*

Chorus

Ca' the yowes to the knowes,
Ca' them where the heather grows,
Ca' them where the burnie rowes,
My bonie dearie.

Hark, the mavis' evening sang
Sounding Clouden's woods amang!
Then a faulding let us gang,
My bonie dearie.

Ca' the, &c.

We'll gae down by Clouden side,
Thro the hazels spreading wide,
O'er the waves, that sweetly glide
To the moon sae clearly.

Ca' the, &c.

Yonder Clouden's silent towers,
Where at moonshine midnight hours,
O'er the dewy bending flowers,
Fairies dance sae chearie

Ca' the, &c.

Ghaist nor bogle shalt thou fear;
Thou'rt to love and heaven sae dear
Nocht of ill may come thee near,
My bonie dearie.

Ca' the, &c.

'Mr Clunie' was really John Clunzie, schoolmaster and precentor
at Markinch in Fife. The Clouden is a tributary of the River Nith,
and the 'silent towers' mentioned are the ruins of Lincluden
Abbey.

To Mary in Heaven

1789

Often called called by its first line, *Thou ling'ring star, with less'ning ray* this song doesn't somehow ring true. Its emotions seem staged, and the impulse governing the work is obviously lacking the inspiration which fired so many of the other love songs. Even the musical setting is questioned. Mackay says it's *Mary weep no more for me* and Henly asserts that it is *Captain Cook's Death* by Lucy Johnstone, afterwards Mrs Oswald of Auchencruive. That apart, much else of the work is ambivalent. Even Burns thought himself '*too much interested in the subject of it, to be a critic*' when he sent the first draft of it to Mrs Dunlop in November 1789 to ask her opinion of it. Burns rarely required the opinion of a second party to judge of his work, but there was almost a guilt element in this composition and whether this has to do with his relationship with its enigmatic subject or with his need to gloss it over, we shall never know.

The Victorians loved nothing better than a funeral. Thanatopsis was the flavour of the age. In literature, their favourite heroine was a dead heroine, especially a young, dead heroine and this was reflected in their enthusiasm for this song by Burns. Today we are not so sure about Mary Campbell, or of the real importance of the exchange of Bibles over the Faile stream, or of Burns's writing this lyric through his tears on the anniverary of her death, but what we do know was that she was involved in his aborted scheme to emigrate to the West Indies, and that she did die in Greenock waiting for him to join her. There is something in all this Highland Mary saga that only Burns knows and he never said anything about it except what he suggested here in a melancholy lyric placed on a lambent musical theme. He was obviously affected by her death, yet still one feels that perhaps Burns protests too much.

Thou ling'ring star, with less'ning ray,
That lov'st to greet the early morn,
Again thou usher'st in the day
My Mary from my soul was torn.
O Mary! dear departed shade!
Where is thy place of blissful rest?
See'st thou thy lover lowly laid?
Hear'st thou the groans that rend his breast?

That sacred hour can I forget,
Can I forget the hallow'd grove,
Where, by the winding Ayr, we met,
To live one day of parting love!
Eternity will not efface
Those records dear of transports past,
Thy image at our last embrace,
Ah! little thought we twas our last!

Ayr, gurgling, kiss'd his pebbled shore,
oerhung with wild-woods, thickening green;
The fragrant birch and hawthorn hoar,
Twin'd amorous round the raptur'd scene:
The flowers sprang wanton to be prest,
The birds sang love on every spray;
Till too, too soon, the glowing west,
Proclaim'd the speed of winged day.

Still oer these scenes my mem'ry wakes,
And fondly broods with miser-care;
Time but th' impression stronger makes,
As streams their channels deeper wear,
My Mary! dear departed shade!
Where is thy blissful place of rest?
See'st thou thy lover lowly laid?
Hear'st thou the groans that rend his breast?

When 'Highland' Mary Campbell's coffin was exhumed at the
Greenock West Kirkyard, it was found that the bottom board of
an infant's coffin lay with it. Whether this was merely an accident
of adjacent burial or whether it was Mary Campbell's baby has
never been proved, and 'Not Proven' remains the verdict to this
day. Nevertheless, it is known that Burns always felt guilty about
Highland Mary Campbell. And we will never really know why.

Comin Thro the Rye

1789

This was yet another refinement of a bawdy original, and once again 'Jenny' is used without reference to a specific, real-life heroine, although mention has been made of a Jenny from Dalry. The 'rye in question may have been a field of rye, the ford of the Rye Water in its course to the Garnock as it flows below Ryefield House, near Dalry. Others think that 'rye' was a long, narrow, cobble-stoned lane leading to the town, where young ladies risked wet petticoats due to the pools of water during rain. Whatever it was, the rye gave a name to this sprightly tune and it has been the favourite of sopranos ever since.

Comin thro the rye, poor body,
Comin thro the rye,
She draigl't a' her petticoatie,
Comin thro the rye!

Chorus
O, Jenny's a' sweet, poor body,
Jenny's seldom dry:
She draigl't a' her petticoatie,
Comin thro the rye!

Gin a body meet a body
Comin thro the rye,
Gin a body kiss a body,
Need a body cry?

O, Jenny's, &c.

Gin a body meet a body
Comin thro the glen,
Gin a body kiss a body,
Need the warld ken!

O, Jenny's, &c.

There are variants in the verses, all in Burns's handwriting, as he amended the lyric from time to time, but basically, the song as it is known today is the song he sent to Johnson during 1789 and 1790.

On 20 June 1796, only weeks before Burns's death, a song was entered at the Stationer's Hall, which claimed to the original song. It has music adapted by J. Sanderson and words by Mr Cross, and was sung in a London pantomime in that year. It began,

If a body meet a body
Going to the fair;
If a body kiss a body
Need a body care?

I daresay by then poor Burns was beyond caring.

The Banks o Doon

1791

This famous song is an extensive revision of a previous song *Ye Flowery Banks*. That particular version had been sent to John Ballantyne, the banker and merchant in Ayr with the following note:

> *While here I sit, sad and solitary, by the side of a fire in a little country inn, & drying my wet clothes, in pops a poor fellow of a sodger & tells me he is going to Ayr – By heavens! say I to myself with a tide of good spirits which the magic of that sound, Auld toon o Ayr conjures up, I will send my last song to Mr Ballantine – here it is –*

Sweet are the banks – the banks o Doon,
The spreading flowers are fair,
And everything is blythe and glad,
But I am fu' o care.
Thou'll break my heart, thou bonie bird,
That sings upon the bough;
Thou minds me o the happy days
When my fause Luve was true:
Thou'll break my heart, thou bonie bird,
That sings beside thy mate;
For sae I sat, and sae I sang,
And wist na o my fate.
Aft hae I rov'd by bonie Doon,
To see the woodbine twine;
And ilka birds sang o its Luve,
And sae did I o mine:
Wi lightsome heart I pu'd a rose,
Upon its thorny tree;
But my fause Luver staw my rose
And left the thorn wi me:

Wi lightsome heart I pu'd a rose,
Upon a morn in June;
And sae I flourished on the morn,
And sae was pu'd or noon!

This next version was the song that Burns told Cunningham he
had '*worked out to a Strathspey reel*' in March 1791 while he was
at Ellisland.

Ye banks and braes o bonie Doon,
How can ye bloom sae fresh and fair?
How can ye chant, ye little birds,
And I sae weary fu' o care!
Thou'll break my heart, thou warbling bird,
That wantons thro the flowering thorn!
Thou minds me o departed joys,
Departed never to return.

Aft hae I rov'd by bonie Doon
To see the rose and woodbine twine,
And ilka bird sang o its luve,
And fondly sae did I o mine.
Wi lightsome heart I pu'd a rose,
Fu sweet upon its thorny tree!
And my fause luver staw my rose –
But ah! he left the thorn wi me.

The reference in the last couplet is to the sad tale of Peggy
Kennedy, daughter of a Carrick laird, Robert Kennedy, to whom
he had been introduced by Gavin Hamilton. The young lady was
only 17 and engaged to Captain McDoual, the younger of Logan,
who at only 25 was the MP for the county. Burns sent her the song
with one of his windiest and wordiest letters. He did much better
with the poem, *Young Peggy*, but his best wishes for her happiness
proved vain as McDoual denied the secret marriage they had
undertaken once he discovered she was pregnant, and he went off
and married a laird's daughter in Dumfries. Peggy was delivered
of his child soon after and her father took her case to the High

Court for 'declarator of Marriage'. Her cause was upheld, her marriage was recognised and her child declared legitimate. She was also awarded damages for seduction, but it was too late. Peggy had died, it is said, of a broken heart. Burns, of all people, would have been drawn to her plight, especially in the light of his own secret betrothal to Mary Campbell, and this song, the third re-working in all of the lyric, was the result.

Bonie Wee Thing

1791

'*Composed on my little idol – the charming, lovely Davies.*' These were the words Burns used in the interleaves of Volume IV of Johnson's *Musical Museum* in 1792. When he sent Miss Davies a copy of the song in March 1793, he wrote,

> *I am a good deal luckier than most poets. When I sing of Miss Davies or Miss Lesley Baillie, I have only to feign the passion – the charms are real.*

Deborah Duff Davies was the daughter of Dr Davies of Tenby in Pembrokeshire, and was related to Captain Riddel of Glenriddel, who probably introduced her to Burns. She was 20 years old, tiny and attractive, and Burns was intrigued by her. He sent her other songs, like *Lovely Davies*, and accompanying letters that were away over the top. Like in August 1791 –

> *Woman is the blood-royal of my life; let them all be sacred. Whether this last sentiment be right or wrong, I am not accountable; it is an original component feature of my mind.*

But his improvised epigrams were right on the mark One day, in Moffat, Burns and a friend saw Miss Davies ride by, accompanied by a large and portly lady. The friend remarked on the difference in size between the two women. Burns said at once,

> *Ask why God made the gem so small*
> *And why so big the granite?*
> *Because God meant mankind should set*
> *The higher value on it.*

He also made on her, a beautiful little person, a beautiful little song.

Chorus
Bonie wee thing, cannie wee thing,
Lovely wee thing, wert thou mine,
I wad wear thee in my bosom,
Lest my jewel it should tine.

Wishfully I look and languish
In that bonie face o thine,
And my heart it stounds wi anguish,
Lest my wee thing be na mine.

Bonie wee thing, &c.

Wit, and Grace, and Love, and Beauty,
In ae constellation shine;
To adore thee is my duty,
Goddess o this soul o mine!

Bonie wee thing, &c.

Unfortunately, like Peggy Kennedy, Deborah Davies was also jilted (by a certain Captain Delany) and like Peggy, died of a decline.

Ae Fond Kiss

1791

In January 1792, Mrs James McLehose sailed from Greenock for Jamaica in the *Roselle*, the very ship Burns had booked to take him to the West Indies just five years before. She was making a final, futile attempt to reconcile with her wayward husband, after the whirlwind passion she had had for Burns had abated. Only a few weeks before, on 6 December 1791, they had parted at Mr Mackay's White Hart Inn in the Grassmarket and he had returned to the West to begin married life with Jean at Ellisland and to take up his commission in the Excise.

His rounds took him by the Post Office in Sanquhar, from where, on 27 December, he posted a song to Nancy, his 'Clarinda'. A song of farewell, of parting love, of 'resigned passion', in Maurice Lindsay's apt phrase, that was to contain some of the finest lines he ever wrote. These words, pouring spontaneously on to the page, were supposedly to wind down their affair as gently as his other words, sparked on to page after page of hysterical letters by the other Burns known as 'Sylvander', had wound them into a tumult of unrequited love four years previously.

Here, however, was no Arcadian *billet doux* but an immediate cry from the very soul. These lines come from a man who knew what love was and what it still means in being remembered, and yet it was dashed off 'to catch the post'. Or so he said. ('*I have just ten minutes before the post goes... I have been rhyming a little of late, but I do not know if they are worth the postage.*')

Every work of Burns of any worth is the result of his polishing, yet one can believe in the spontaniety of this lyric. It doesn't have the artifice of craft, even good craft, but simply states its case in immediate and hearty-searing verse that virtually sings its own meaning. If it were meant to ease the pain of parting, it surely failed, for any woman receiving lines like these she could not fail to fall in love all over again.

Ae fond kiss, and then we sever;
Ae fareweel, alas, for ever!
Deep in heart-wrung tears I'll pledge thee,
Warring sighs and groans I'll wage thee.
Who shall say that Fortune grieves him,
While the star of hope she leaves him?
Me, nae cheerful twinkle lights me;
Dark despair around benights me.

I'll ne'er blame my partial fancy,
Naething could resist my Nancy:
But to see her was to love her;
Love but her, and love for ever.
Had we never lov'd sae kindly,
Had we never lov'd sae blindly,
Never met – or never parted,
We had ne'er been broken-hearted.

Fare-thee-weel, thou first and fairest!
Fare-thee-weel, thou best and dearest!
Thine be ilka joy and treasure,
Peace, Enjoyment, Love and Pleasure!
Ae fond kiss, and then we sever!
Ae fareweeli alas, for ever!
Deep in heart-wrung tears I'll pledge thee,
Warring sighs and groans I'll wage thee.

Nancy survived Burns by 45 years, dying in Edinburgh in 1841 at the age of 83, the very age Burns himself would have been had he lived. She kept every letter he had written to her in a little wooden box covered in wallpaper, and after her death her son sold them at auction for three shillings – including the box. She never forgot her Sylvander, and would talk to everyone about him at the slightest opportunity. In her diary, kept right up to the last decade of her life, the entry for 6 December 1831 read:

> *This day I can never forget. Parted with Burns in 1791, never more to meet in this world. May we meet in heaven.*

The Deil's Awa wi th' Exciseman

1792

Lockhart claims, on the authority of Joseph Train, that Burns composed this song *extempore* on 27 February while waiting on the Solway to board a French brig, the *Rosamond*, which had run aground, but still had its guns intact. Britain was at war with France at this time, and the ship could be regarded as legitimate bounty if the Excise could seize it as a prize of war. John Lewars was sent back to Dumfiries for reinforcements and heavier arms, and before dawn Officer Burns led a company to the vessel. They were able to surprise the crew and Burns, using his 'schoolroom French' was able to instruct the captain to bring the ship into Dumfries harbour. Next day, at the public auction of the ship's effects, Burns bought the two cannon from the brig and returned them to the French revolutionists – 'with his Poet's compliments'.

This story, with all respect to Mr Train, is quite untrue – but it is still a good story.

> The deil cam fiddlin thro the town,
> And danc'd awa wi th' Exciseman,
> And ilka wife cries, 'Auld Mahoun,
> I wish you luck o the prize, man.'

> *Chorus*
> The deil's awa, the deil's awa,
> The deil's awa wi th' Exciseman,
> He's danc'd awa, he's danc'd awa,
> He's danc'd awa wi th' Exciseman.

> We'll mak our maut, and we'll brew our drink,
> We'll laugh, sing, and rejoice, man,
> And mony braw thanks to the meikle black deil,
> That danc'd awa wi th' Exciseman.

> The deil's awa, &c.

There's threesome reels, there's foursome reels,
There's hornpipes and strathspeys, man,
But the ae best dance ere came to the land
Was – the deil's awa wi the Exciseman.

The deil's awa, &c.

The real truth of the composition of this rollicking song is that it was written by Burns at a dinner held for Excise Officers in Dumfries the following month. He scribbled the words, all three verses, on the back of an envelope, in the true tradition of song-writing, and when asked to speak from his place by the President, he rose up and sang the whole thing through.

Whistle and I'll Come to Ye, My Lad

1793

The first set of words composed by Burns to the traditional chorus was sent to Johnson in time for his second volume of songs in 1788, but Burns re-worked the lyric in 1793, for Thomson, then made further minor changes in 1795. The version published in Thomson's 1799 Collection is the set of lyrics now commonly used.

The heroine of the song is a much under-estimated part of Burns's love-life, Jean Lorimer, also known as 'Chloris' and, because of her yellow hair, the '*The Lassie wi the lint-white locks*'. She was the reason for one of the changes as he wanted to insert her name in the chorus, but Thomson, for once, rightly objected. Burns sent off one of his flowery protests, in which he studiedly mentioned Jean as the muse.

> *In fact, a fair dame, at whose shrine I, the Priest of the Nine, offer up the incense of Parnassus; a dame whom the Graces have attired in witchcraft, and whom the Loves have armed with lightning; a fair one, herself the heroine of the song, insists on the amendment, and dispute her commands if you dare.*

Thomson dared, and suggested other small changes, but Burns demurred and the lyric remained as he originally wrote it. Jean Lorimer was the first to sing it, and she did so, according to Cromek, '*in the spirit of arch-simplicity it requires*'.

Chorus
O Whistle, an I'll come to ye, my lad,
O whistle, an I'll come to ye, my lad,
Tho father an mother an a' should gae mad,
O whistle, an I'll come to ye, my lad.

But warily tent when ye come to court me,
And come nae unless the back-yett be a-jee;
Syne up the back-stile, and let naebody see,

And come as ye were na comin to me,
And come as ye were na comin to me.

O whistle an I'll come, &c.

At kirk, or at market, whene'er ye meet me,
Gang by me as tho that ye car'd na a flie;
But steal me a blink o your bonie black ee,
Yet look as ye were na lookin to me,
Yet look as ye were na lookin to me.

O whistle an I'll come, &c.

Aye vow and protest that ye care na for me,
And whiles ye may lightly my beauty a-wee;
But court na anither, tho jokin ye be,
For fear that she wile your fancy frae me,
For fear that she wile your fancy frae me.

O whistle an I'll come, &c.

In writing to Burns in 1794, Thomson wondered how a woman could be beautiful with 'lint-white locks' but Burns defended his description as the 'fair one' was flaxen-haired, derived from flax, made from lint, a plant with a white flower. Jean, in other words, was like Clarinda, a blonde, and Burns preferred blondes. There was no doubt also that Jean had a place in his catalogue of genuine female friends. He might have married Ellison Begbie had she agreed, then Jean Armour appeared. He might have really emigrated with Mary Campbell, but the book came out. He might then have married Nancy McLehose had she not been married already, and, finally, he fell in love with Jean, who was just 17, and fascinated by this poetic Exciseman, who was happily married himself at the time. In all the talk of his reputed womanising, these ladies just mentioned are the only ones to deserve any real consideration as objects of his true, and lasting, affection as well as providing the necessary inspiration. As he said himself,

> *Whenever I want to be more than ordinary in song... I put myself in the regimen of admiring a fine woman.*

And few came finer than Jean Lorimer, the one he chose to call his 'Chloris', the Goddess of Flowers. The name is unusual, and one he was unsure of in February 1796 when he confided to Thomson,

> *In my past by-songs I dislike one thing – the name Chloris.*
> *I meant it as the fictitious name of a certain lady, but on*
> *second thoughts, it is a high incongruity to have a Greek*
> *appelation to a Scot pastoral ballad.*

Burns wrote no less than 14 songs for this 'certain lady' – *'the lovely goddess of my inspiration'*. He wrote far more songs for her than he ever wrote for any other one girl, even Jean Armour, although the 'Jeans' mentioned in some songs may have been interchangable. They were actually the best of friends in real life, and Burns had for both, the 'white-flower love' he had for all his heroines in song.

When she was young, Jean Lorimer never lacked for suitors around Moffat. Burns was only one of her many admirers. To everyone's surprise, however, she suddenly eloped to Gretna Green with a wastrel called Whelpdale, who abandoned her when he fled the district soon after to escape his creditors. She spent most of her life from 1822 on the streets of Edinburgh, but, thanks to the efforts of Burns admirers, and a fund they raised for her, she ended her years respectably as 'Mrs Lorimer', and remembered by all, even in her faded beauty, as 'Burns's Chloris'. She died in 1831, aged 56. In 1901, the Edinburgh Ninety Club put a memorial stone on her grave in Newington. She deserves to be so remembered for she was an important part of the Robert Burns song-story.

Scots Wha Hae

1793

They are most welcome to my ode, only let them insert it as a thing they have met with by accident and unknown to me.

This was Burns's reaction to a request by James Perry in London to print *Scots Wha Hae* in the London *Morning Chronicle* in May 1794. His reluctance to be named was due more to political prudence than modesty. and Perry printed it with a suitably arch prefatory note. Burns was right in taking precautions in dangerous times, but he was wrong in thinking no one would guess that he was the author. His stamp was all over it, and Perry was right in thinking Burns ought to have put his name to it.

There are various stories as to its genesis. Syme says Burns wrote it while on a tour with him in Galloway but Burns begs to differ. Writing to Thomson in 1793, he mentioned that tradition had it that *Hey Tutti Taiti*, the air to which the music was set, was Bruce's march at the Battle of Bannockburn.

This thought, in my yesternight's evening walk, roused me to a pitch of enthusiasm on the theme of liberty and independence, which I threw into a kind of Scots ode, fitted to the air, that one might suppose to be the gallant royal Scot's address to his heroic followers on that eventful morning.

Scots, wha hae wi Wallace bled,
Scots, wham Bruce has aften led,
Welcome to your gory bed
Or to victorie!
Now's the day, and now's the hour;
See the front o battle lour,
See approach proud Edward's power –
Chains and slaverie!

Wha will be a traitor knave?
Wha can fill a coward's grave?

Wha sae base as be a slave? –
Let him turn, and flee!
Wha for Scotland's King and Law
Freedom's sword will strongly draw,
Freeman stand, or Freeman fa',
Let him follow me!

By oppression's woes and pains,
By your sons in servile chains
We will drain your dearest veins,
But they shall be free!
Lay the proud usurpers low!
Tyrants fall in every foe!
Liberty's in every blow! –
Let us do, or die!

Burns visited the field of Bannockburn, near Stirling, on 26 August 1787, and noted:

> *I said a fervent prayer for Old Caledonia over the hole in a blue whinstone where Robert de Bruce fixed his royal standard... I had no idea of giving myself any trouble on the subject, till the accidental recollection of that glorious struggle for freedom... roused my rhyming mania.*

Thomson had his usual ideas for changes both as to tune and lyric, but this time Burns was firm –

> *I have scrutinized it over and over; and to the world, some way or other, it shall go as it is.*

My Love is Like a Red, Red Rose

1794

This is one of the most derivative of all Burns's songs, (the other being *Auld Lang Syne*). There were many old versions of the *Red Rose* theme, and most of these would have been known to him, but none has quite the finish of the delectable song he finally formed. It may have been in the air for centuries, and every stanza might have the mark of an old fragment, but it was his high musical-poetic touch that finally put it all together on the page in the master-form of the song we now know. It is certainly something of an amalgam, but what a jewel of one it is.

> O my Luve's like a red, red rose,
> That's newly sprung in June;
> O my Luve's like the melodie,
> That's sweetly play'd in tune.
>
> As fair art thou, my bonie lass,
> So deep in luve am I;
> And I will luve thee still, my dear,
> Till a' the seas gang dry.
>
> Till a' the seas gang dry, my dear,
> And the rocks melt wi the sun;
> And I will luve thee still, my dear,
> While the sands o life shall run.
>
> And fare-thee-weel, my only Luve!
> And fare-thee-weel, a while!
> And I will come again, my Luve,
> Tho twere ten thousand mile!

This Burns version was first published by the Italian singer and music teacher, Pietro Urbani, in his *Scots Songs*, published by Urbani and Liston in April 1794. This would not have happened had not Thomson and Burns disagreed violently about *Red Rose*.

What to me appears the simple and the wild, to him...will be looked on as the ludicrous and the absurd.

He had no great opinion of Signor Urbani either.

He is... a narrow, contracted creature... but he sings so delightfully... that whatever he introduces... must have instant celebrity.

Johnson gave the singer permission to use anything he found in the Museum, but he was expressly forbidden to use Burns's name. Despite this, he did, and their friendship ended. Urbani's publishing business failed in 1809 and he went to Dublin where he died destitute. However, he is to be remembered as the man to whom Burns gave this immortal song in its original setting by Niel Gow, entitled *Major Graham*, which Burns himself had specified. Thomson eventually published his own version in *Original Scottish Airs* in 1799 set to *Wishaw's Favourite* by William Marshall, but it was not a success. It was not until it was put out by Paisley's Robert Archibald Smith in his *Scottish Minstrel* in 1821 to the traditional tune, *Low down in the broom*, that it achieved the world-wide fame it enjoys to this day.

A Man's A Man

1795

Burns to Thomson, January 1795:

> *A great critic on Song says that Love and Wine are the
> exclusive themes for song-writing. The following is on nei-
> ther subject, and consequently is no song...*
>
> *I do not give you the foregoing for your book, but merely by
> way of 'vive la bagatelle'; for the piece is not really poetry.*

Perhaps so, but what this song lacks in poetry it makes up for in
passion. It is the nearest Burns got to articulating his essential rad-
icalism, and considering the time in which it was written, it is a
call to revolution, but with a cautious, philosophical Scottish
note. It is only in the last line that brotherhood breaks out as if it
could not be suppressed any longer.

Is there for honest Poverty
That hings his head, an a' that;
The coward slave – we pass him by,
We dare be poor for a' that!
For a' that, an a' that.
Our toils obscure an a' that,
The rank is but the guinea's stamp,
The Man's the gowd for a' that.

What though on hamely fare we dine,
Wear hoddin grey, an a that;
Gie fools their silks, and knaves their wine;
A Man's a Man for a' that:
For a' that, an a' that,
Their tinsel show, an a' that;
The honest man, tho e'er sae poor,
Is king o men for a' that.

Ye see yon birkie, ca'd a lord,
Wha struts, an stares, an a' that;
Tho hundreds worship at his word,
He's but a cuff for a' that:
For a' that, an a' that,
His ribband, star, an a' that:
The man o independent mind
He looks an laughs at a' that.

A prince can mak a belted knight,
A marquis, duke, an a' that;
But an honest man's abune his might,
Guid faith, he maunna fa' that!
For a' that, an a' that,
Their dignities an a' that;
The pith o sense, an pride o worth,
Are higher rank than a' that.

Then let us pray that come it may,
(As come it will for a' that,)
That Sense and Worth, oer a' the earth,
Shall bear the gree, an a' that.
For a' that, an a' that,
It's coming yet for a' that,
That Man to Man, the world o'er,
Shall brothers be for a' that.

It was well-known in Dumfries that the poet's private sympathies
were with the French Revolution and he was frequently in trouble
with the authorities on account of them. On one occasion there
were calls for *Ca Ira*, the revolutionists' song, rather than *God
Save the King*, the Hanovarian National in the Theatre Royal,
Dumfries and a near-riot ensued. Burns sat through the uproar
with his arms folded and his hat on, and next day was hauled
before his superiors on suspicion of seditious behaviour. Only a
well-worded aplogy saved his job. Similarly, his toasts to
Washington and other colonial revolutionists often offended the
Dumfries establishment, as did his close friendship with Syme and

Maxwell, who were open in their socialist views. All three were
forced to join the local Volunteer Militia as a gesture of appease-
ment and they made much fun of what Burns called the 'awkward
squad'. On his deathbed, he begged that they should not, under
any circumsances, fire a salvo over his grave. But they did. With
near-fatal results to those by-standers in the vicinity.

More seriously, it was on this slight connection to the Army
that Burns was given a military funeral with full honours, but it
is also thought by many that the large Army presence on that day,
with soldiers with fixed bayonets lining the High Street between
the Mid-Steeple and St Michael's, and *facing the citizens* and not
the passing cortege and procession, was an act of authorities who
were taking no chances. In addition to the theatre disturbance,
there had been bread riots in the street. The funeral might have
ignited an explosive spark in the ordinary people. Even when dead,
Burns was dangerous.

O, Wert Thou in the Cauld Blast

1796

Jessie Lewars was the last of Burns's song heroines. She lived with her brother John, who was in the Excise with the poet. Their house in the Mill Vennel (now Burns St) in Dumfries was exactly opposite the Burns family, and Jessie and her brother often visited. On one occasion, Burns heard Jessie singing *The Robin cam to the Wren's Nest* and promised to write a song for her, but it was not until he was dying that he was able to do so. Even though he was then helpless himself, the burden of the lyric was how he might help this young girl who had come in to look after him while Jean lay in the next room expecting the birth of his last son, Maxwell. Even with death so near, he imagined himself in love again, and a poignant and splendid song was the result.

O wert thou in the cauld blast,
On yonder lea, on yonder lea,
My plaidie to the angry airt,
I'd shelter thee, I'd shelter thee;
Or did Misfortune's bitter storms
Around thee blaw, around thee blaw,
Thy bield should be my bosom,
To share it a', to share it a'.

Or were I in the wildest waste,
Sae black and bare, sae black and bare,
The desert were a Paradise,
If thou wert there, if thou wert there;
Or were I Monarch o the globe,
Wi thee to reign, wi thee to reign,
The brightest jewel in my Crown
Wad be my Queen, wad be my Queen.

Jessie married James Thomson, a writer in Dumfries in June 1799, and bore him seven children, but only after she had looked after the Burns boys for a year after their father's death. It was she who gave a very sympathetic account of Burns to Chambers. She testified to Burns's simple, but in cases, quite definite needs –

> *as far as circumstances left [him] to his own inclinations. He was always anxious that his wife should have a neat and genteel appearance. In consequence, as she alleged, of the duties of nursing, and attending to her infants, she could not help being sometimes a little out of order. Burns disliked this, and not only remonstrated against it in a gentle way, but did the utmost that in him lay to counteract it by buying for her the best clothes he could afford. She was, for instance, the first person in Dumfries who appeared in a dresss of gingham – a stuff now common, but, at its first introduction, rather costly, and almost exclusively used by persons of superior conditions.*

Auld Lang Syne

1788 (revised 1793)

*One song more and I have done, Auld Lang Syne. The air
is mediocre; but the following song – the old song of olden
times, and which has never been in print, not even in man-
uscript, until I took it down from an old man's singing – is
enough to recommend any air.*

This was how Burns introduced the famous dismissory song to
Thomson in 1793 for his *Select Scottish Airs*. Thomson thought
he had written this explanation *'merely in a playful humour'* and
he delayed printing it until 1822, 26 years after the poet's death.
This was probably because Thomson was aware that the same
title had been published in Johnson's *Museum* twice before, once
with Burns's words in 1796 and one with words by Alan Ramsay,
dating from his *Scots Songs* of 1720 to an air dating from 1700,
and containing the key phrase, *'should auld acquaintance be forgot'*.
These same words can be traced back to Watson's *Scots Poems* of
1711, and before that to the Bannantyne Manuscript of 1568. So
it is a phrase that has a pedigree, and Burns would certainly have
known of this provenance. In sending his first draft to Mrs Dunlop
in 1788, he said,

*Is not the phrase Auld Lang Syne exceedingly expressive?
Light be the turf on the breast of the heaven-inspired poet
who composed this glorious fragment...*

That first poet might have been Sir Robert Aytoun, who was in the
court of King James VI and I, but it matters little now. What mattered
was that another poet took up this first inspiration and began the del-
icate work of salvaging an auld sang. It shows the poet once again
not only as song-maker but as musicologist. His work in this field is
quite staggering. In November 1794, he tried to reassure Thomson.

*The two songs you saw in Clarke's are neither of them worth
your attention. The words... are good, but the air is an old air,
the rudiments of the modern tune of that name. The other
tune you may hear as a common Scots country dance.*

This last is probably the one that is best known today, the one known to every function secretary and popularised between the wars by Guy Lombardo and his Orchestra each New Year's Eve from the Rockefeller Centre in New York. It has now become the song that everybody has heard of but nobody knows.

So, for the record, this is what Burns wrote first in 1788, and again, with only minor amendments, like the omission of '*days o*' in the last line of the 1793 revision.

> *Should auld acquaintance be forgot*
> *And never brought to mind?*
> *Should auld acquaintance be forgot*
> *And days o lang syne?*

There is more than mere sentimentality here. There is genuine sentiment, in the 18th-century sense, almost a 'presentiment'. We need to remember the past so that we can freely embrace the future. It has a real practicality. Memories, like dreams, have a purpose. They clear things up. They get rid of the rubbish. In the same way, a 'guid greet' can do you the world of good. Like a good fart, it's always better out than in. The final line in the verse is generally rendered as – '*For the days of auld lang syne*' – which is not in the original manuscript. And the the sibilant '*s*' in '*syne*' is always being replaced by the lazier '*z*'. Especially by English-speakers. But this is mere usage. The modern chorus uses '*my dear*' rather than '*my jo*' from the first draft.

> *For auld lang syne, my jo,*
> *For auld lang syne,*
> *We'll tak a cup o kindness yet,*
> *For auld lang syne!*

'*Auld lang syne*' is literally 'old long ago or 'in days gone by', that memory-haven where the best of the past is stored in all of us, to be available as needed. This is where nostalgia lives, a gentle remembering that grows more poignant as we get older. It is this that sweetens Burns's 'cup o kindness' – a lovely phrase.

> *And surely you'll be your pint-stowp,*
> *And surely I'll be mine,*

> *And we'll tak a cup o kindness yet*
> *For auld lang syne!*

A pint-stowp was a tin measure of two-quarts – half-a-gallon.
Burns's point here was that each of us can afford to stand our
own round, or pay for each other at least. It's surely a poor world
if you can't stand a friend a drink – and better still join him in it.
The pub or tavern was a man's world in Burns's day.

> *We twa hae run aboot the braes*
> *And pu'd the gowans fine,*
> *And we've wander'd mony a fit,*
> *Sin auld lang syne.*

This verse sounds like the nucleus from which Burns made the
song. He always said he only composed two stanzas out of the five,
and he would surely have known that there were few braes (hills)
in Ayrshire. Although he did know about gowans – that *modest,
crimson-tipped flow'r'* otherwise known as the daisy. He is here a
man remembering boyish friendships – the kind that last forever.

> *We twa hae paidl'd in the burn*
> *Frae morning sun till dine*
> *But seas between us baith hae roar'd*
> *Sin auld lang syne.*

Again the theme is male nostalgia – wading in a stream, even with
kirtled, or lifted skirts wasn't such a free experience for girls –
even sonsie, robust Ayrshire farm girls. '*Dine*' is 'dinner', mean-
ing the evening meal, although, in Burns's time, and for many
Scots yet, dinner is taken at noon. The '*seas between*' suggests the
exile which Burns never became. Except in his last years at
Dumfries perhaps? '*Sin*' in the last line is again a contraction of
'since' for ease of singing.

> *And there's a hand, my trusty fiere,*
> *And gie's a hand o thine,*
> *And we'll tak a right guid-willie waught*
> *For auld lang syne.*

This is the real stuff of Burns. A firm, honest, open handclasp
between men. '*Fiere*' is a standard of any kind, a guage by which

Burns compares one man to another, hence in this instance, a standard-bearer. The term comes from a spinning process, and no doubt reflects Burns's brief involvement with heckling flax at Irvine in 1771. '*Guid-willie*' is 'goodwill' and '*waught*' is a generous swig of any liquid, so Burns here is telling us to get it over in one good gulp without any reserve or inhibitions. This is the only way real friends can drink together. No timid sipping at the lip, but a good trusting swallow. It is then, with head laid back and eyes closed, we are at our most vulnerable.

This then is the song and its *verbatim* translation, but of course it means a lot more than it says, as was Burns's way in so much of his work. Here he was working as a song-maker, using perhaps the greatest of his word skills as a song-saver in an act of artistic rescue. In the case of *Auld Lang Syne*, he took what was little more than couplet, a mere wisp of a thread of an idea, and he wove it into a brand-new coat which it still wears proudly to this day.

Should auld acquaintance be forgot
And never brought to mind?
Should auld acquaintance be forgot
And days o lang syne?

Chorus
For auld lang syne, my jo,
For auld lang syne,
We'll tak a cup o kindness yet,
For auld lang syne!

For Auld, &c.

And surely you'll be your pint-stowp,
And surely I'll be mine,
And we'll tak a cup o kindness yet
For auld lang syne!

For Auld, &c.

We twa hae run aboot the braes
And pu'd the gowans fine,
And we've wander'd mony a fit,
Sin auld lang syne.

For Auld, &c.

We twa hae paidl'd in the burn
Frae morning sun till dine
But seas between us baith hae roar'd
Sin auld lang syne.

For Auld, &c.

And there's a hand, my trusty fiere,
And gie's a hand o thine,
And we'll tak a right guid-willie waught
For auld lang syne.

For Auld, &c.

A final thought on the songs. It is little appreciated how much fine tuning his writing generally owes to his letter-writing. The letters, hundreds of them, were superb efforts of sagacity and penmanship. He had a prose style that would have done credit to any Augustan classicist and in reading them, one is reminded of what a master of language Burns was. It was this mastery he applied to his songwriting. His was the written English of Addison, and of a whole school of English poets of that period, but the songs could only have been his own. They were of his very skin and bone, as Scotland itself was. The stuff of his songs came out of his marrow.

Whether for James Johnson's *Musical Museum* or for George Thomson's *Select Collection of Scottish Airs*, or even for the wayward Cunningham, these songs were masterworks of their kind, with lyrics ringing true with thought and winging unerringly from heart to heart as if carried on a sunbeam. A small work, yes, a song lyric, but when it is right, it is a gem, a jewel. And Burns mostly got it right. Like Schubert, he was able to catch the ache of real feeling in miniature.

He had gone back to Nature – his own nature. These songs are capsulated radiance. And most of them were written in that final, glorious, sunburst of poetic genius as his body was giving out until, after the last line of his last song, the pen dropped from his lifeless fingers. The love songs had become his threnody.

The Heron Memoir
1797
Some comments and selected excerpts

The importance of Robert Heron's Memoir of the Life of the Late
Robert Burns goes without saying, as it is the first biographical
writing about him, written less than a year after his death.
Whatever its literary merits, it is a vital document and must be
seriously considered by any who seek to know Burns from the
point of view of his own times. One could only have wished for
a writer worthier of the task.

Heron begins,

*Biography is, in some instances, the most trifling and con-
temptible, in others, the most interesting and constructive
of all the species of literary composition. It would be diffi-
cult to persuade one's self to agree with several late histori-
ans of the late poets, philosophers and statesmen; that the
mere industrious acumulation of dates, anecdotes, and wit-
ticisms, of transactions in which no peculiarities of genius
and character were displayed, or of obscure events by which
the habits of feeling, thought or action, were in no way
remarkably influenced; can deserve to be ambitiously stud-
ied, or admired as the perfection of biographical writing.*

*The following memoir of one who was a great man, solely
of God Almighty's making such; has been composed under
the direction of a very different, although perhaps not a
more correct, critical principle. If, however, this principle is
just; it is the proper business of the biographer to trace the
gradual development of the character and talents of his
hero, with all the changes which these things undergo from
the influnce of external circumstances, between the cradle
and the grave; and at the same time, to record all the emi-
nent effects which the display of that character, and the*

exercise of those talents, have produced upon nature and on human society, in the sphere within which they were exhibited and employed.

The writer's wishes will be amply gratified; if this trifle shall be found to afford any exposition of the nicer laws of the formation and progress of human character, such as shall not be scorned as data by the moral philosopher, or, as facts to enlighten his imitations, by the dramtist; if it shall be received by the world in general, as an honest though humble tribute to illustrious genius; and, above all, if it shall be regarded by the candid and the good, as presenting some details and reflections, of which the direct tendency is, to recommend that steady virtue, without which even genius in all its omnipotence is soon reduced to paralytic imbecility, or to maniac mischievousness.

And having started off in such a style, so he goes on, through a welter of commas and semi-colons, never missing a digression if he can help it, and with only the occasional respite of a full stop. He posts his intention early, that is, as far as Robert Burns is concerned, to make this a search for the dirt rather than the uncovering of a deity. Despite this, he does make some good points. For instance, in dealing with Burns's early life he had a whole page on parish schools and how important these single-teacher establishments were in rural Scotland, and how they benefited '*the peasant youth*' if only for a time in summer. He goes on,

It was so with Burns. He returned from labour to learning, and from learning went again to labour; till his mind began to open to the charms of taste and knowledge; till he began to feel a passion for books, and for the subjects of books which was to give a colour to the whole thread of his future life.

This was certainly true. Reading was the first gift given him, and it was the key to everything else, and Heron recognised this at least. Except that he imagined Burns was sparked to poetry by the diligent reading of other poets, whereas we know better, from

Burns himself, that it had a lot to do with puberty and matura-
tion. Heron saw the Masons as nothing more than a means of
introducing Burns to drink. The recognition of his own power
with words and way with girls made Burns a reckless, if enthusi-
astic, lover. He also hints that the youth's untypical learning for
one of his class made him discontented with his station in life.
There is some truth in this. Heron saw him, nevertheless, as a
sagacious observer of the peasant life, where he celebrated the
humble and artless rustic who never aspired to grandeur.
However, Burns had such aspirations from the time of his local
fame as a writer. Heron gave an account of the excitement in the
countryside when the poems first came out in print.

> *I was at that time resident in Galloway, contiguous to*
> *Ayrshire; and I can well remember, how that even plough-*
> *boys and maidservants would have gladly disposed the*
> *wages which they earned the most hardly, and which they*
> *wanted to purchase necessary clothing, if they might but*
> *procure the work of Burns.*

Heron was given a copy by a friend, and opened it as he was
about to go to bed. He did not close it till he had read 'every syl-
lable it contained'. He then added, '*Ex illo Corydon, Corydon est*
tempore nobis! Virg. Ec.7.' He was won over, bowled over in fact,
so that when he met Burns at Dr Blacklock's in the early winter
of 1786–87, he was ready to be impressed, but he was aware that
Burns was, in many Edinburgh circles, for all his obvious gifts, no
more than the latest novelty. For all the attention he received from
the gentry, it was not the real praise he had known in Ayrshire.
This is an acute observation by Heron, but he goes on to suggest
that Burns succumbed too easily to the heady sensation of being
'*the idol of fashion*', but what else could he do? He was only there
to get his second edition out, everything else was just so much
empty noise around this main aim. He perhaps might have been
better advised about giving away his copyright to publisher,
Creech, but he thought if he got out of the capital and back to the
west with a few hundred pounds in his pocket, he would be doing

well. He did just that, he got more than seven hundred pounds, in his pocket (according to Heron, that is), but with one thing and another, it didn't turn out to be the windfall it ought to have been for a ploughboy turned poet. Heron makes another point about Burns in his new situation.

> The conversation of the most eminent authors, is often found to be so unequal to the fame of their writings, that he who read with admiration, can listen with none but sentiments of the most profound contempt. But, the conversation of Burns was, in comparison with the formal and exterior circumstances of his education, perhaps even more wonderful than his poetry...

It was the sheer common sense or *mother-wit* in the poet's talk that astounded all who heard him, even Heron. He affected no airs, because he knew his own value, and therefore could meet any minds on level ground. It was in the social scene that Burns often found himself at a disadvantage. He wasn't the crude rustic they had all expected and this discomfited them more than it did him. Heron points out that Burns could not adopt the supercilliousness that was the mark of fashionable conversation and that this made Burns retreat to more congenial company a little lower on the social ladder. The truth was that Burns was soon bored with tittle-tattle, but Heron does not see it this way. He has the authority of a Mr Arthur Bruce to say that Burns would have to have been superhuman to resist the temptations put in his way in Edinburgh, and that the bucks of Edinburgh succeeded where the boors of Ayrshire had failed. He yielded to the tavern and the brothel, and from this point on began to exhibit '*a new arrogance in his conversation*' and began to accustom himself to be '*what is vulgarly, but expressively, called the cock of the company.*' According to Heron, the rot set in at Edinburgh and was to grow steadily worse all the way to Dumfries.

The tours were dismissed as no more than escapee jaunts and Heron wondered why Burns lingered on in Edinburgh so long after the publication of his second and third editions, but it didn't seem to occur to him that Burns was waiting for his money from Creech. The publisher so prevaricated in this that Burns threatened to take a cudgel to the man. Burns was as much sinned against in Edinburgh as sinning. While there is a little truth in what he says, it is not, by any means, the full story. The translation of a farmer to a man of letters brings its own problems, and perhaps the truth is if Burns had *stayed* in Edinburgh he might have managed this transition better. It is often forgotten that he returned to Ayrshire for Jean Armour's sake (whom Heron, by the way, calls Jane). He also calls Patrick Miller of Dalswinton, Peter.

The whole memoir slides down the gradual, but irresistible slope of vagueness and error suited to his thesis that the man is only as good as the company he keeps. Added to which, Burns, he says, was victim to the good intentions of well-meaning friends. There could have been something in this, especially if one thinks of the poor advice on Ellisland Farm, and the unexpected rigours of his Excise routine forced on him by doltish superiors. Burns had got out of he way of hard, manual labour. He had deliberately tried to write his way out of it, but in the end, he had to yield to the need to keep '*wife and weans*' and the strain took its toll.

The path from Edinburgh to Dumfries, from Heron's point of view, was down all the way, yet how was it that Burns was able find time to write all those letters, in exquisite penmanship, save all those songs, throw off a *Tam o Shanter* and ride all over the countryside '*searchin auld wives barrels*'? He did not '*sink rapidly into disgrace and wretchedness*'. Would such a man worry about a new, gingham dress for Jean or pull every string to get his three sons a good education? The picture that Heron here paints of a man –

> *crippled, emaciated, having the very power of animation wasted by disease, quite broken-hearted by the sense of his errors, and of the hopeless miseries in which he saw himself and his family depressed*

is quite at odds with a concerned husband father whose boyhood was now killing him, rather than any excesses, and whose only

regret was that he knew he was going to die still full of songs. At
the conclusion of his long memoir, Robert Heron had to admit,

> From the preceding detail of the particulars of this poet's
> life, the reader will naturally, and justly infer him to have
> been an honest, proud, warm-hearted man; of high pas-
> sions, a sound understanding, a vigorous and excursive
> imagination. He was never known to descend to any act of
> deliberate meanness. In Dumfries, he retained many
> respectable friends, even to the last. It may be doubted
> whether he has not by his writings, exercised a greater
> power over the minds of men, and by consequence, on their
> conduct, upon their happiness and misery, upon the general
> system of life, than has been exercised by any half dozen of
> the most eminent statesmen of the present age.

However the sensibilities of former admirers might be offended
by the circumstance of his heros death, Burns knew that posterity
would get it right, as it always does. He told his wife at the end,

> Don't be afraid. I'll be more respected a hundred years after
> I am dead than I am at present.

Postscript

The Kilmarnock Edition of *Poems, Chiefly in the Scottish Dialect* issued on Monday, 31 July 1786, octavo in blue papers, price stitched, three shillings, showed 33 entries in the Contents. These comprised 19 Poems, 8 Epitaphs, 7 Epistles, 3 Songs, 2 Epigrams, one Ode, one Lament, a Prayer and an Inscription, which, in total, make 43 items. Even if one adds four pages of Preface and five for a Glossary, it is not a huge work by any means. Yet it was this little acorn of a publication which grew into the vast oak of Burnsiana, which in turn, has become the veritable forest of books about him, of which this is yet another one.

> *The simple bard. unbroke by rules of art,*
> *He pours the wild effusions of the heart:*
> *And if inspired, tis Nature's pow'rs inspire;*
> *Her's the melting thrill, and her's the kindling fire.*

This quatrain on the title page is anonymous, and it is just as well. Its quality is misleading and its sense even more so. If nothing else, this present book has shown us just how much Burns was broken by the rules of art. No writer could have worked harder to make himself proficient in letters, but once again, the false modesty of the seller intrudes, and a self-deprecating tone adopted to intrigue the potential buyer. An excess of modesty is the resort of the self-centred. A shy person is often afraid to enter a crowded room because he or she is convincinced that everyone will be looking at them. What egotism. Any artist, if he is honest, has an erring sense of his own worth – as an artist. And Robert Burns was an artist. He was also honest, with himself, if not always with others. He wrote,

> *The honest man has nothing to fear. If we lie down in the grave, a piece of broken machinery, well so be it. At least there's an end of pain and care and want. The whole man still lives in how folk will remember him...*

The world will remember Burns the artist long after the man. By his works, so shall ye know him, and by and large, these were good works he left us. He also said, of himself,

> *If he has been in his life the sport of his own instincts, he goes to a God who gave him these instincts, and well knows their force...*

Let us, therefore, thank that same God then, for the life-work of that same young man whom I like to remember best by the unforced and unpretentious couple of verses which combined two of the things he valued in his life, good wine and good friends, and with a little philosophical nub for good measure.

> *Here's a bottle and an honest man!*
> *What wad ye wish for mair, man?*
> *Wha kens, before his life may end,*
> *What his share may be o care, man?*
>
> *Then catch the moments as they fly,*
> *And use them as ye ought, man!*
> *Believe me, Happiness is shy,*
> *And comes not ay when sought, man!*

Myths and Misconceptions

Some of the best things written about Robert Burns were the lies told about him. The spurious is always interesting, and even if 'facts are chiels that winna ding' some canards survive because people would like to believe them. In Burns's case, the below are only a few of the questions that are repeatedly asked about him, and it is a pleasure to print them here, if only for the opportunity it gives to nail the untruths to the page. It probably will make little difference. Human nature being what it is, people prefer to believe the worst, and no one one would undertsand that better than Burns himself.

To begin with, Robert Burns did NOT

a) populate Scotland single-handedly.
This is almost the greatest fallacy about the poet. If everything that was said about his reputed sex life were only half-true, he would never have had time to draw breath never mind write what he did and keep two full-time jobs going. The facts are these. He sired 13 children in all between 1785 and 1796, including two sets of twins. That works out at a child and a bit every year till his death. His 'bit on the side', as it were, resulted in four 'bastard weans', two of whom were brought up by Jean Armour. Two of her own children died at birth, and two in infancy. Of the nine remaining, only three sons survived into adulthood

b) marry Highland Mary secretly.
Contemporary Burns scholarship is not even sure that Mary Campbell was a serious part of the Burns story, although it is true that Bibles were exchanged '*upon the second Sunday in May*' in 1786 when he was planning to go to the Indies. This exchange might have been an engagement rite, but there there was no marriage. Mary died at Greenock and, for some reason,

Burns was always to feel guilty about her. Hence his poignant song, *To Mary In Heaven*, so dearly loved by the Victorians.

c) write *Annie Laurie* or *The Bonny, Bonny Banks of Loch Lomond.*

There was a time when every Scots song ever written was either ascribed to Burns or Harry Lauder, but neither of them wrote either of the above. However, what is interesting from a Burns point of view is that while the music of both songs was written by Alicia Anne Spottiswoode (Lady John Scott), the words of *Annie Laurie* were written by Alan Cunningham, a good friend, but somewhat doubtful biographer, of Robert Burns.

d) die a pauper – or of drink or of venereal disease.

Lying by his bedside on his death was a book of plays in French, and two banker's orders which he had not cashed. He also had money owing to him from his brother, Gilbert, and from friends whom he had helped, as well as some remaining book residuals, not to mention a library of some worth and some valuable articles given him by admirers. He could have raised money on all of this at short notice. He was by no means a pauper, but in his dying straits the poor man was convinced that, because he received an ordinary reminder about a tailor's bill, he was being dunned by creditors and so panicked about leaving his family penniless. Which was not the case at all. Had he been well he would have seen this clearly. In addition, he was already marked for promotion in the Excise. While he enjoyed 'the social hour', he could not hold his drink because of his weak stomach, therefore he was rarely totally drunk, but he often pretended to be, just to be part of the company. He had a horror of sexually transmitted diseases (see his letter to his young brother, William, in London) and there is no record of his ever being affected. He died prematurely from natural causes exacerbated by the combination of a cruel boyhood, unlucky professional circumstances and a doctor's ineptitude.

That being said, Robert Burns DID

marry his first love, Jean Armour;

write a book of Poetry in the Scottish Dialect, thus preserving an ancient tongue;

single-handedly collect and revise more than 300 Scots songs, write more than 700 letters in superb English;

and die too soon. Much too soon.

He knew that himself. He was only 37. Who knows what was in him yet?

As I cam ower Glenap, I met an ancient woman
Wha bade me yet keep up my heart
For the best o my days is comin.

His tragedy was that he was never to see his 'best days'.
It is ours too.

Some Burns Contemporaries

George Washington
Benjamin Franklin
Thomas Jefferson
Denis Diderot
Joseph Haydn
Thomas Paine
Oliver Goldsmith
Edmund Burke
Thomas Muir
Captain Cook
Adam Smith
James Watt
James Boswell
Dr Johnson
David Garrick
Maximilien Robespierre
Marie Antoinette
Thomas Gainsborough
William Pitt
Catherine the Great
Sir Alexander MacKenzie
Jean Jacques Rousseau
Wolfgang Amadeus Mozart
Beau Brummell
William Blake
Sarah Siddons
Sir John Moore
Friederich von Schiller
William Murdoch
Sir Joshua Reynolds
Edward Jenner
Mary Wollstonecraft

Napoleon Bonaparte
Horatio Nelson
Mungo Park
Josiah Wedgwood
Edmund Kean
Duke of Wellington
Jane Austen
King George the Third

APPENDIX III

The Posthumous Burns

Memoir of Robert Burns by Robert Heron, 1797.
First American Edition of *Poems*, 1798.
Dr James Currie appointed first biographer, 1800.
First Glasgow Edition of *Poems*, 1800.
First Burns Supper organised by Rev Hamilton Paul, 1801
First Burns Club founded at Greenock, 21 July 1801.
Burns re-interred in new mausoleum at Doon, 19 September 1815.
First French Edition of *Poems*, 1826.
Life of Burns by J. G. Lockhart, 1828.
Jean dies at Dumfries on 26 March 1834 and is buried with Burns.
Life and Land of Burns by Alan Cunningham, 1835.
First German Edition of *Poems*, 1839.
First Burns Festival, Ayr 1844.
Works tranlated into Latin, 1862.
Essay on Burns by Robert Louis Stevenson, 1879.
Burns Federation founded at Kilmarnock, 1885.
Works translated into English (by William Corbett), 1892.
Centennial Edition of Burns by W. E. Henley, 1896.
Rosebery Centennial Burns Celebrations UK, 1896.
Works translated into Gaelic, 1910.
Works translated into Esperanto by Montagu C. Butler, 1926.
Loves of Robert Burns, a film with Joseph Hislop, UK, 1929.
Life of Robert Burns by Franklyn Bliss Snyder, USA, 1932.
First Japanese Edition of *Poems*, 1934.
Auld Lang Syne, a film with Andrew Cruikshank, UK, 1937.
Pride and Passion, by John deLancey Ferguson, New York, 1939.
James Barke's novels on Burns published from 1946 to 1959.
First Russian Edition of *Poems*, 1950.
Robert Burns by David Daiches, 1952.
Works translated into Hcbrew, 1956.
The Burns Encyclopaedia by Maurice Lindsay, 1959.
Burns – his Poems and Songs by Thomas Crawford, 1960.

There Was A Man opened at Traverse Theatre, Edinburgh, 1965.
Burns – Serial – Scottish Television, 1968
Robert Burns and his World by David Daiches, London, 1971.
The Songs of Robert Burns recorded by Jean Redpath, USA, 1974
Burns Festival, Ayr, 1975.
Works of Burns, edited by James A. Mackay, Alloway, 1986.
Letters of Burns, edited by James A. Mackay, Alloway, 1987.
Burns by James A. Mackay, Edinburgh, 1992.
The Dirt and the Deity by Ian McIntyre, 1995.
On the Trail of Robert Burns by John Cairney, Edinburgh, 2000

APPENDIX IV

Chronology of Complete Works

(With settings and original publications)

1774–1796

Date Written	Title	Tune	Published
1774 at Mount Oliphant Farm, near Ayr			
SONG	Handsome Nell	*I am a man unmarried*	Currie 1800
1775 at Kirkoswald School			
SONG	Now Westlin Winds	*Port Gordon*	Kilmarnock 1786
1776			
SONG	I dream'd I lay	*The young man's dream*	Johnson 1788
1777			
FRAGMENT	Villain as I am		Cromek 1808
1778 at Lochlea Farm, Tarbolton			
FRAGMENT	One night as I did wander		Cromek 1808
SONGS	The Tarbolton Lassies	Trad	Chambers 1851
	O, Tibbie, I hae seen the day	*Invercauld's Reel*	Johnson 1788
	O, woe is me, my mother dear	*Invercauld's Reel*	Glenriddel mss 1874
1779			
SONGS	Montgomerie's Peggy	*Galla Water*	Cromek 1808
	The Ploughman's Life	*Rinn m'eudail mo mhealladh*	Cromek 1808
1780			
POEM	The Ronalds of the Bennals		Chambers 1851
SONGS	Here's to thy health	*Laggan Burn*	Johnson 1796
	The Lass of Cessnock Banks	*The Butcher Boy*	Aldine Edition 1839
	Bonie Peggy Alison	*The Braes o Balquhidder*	Johnson 1788
	Mary Morison	*Duncan Davison*	Currie 1800
1781			
POEMS	To Ruin		Kilmarnock 1786
	A prayer in the prospect of death		Kilmarnock 1786
	Stanzas on the same occasion		Edinburgh 1787
	Paraphrase of the first Psalm		Edinburgh 1787
	Ninetieth Psalm versified		Edinburgh 1787
SONGS	Winter: A Dirge	*MacPherson's Rant*	Kilmarnock 1786
	Farewell to Eliza	*Gilderoy*	Kilmarnock 1786
1782			
POEM	I'll go and be a sodger		Currie 1800
SONGS	Raging Fortune	Trad	Cromek 1808

Date Written	Title	Tune	Published
	Fickle Fortune	*I dream'd I lay*	Cromek 1808
	No churchman am I	*Prepare, my dear brethen*	Edinburgh 1787
	My father was a farmer	*The Weaver and his shuttle-O*	Cromek 1808
	John Barleycorn	*Lull me beyond thee*	Edinburgh 1787
1783			
EPITAPH	On James Grieve		Scott Douglas 1877
POEMS	Remorse		Currie 1800
	The death and dying words of poor Mailie		Kilmarnock 1786
SONGS	My Nannie-O	Trad	Edinburgh 1787
	The Ruined Farmer	*Go from my window, love, do*	Chambers 1852
	Rigs o Barley	*Corn Rigs*	Kilmarnock 1786
	Green Grow the rashes-O	*Cou thou me the raschyes grene*	Edinburgh 1787
	'Indeed, will I,' quo Findlay	*Lass, an I come near thee*	Johnson 1792

1784 at Mossgiel Farm, Mauchline

EPISTLE	To John Rankine		Kilmarnock 1786
REPLY	To An announcement by John Rankine		
	(I am the keeper of the law)		Stewart 1801
EPITAPHS	On John Rankine		Stewart 1801
	On William Muir of Tarbolton Mill		Currie 1800
	On William Hood		Kilmarnock 1786
	On my honoured father		Kilmarnock 1786
	On a noisy polemic		Kilmarnock 1786
	On a henpecked squire		Kilmarnock 1786
EPIGRAM	On a henpecked squire	(2)	Kilmarnock 1786
POEMS	Prayer under the pressure of violent anguish		Edinburgh 1787
	On Tam the Chapman		Aldine 1839
	Lines on the Author's death		Stewart 1801
	The Twa Herds, or the Holy Tulzie		Stewart and Meikle 1799
BALLAD	On the American War	*Killiecrankie*	Edinburgh 1787
SONGS	The Mauchline Lady	*I had a horse and I had nae mair*	Johnson 1788
	O Leave novels	*Donald Blue*	Currie 1801
	The Belles of Mauchline	*Bonie Dundee*	Currie 1801
	My girl she's airy	*Black Joke*	Scott Douglas 1877
	Man was made to mourn	*Peggy Bawn*	Kilmarnock 1786

1785

EPISTLES	To Davie, a brither-poet		Kilmarnock 1786
	Also second epistle		Kilmarnock 1786
	To J. Lapraik		Kilmarnock 1786
	Also second and third epistles		Kilmarnock 1786
	To William Simpson		Kilmarnock 1786
	To John McMath		Cromek 1808
	To John Goldie		Glenriddel MSS 1874

Date Written	Title	Tune	Published
ELEGY	On the death of Robert Ruisseaux		Cromek 1808
EPITAPHS	On John Dove		Stewart and Meikle 1799
	On James Smith		Stewart 1801
FRAGMENTS	Her flowing locks		Cromek 1808
	My Jean		Johnson 1788
POEMS	Poor Mailie's Elegy		Kilmarnock 1786
	Holy Willie's Prayer		Stewart and Meikle 1799
	A Poet's welcome to his love-begotten daughter		Stewart 1799
	Epitaph on Holy Willie		Stewart 1801
	Death and Dr Hornbook		Edinburgh 1787
	To a Mouse		Kilmarnock 1786
	Halloween		Kilmarnock 1786
	The Mauchline Wedding		Bicentenary 1986
	Address to the Deil		Kilmarnock 1786
	Scotch Drink		Kilmarnock 1786
	Adam Armour's Prayer		Hogg and Motherwell 1834
	The Cotter's Saturday Night		Kilmarnock 1786
SONGS	Brose and Butter	Trad	Bicentenary 1986
	Farewell to Ballochmyle	Trad	Johnson 1790
	The Fornicator	*Clout the Caldron*	Bicentenary 1986
	Young Peggy	*The last time I came oer the moor*	Johnson 1787
	Rantin, Rovin Robin	*Dainty Davie*	Cromek 1808
	The Braes o Ballochmyle		(Music: Allan Masterton 1787)
	Kissin my Katie	*The Bob o Dumblame*	Johnson 1790
	Tho Women's Minds	*For a' that*	Johnson 1790
CANTATA	The Jolly Beggars	Trad	Stewart and Meikle 1799

1786

	Title		Published
EPISTLES	To James Smith		Kilmarnock 1786
	To John Kennedy		Cunningham 1834
	To Major Logan		Cunningham 1834
	To Gavin Hamilton (Stanzas on naething)		Alex Smith's Edition 1865
	To Dr McKenzie		Hogg and Motherwell 1835
	To a Young Friend		Kilmarnock 1786
ADDRESSES	To the Unco Guid		Edinburgh 1787
	Address to Edinburgh		Edinburgh 1787
	To a Haggis		Caledonian Mercury 1786
ODE	Despondency		Kilmarnock 1786
DEDICATION	To Gavin Hamilton		Cromek 1808
PAMPHLET	The Court of Equity or Libel Summons		
	Hastie and Egerton MSS		circa 1810
EPIGRAM	On rough roads		Kilmarnock 1786

Date Written	Title	Tune	Published
PRAYER	O Thou, dread power		Edinburgh 1787
EPITAPHS	On Robert Aitken		Kilmarnock 1786
	On Gavin Hamilton		Kilmarnock 1786
	On Wee Johnie		Kilmarnock 1786
INSCRIPTION	On a work of Hannah More's		Bicentenary 1986
FRAGMENT	The night was still		Blackie's *Land o Burns* 1840
POEMS	The Auld Farmer's New-Year Morning Salutation		Kilmarnock 1786
	The Twa Dugs		Kilmarnock 1786
	The Author's earnest cry and prayer		Kilmarnock 1786
	The Vision		Kilmarnock 1786
	To a Mountain Daisy		Kilmarnock 1786
	To a Louse		Kilmarnock 1786
	The Holy Fair		Kilmarnock 1786
	On a Scotch Bard gone to the Indies		Kilmarnock 1786
	A Dream		Kilmarnock 1786
	The Farewell to the brethren of St James's Lodge		Kilmarnock 1786
	A Bard's Epitaph		Kilmarnock 1786
	The Ordination		Edinburgh 1787
	Tam Samson's Elegy		Edinburgh 1787
	The Brigs of Ayr		Edinburgh 1787
	The Calf		Edinburgh 1787
	A Winter Night		Edinburgh 1787
	Sketch		Currie 1800
	The Inventory		Currie 1800
	On meeting with Lord Daer		Currie 1800
	Lines to an old sweetheart		Currie 1800
	Address of Beelzebub		Edinburgh Magazine 1818
	Willie Chalmers		Lockhart's Life of Burns 1829
	Reply to a trimming epistle		Stewart and Meikkle 1799
	Nature's Law		Aldine 1839
	Lines written on a banknote		Gilbert Burns 1820
	The Farewell		Rev Hamilton Paul 1819
SONGS	The Rantin dog, the Daddie oit	*Whare'll our gudeman lie?*	Johnson 1790
	The Lass o Ballochmyle	*Ettrick Banks*	Currie 1800
	My Highland Lassie-O	*MacLauchlin's Scots Measure*	Johnson 1788
	Where, braving angry winter's storms	*Niel Gow's Lament for Abercairney*	Johnson 1788
	Again rejoicing Nature sees	*Johnny's grey breeks*	Edinburgh 1787
	The gloomy night is gath'ring fast	*Roslin Castle*	Edinburgh 1787
	Will ye go to the Indies, my Mary?	*Ewe-bughts, Marion*	Currie 1800
	Yon wild mossy mountains	*Phebe*	Johnson 1792
	Masonic Song	*Shawn-boy/oer the water to Charlie*	Cunningham 1834

Date Written	Title	Tune	Published

1787 at Edinburgh and on tours

PROLOGUE	Spoken by Mr Woods on his benefit-night		Edinburgh Courant 1787
EPISTLE	To Mr McAdam of Craigen-Gillan		Cromek 1808
ADDRESS	To Wm Tytler Esq		Currie 1800
EPIGRAMS	At Roslin Inn		Hogg and Motherwell 1835
	Addressed to an artist		Chambers 1852
INSCRIPTIONS	For the headstone of Fergusson		Currie 1800
	For the portrait of Fergusson		Cromek 1808
LAMENT	For the absence of Mr Creech		Cromek 1808
ELEGIES	On the death of Sir James Hunter Blair		Currie 1800
	On the death of John McLeod Esq		Edinburgh 1793
	On the death of Lord President Dundas		Cunningham 1834
	On Stella		Alex Smith 1865
EPITAPH	On Mr Cruikshank		Hogg and Motherwell 1845
POEMS	To Miss Logan		Edinburgh 1787
	William Smellie – a sketch		Currie 1800
	Castle Gordon		Currie 1800
	Extempore in the Court of Session		Cromek 1808
	Written on the window of an Inn a Stirling		Cunningham 1834
	Reply to a censorious critic		Cunningham 1834
	The Libeller's self-reproof		Cunningham 1834
	The book-worms		Cunningham 1834
	Verses under a noble Earl's picture		Cunningham 1839
	A bottle and a friend		Cromek 1808
	On Elphinstone's translation of Martial		Stewart 1801
	Lines on the celebrated Miss Burns		Stewart 1801
	A Highland Welcome		Stewart 1801
	At Inveraary		Stewart 1801
	On Carron Iron-Works		Stewart 1801
	To Mr Renton of Lamberton		Chambers 1851
	To Miss Ferrier		Chambers 1852
	On the death of John McLeod		Edinburgh 1793
	Verses written in the Inn at Kenmore		Edinburgh 1793
	The Humble Petition of Bruar Water		Edinburgh 1793
	Lines on the Fall of Fyers		Edinburgh 1793
	On scaring some water-fowl at Loch Turit		Edinburgh 1793
	To the Guidwife of Wauchope House		Elizabeth Scott's Poems 1801
	Strathallan's Lament		Johnson 1788
	Interpolation *Your friendship much can make me blest*		Johnson 1788
	Sylvander to Clarinda		Glenriddel MSS 1874
	Birthday Ode for 31 December 1787		Glenriddel MSS 1874
SONGS	My Peggy's charms	Trad	Currie 1800
	Rattlin, roarin Willie	Trad	Johnson 1788

Date Written	Title	Tune	Published
	The Birks o Aberfeldie	*The Birks o Abergeldie*	Johnson 1788
	A Rosebud by my early walk	*A rosebud*	Johnson 1788
	The young Highland rover	*Morag*	Johnson 1788
	Lady Onlie, Honest Lucky	*The Ruffian's Rant*	Johnson 1788
	Blythe was she	*Andro and his Cutty Gun*	Johnson 1788
	The Banks of the Devon	*Bhannerach dhon na chri*	Johnson 1788
	And maun I still on Menie doat?/ Again rejoicing Nature sees	*Johnny's grey breeks*	Edinburgh 1787
	Bonie Dundee	*Adew Dundee*	Edinburgh 1787
	Highland Harry back again	*The Highland Watch's Farewell to Ireland*	Johnson 1790
	My Lord a-hunting he is gane	*My lady's gown there gairs upon it*	Johnson 1803
	Theniel Menzies' Bonie Mary	*The Ruffian's Rant or Roy's Tune*	Johnson 1803
	The bonie lass of Albanie	*Mary's dream*	Chambers 1852
	The Bonie Moor-hen	*Beware of the Ripells*	Cromek 1808

1788 at Ellisland, near Dumfries

EPISTLES	To Hugh Parker	Cunningham 1834
	To James Tennant of Glenconnor	Cunningham 1834
EPIGRAM	To Miss Ainslie in Church	Bicentenary 1986
ODE	To the memory of Mrs Oswald of Auchincruive	Edinburgh 1793
EPITAPHS	On William Nicol	William Clark 1831
	On William Michie	Cromek 1808
FRAGMENTS	The Poet's progress	Scott Douglas 1877
	Sapho Redivivus	Scott Douglas 1877
	When Guilford good	Johnson 1788
POEMS	O, were I on Parnassus Hill	Johnson 1790
	A new Psalm for the chapel of Kilmarnock	Hately Waddell 1867
	Verses in Friar's Carse Hermitage (2)	Currie 1800
	Verses to Clarinda	Cromek 1808
	To Alex Cunningham Esq	Scott Douglas 1877
	A mother's lament	Johnson 1790
	The lazy mist hangs	Johnson 1790
	Louis, what reck I by thee	Johnson 1796
	The virgin kiss	Chambers 1838
	The henpecked husband	Stewart 1801
	Versicles on sign-posts	Alex Smith 1867
	(With) Pegasus at Wanlockhead (upon a day)	Cunningham 1835
	Impromptu on Captain Riddell	Cromek 1808
	Reply to a note from Captain Riddell	Scott Douglas 1877
	To Miss Cruikshank	Edinburgh 1793

Date Written	Title	Tune	Published
SONGS	I'm oer young to marry yet	Trad	Johnson 1788
	To the weavers gin ye go		Johnson 1788
	Musing on the roaring ocean	*Druimionn dubh*	Johnson 1788
	Stay, my charmer	*An gille Dubh*	Johnson 1788
	My Hoggie	*Moss Platt*	Johnson 1788
	Duncan Davison		Johnson 1788
	Jumpin' John		Johnson 1788
	Clarinda, mistress of my soul	*Music by J.G.C.Schetky*	Johnson 1788
	McPherson's Farewell	McPherson's Rant	Johnson 1788
	Up in the morning early	Trad	Johnson 1788
	For thee is laughing Nature gay	Trad	Johnson 1788
	To daunton me	Trad	Johnson 1788
	Hey, the dusty miller	Trad	Johnson 1788
	The winter it is past	Trad	Johnson 1788
	The bonie lad's that's far awa	Trad	Johnson 1788
	Hey ca thro	Trad	Johnson 1790
	I hae a wife o my ain	Trad	Johnson 1790
	Ca the ewes to the knowes	Trad First Version	Johnson 1790
		Trad Second Version	Thompson 1794
	Beware o bonie Ann		Johnson 1790
	The Blue-eyed Lassie		Johnson 1790
	Whistle oer the lave ot		Johnson 1790
	Of a' the airts		Johnson 1790
	(Miss Admiral Gordon's Strathspey)	Trad	Johnson 1790
	The gard'ner wi his paidle	*The Gardener's March*	Johnson 1790
	The day returns	*Seventh of November*	Johnson 1790
	She's fair and fause	*(The lads o Leith)*	Johnson 1792
	Sweet Afton	Trad	Johnson 1792
	Auld Lang Syne		Johnson 1796
		Revised version	Thomson 1793
	Raving Winds around her blowing		
	M'Grigor of Roros Lament		Johnson 1788
	The Chevalier's Lament	*Captain oKean*	Currie 1800
	Robin shure in hairst	*Robin shear'd in hairst*	Johnson 1803
	How long and dreary is the night	*Cauld kail*	
		First version	Johnson 1788
		Second version	Thomson 1794
1789			
EPISTLES	To Dr Blacklock		Currie 1800
	To Robert Graham of Fintry		Currie 1800
SONNET	To Robert Graham of Fintry		Currie 1800
ODES	On the departed Regency Bill		Glenriddel MSS 1874
	Delia		Lives of the Scottish Poets 1822

Date Written	Title	Tune	Published
INSCRIPTION	To the Honourable C. J. Fox		Currie 1800
ELEGIES	On the Year 1788		Stewart 1801
	On Captain Matthew Henderson		Edinburgh 1793
FRAGMENT	Kirk and State excisemen		Stewart 1801
POEMS	The Kirk's Alarm		Stewart 1801
	The wounded hare		Edinburgh 1793
	On the late Captain Grose's peregrinations		Edinburgh 1793
SONGS	My wife's a wanton/winsome wee thing		Currie 1800
	The Whistle – a Ballad		Johnson 1792
	Sweet Tibbie Dunbar	Trad	Johnson 1790
	Ay waukin O	Trad	Johnson 1790
	John Anderson, my jo	Trad	Johnson 1790
	Johnie Cope	Trad	Johnson 1790
	Carl, an the King come	Trad	Johnson 1790
	Willie brew'd a peck omaut	Trad	Johnson 1790
	Awa, Whigs, awa	Trad	Johnson 1790
	Waukrife Minnie	Trad	Johnson 1790
	The Captive Ribband	Trad	Johnson 1790
	On a bank of flowers	*The bashful lover*	Johnson 1790
	My heart's in the Highlands	*Failte na miosg*	Johnson 1790
	The Battle o Sherramir	*The Cameron Rant*	Johnson 1790
	There's a youth in this city	*Music: Niel Gow*	Johnson 1790
	Eppie Adair	*My Appie*	Johnson 1790
	My love, she's but a lassie yet	*Miss Farquerson's Reel*	Johnson 1790
	To Mary in Heaven	*Mary weep no more for me*	Johnson 1790
	The Silver Tassie	*The secret kiss*	Trad Johnson 1790
	Tam Glen	*The Merry Beggars*	Johnson 1790
	Where Helen lies	*Kirkconnel Lea*	Bicentenary 1986
	Comin thro the Rye	Trad	It is na, Jean, thy bonie face Johnson 1796
The Maid's Complaint			Johnson 1792
	Anna, thy charms	*Bonny Mary*	The Edinburgh Star
	The Fete Champetre	*Killiecrankie*	Gilbert Burns 1820
	The Five Carlins	*Chevy Chase*	Lockhart's *Life of Burns* 1828
	I'll tell you a tale of a wife	Auld Sir Symon	Bicentenary 1986
	Election Ballad for Westerha'	*Up an waur them a' Willie*	Cunningham 1834

1790

PROLOGUES	Spoken at the theatre of Dumfries		Currie 1800
	For Mrs Sutherland (in Scots)		Stewart 1801
ADDRESS	New Year's day 1790		Currie 1800

Date Written	Title	Tune	Published
ADDRESSES	Election Ballad to Graham of Fintry		Scott Douglas 1877
ELEGIES	On Willie Nicol's Mare		Cromek 1808
	On the late Miss Burne		Currie 1800
EPITAPH	For Captain Matthew Henderson		Edinburgh 1793
LAMENT	For Mary, Queen of Scots		Edinburgh 1793
VERSES	For Captain Grose		Currie 1800
POEMS	Tam o Shanter		Grose's Antiquities 1791
	Lines to a gentleman who had sent a newspaper		Currie 1800
	On the birth of a posthumous child		Edinburgh 1793
	Out over the Forth		Johnson 1796
SONGS	Gudewife, count the lawin	Trad	Johnson 1796
	The Campbells are comin		Bicentenary 1986
	There'll never be peace till Jamie comes hame		Johnson 1792
	The Banks oDoon	Trad	
	First version		Scott Douglas 1877
	Second version		Cromek 1808
	Third version		Johnson 1792
	At the Glove Tavern, Dumfries /I murder hate		
		Killiecrankie	Kilmarnock 1876
	Killiecrankie	*An ye had been whare I had been*	
			Johnson 1790
	Yestreen I had a pint o wine	*Banks of Banna*	Cromek 1810

1791 at the Wee Vennel (Bank St), Dumfries

Date Written	Title	Tune	Published
EPISTLES	To William Stewart		Lockhart's Life of Burns 1829
	To John Maxwell of Terraughtie		Cromek 1808
	To Robert Graham of Fintry		Edinburgh 1793
EPIGRAMS	On Miss Davies		Stewart 1801
	At Brownhill Inn		Chambers 1838
	The Toadeater		Lockhart 1828
ADDRESS	To the shade of Thomson		Edinburgh 1793
ODE	On sensibility		Currie 1800
LAMENT	For James, Earl of Glencairn		Edinburgh 1793
FRAGMENTS	Damon and Sylvia		Aldine 1839
	The Keekin'-Glass		Chambers 1852
	Cock up your beaver	[Herd MS]	Johnson 1792
GRACES	Before Dinner		Currie 1800
	After Dinner		Stewart 1801
POEMS	On Pastoral Poetry		Currie 1800
	Verses on the destruction of Drumlanrig Woods		Scots Magazine 1803

Date Written	Title	Tune	Published
	Grim Grizzel		Hogg and Motherwell 1834
	Lines to Sir John Whitefoord		Edinburgh 1793
	On Glenriddell's fox breaking his chain		Glenriddel mss 1874
	Nithsdale's Welcome Hame		Johnson 1792
	The Kirk of Lamington		Lockhart 1828
SONGS	Lovely Davis	Trad	Johnson 1792
	O for Ane-and-Twenty, Tam	Trad	Johnson 1792
	Such a parcel o rogues in a nation	Trad	Johnson 1792
	Bonie wee thing	Trad	Johnson 1792
	The Posie	Trad	Johnson 1792
	The Gallant Weaver	Trad	Johnson 1792
	My Eppy McNab	Trad	Johnson 1792
	Altho he has left me	Trad	Johnson 1792
	My tocher's the jewel	Trad	Johnson 1792
	For ane an twenty, Tam	Trad	Johnson 1792
	Turn again, thou fair Eliza	Trad	Johnson 1792
	My Bonie Bell	Trad	Johnson 1792
	Ye Jacobites by name	Trad	Johnson 1792
	Bonie laddie, Highland laddie	Trad	Johnson 1792
	Kenmure's on and awa, Willie	Trad	Johnson 1792
	Craigieburn Wood	Trad	Johnson 1792
	Frae the friends and Land I love	Trad	Johnson 1792
	Ae fond kiss	*Rory Dall's Port*	Johnson 1792
	Gloomy December	*Rory Dall's Port*	Edinburgh 1796
	What can a young lassie do wi an auld man?	Trad	Edinburgh 1796
	The Dearest of the quorum	Trad	Edinburgh 1796
	As I cam oer the Cairney mount	Trad	Edinburgh 1796
	Lovely Polly Stewart	*You're Welcome, Charlie Stewart*	Johnson 1796
	Sae far awa/ O, sad and heavy should I part	*Dalkeith Maiden Bridge*	Johnson 1796
	Caledonia *Caledonian Hunt's Delight of Mr Gow*		Johnson 1796
	The Song of Death	*Oran an Aoig*	Johnson 1796

1792 at the Wee Vennel (Bank St), Dumfries

ADDRESS	The Rights of Women		Currie 1800
	Spoken by Miss Fontanelle		Currie 1800
EPIGRAM	On Miss Fontenelle		Cunningham 1834
FRAGMENTS	No cold approach		Johnson 1792
	Love for love		Johnson 1792
	How gracefully Maria		Johnson 1792
POEMS	On Fergusson		Chambers 1852
	On the Duke of Brunswick's breaking up his camp		Scott Douglas 1877
SONGS	Saw ye bonie Lesley?	*The Collier's Bony Dochter*	Thomson 1798

Date Written	Title	Tune	Published
	I do confess thou art so fair	Trad	Johnson 1792
	The weary pund o tow	Trad	Johnson 1792
	When she cam ben, she bobbed	Trad	Johnson 1792
	The Collier Laddie	Trad	Johnson 1792
	Kellyburn Braes	Trad	Johnson 1792
	The Lands o Virginia-O	Trad	Johnson 1792
	O can ye labour lea, young man	Trad	Johnson 1792
	The deuk's dang oer my daddie	Trad	Johnson 1792
	Lady Mary Ann	Trad	Johnson 1792
	The Deil's awa wi th' Exciseman	*The hemp-dresser*	Johnson 1792
	Willie Wastle	Trad	Johnson 1792
	Here's a health to them that's awa		Cromek 1808
	Scroggam		Johnson 1803
	The Country Lass/In simmer when the hay was mown		Johnson 1803
	Bessy and he spinnin-wheel		
		Sweet's the lass that loves me	Johnson 1792
	Auld Rob Morris	Trad	Thomson 1793
	Duncan Gray	Trad	Thomson 1798
	Highland Mary	*Katherine Ogie*	Thomson 1799
	My wife's a winsome wee thing		
		My wife's a wanton wee thing	Currie 1800
	The Lea-rig	*My ain kind dearie-O*	Currie 1800

1793 at Mill St (Burns St), Dumfries

EPISTLE	To Robert Graham of Fintry [Second]		Edinburgh 1793
ADDRESS	For Miss Fontenelle		Currie 1800
EPIGRAMS	On the Earl of Galloway		Cromek 1808
	On the Laird of Laggan		Currie 1800
	Maria Riddell		Scott Douglas 1877
GRACES	After meat		Stewart 1801
	Before and after meat		Chambers 1852
FRAGMENTS	Ye true, loyal natives		Cromek 1808
	On Commissary Goldie's brains		Cunningham 1834
	Lines inscribed in a lady's almanac		Stewart 1801
	Thanksgiving for a national victory		Bicentenary 1986
	Reply to an invitation		Cunningham 1801
	Grace before and after meat		Chambers 1852
	Lines on John McMurdo, Esq		Cunningham 1834
	Remorseful apology		Currie 1800
EPITAPH	On a lap dog		Currie 1800
POEMS	On hearing a thrush sing		Currie 1800
	On the commemoration of Rodney's victory		Stewart 1801
	Thou greybeard, old Wisdom		Stewart 1801

Date Written	Title	Tune		Published
	On General Demourier's desertion			Cromek 1810
	On Mrs Riddell's birthday			Currie 1800
	On Commemoration of Thomson			Chambers 1856
SONGS	Behold the Hour	Trad	First version	Thomson 1794
		Trad	Second version	Currie 1800
	Wandering Willie	Trad	First version	Currie 1800
		Trad	Second version	Thomson 1793
	Braw Lads of Galla Water	Trad		Thomson 1793
	The Soldier's Return	Trad		Thomson 1793
	Portith Cauld	Trad		Thomson 1798
	Lord Gregory	Trad		Thomson 1798
	Lovely Young Jessie	Trad		Thomson 1798
	Whistle an I'll come to ye, my lad	Trad		Thomson 1799
	By Allan Stream	Trad		Thomson 1799
	Dainty Davie	Trad		Thomson 1799
	Meg o the Mill	Trad	First version	Currie 1800
		Trad	Second version	Johnson 1803
	Phillis the fair	Trad		Currie 1800
	Bonie Jean/There was a lass	Trad		Currie 1800
	The last time I cam oer the moor	Trad		Chambers 1852
	Thine am I, my faithful Fair	*The Quaker's wife*		Thomson 1799
	Deluded swain	*The collier's dochter*		Currie 1800
	Where are the joys?	*Saw ye my father?*		Currie 1800
	As down the burn	*Down the burn, Davie lad*		Currie 1800
	Adown winding Nith	*The mucking o Geordie's byre*		Currie 1800
	Had I a cave	*Robin Adair*		Thomson 1799
	By Allan stream	*Allan Water*		Thomson 1799
	Blythe hae I been on yon hill	*Merrily dance the Quaker*		Thomson 1799
	O, open the door	*Open the door softly*		Thomson 1793
	Logan Braes	*Logan Water*		Currie 1800
	O were my love yon lilac fair	*Hughie Graham*		Currie 1800
	Thou has left me ever, Jamie	*Fee him, Father, fee him*		Thomson 1799
	Come, let me take you to my breast	*Alley Croker*		Thomson 1799
	Scots Wha Hae	*Hey Tutti Taitie*		Thomson 1799
	Husband, husband cease your strife	*My jo, Janet*		Thomson 1799

1794

EPISTLE	From Esopus to Maria	Cunningham 1834
ODE	For George Washington's Birthday	Kilmarnock 1876
SONNET	On the death of Robert Riddell	Currie 1800
INSCRIPTION	To Miss Graham of Fintry	Currie 1800

Date Written	Title	Tune	Published
EPIGRAMS	At Brownhill Inn		Bicentenary 1986
	On a country laird		Morisson 1811
	On a country seat of the same		Scott Douglas 1877
	On the Rev Dr Babbington's looks		Cromek 1808
	On a suicide		Cunningham 1834
	On swearing Burton		Cunningham 1834
	On 'The Marquis.'		Cunningham 1834
	On Andrew Turner		Cunningham 1834
EPITAPH	For Mr Walter Riddell		Stewart 1801
	On a noted coxcomb		Aldine 1839
FRAGMENTS	Monody on a lady		Currie 1800
	Pinned to Mrs Riddell's carriage		Cunningham 1834
	On Captain Lascelles		Glenriddell mss 1874
	On William Graham		Cunningham 1840
	On John Bushby		Cunningham 1840
	To Dr Maxwell		Currie 1800
	To the beautiful Miss Eliza J-n		Scott Douglas 1877
	On Chloris		Stewart 1801
	On seeing Mrs Kemble in 'Yarico'		Stewart 1801
SONGS	The flowery banks o Cree	Trad	Thomson 1798
	Charlie, he's my darling	Trad	Johnson 1796
	Bannocks o bear meal	Trad	Johnson 1796
	The Highland widow's lament	Trad	Johnson 1796
	It was a' for our rightfu' King	Trad	Johnson 1796
	The winter of life	Trad	Johnson 1796
	The tear-drop	Trad	Johnson 1796
	For the sake o somebody	Trad	Johnson 1796
	My luve is like a red, red rose	Major Graham	Urbani and Liston 1794
	Young Jamie, the pride o the plain		
	The carlin o the the glen		Johnson 1796
	The Highland balou	*Cagaran Gaolach*	Johnson 1796
	The Lovely lass o Inverness	*Drumossie*	Johnson 1796
	Wilt thou be my dearie?	*The Sutor's Dochter*	Johnson 1796
	Sae flaxen were her ringlets	*Oonagh's Waterfall*	Johnson 1796
	As I stood by yon roofless tower		
	Cumnock Psalms	First version	Johnson 1796
		Second version	Currie 1800
	Pretty Peg	Trad	Aldine 1834
	Let not women e'er complain	*Duncan Gray*	Thomson 1798
	Youthfu' Chloe, charming Chloe	Trad	Thomson 1799
	Philly and Willy	*The sow's tail to Geordie*	Currie 1800
	O, saw you my dear, my Philly	*When she cam ben, she bobbet*	
			Currie 1800

Date Written	Title	Tune	Published
	Ah, Chloris	Major Graham	Aldine 1834
	Amang the trees	*The King o France he rade a race*	Cromek 1808
	On the seas and far away	*O'er the hills and far away*	Currie 1800
	Sleepst thou or wak'st thou...?	*Deil tak the wars*	Currie 1800
	Lassie wi the lint-white locks	*Rothiemurchie's Rant*	Currie 1800
	The charming month of May	*Dainty Davie*	Thomson 1794
	Behold, my love	*My lodging is on the cold ground*	Thomson 1794
	Canst thou leave me thus, my Katie?	*Roy's wife*	Thomson 1799
	Contented wi little and cantie wi mair	*Lumps o puddins*	1799
	My Nannie's awa		
		There'll ne'er be peace till Jamie comes hame	Thomson 1799
	Farewell, thou stream	*Nansie to the greenwood gane*	Thomson 1799

1795

ADDRESS	To the toothache		Currie 1800
APOLOGY	For declining an invitation		Currie 1800
INSCRIPTIONS	On a goblet		Cunningham 1834
	For an altar to Independence		Currie 1800
	On a blank leaf of his 'Poems'		Thomson 1799
EPIGRAM	On Mr James Gracie		Kilmarnock 1871
EPITAPH	For Mr Gabriel Richardson		Cunningham 1834
FRAGMENTS	The Solemn League and Covenant		Cunningham 1834
	To John Syme of Ryedale		Currie 1800
	On Mr Pitt's hair-powder tax		Bicentenary 1986
	Over sea, over shore		Johnson 1803
	The wren's nest		Johnson 1796
POEM	To Collector Mitchell		Currie 1800
BALLADS	On Mr Heron's Election		Cunningham 1834
SONGS	Bonie Peg-a-Ramsay	Trad	Johnson 1803
	Wee, Willie Gray	Trad	Johnson 1803
	Oy, ay my wife she dang me	Trad	Johnson 1803
	O, gude ale comes and gude ale goes	Trad	Johnson 1803
	O, steer her up and haude her gaun	Trad	Johnson 1803
	O, that I had ne'er been married	Trad	Johnson 1803
	O wat ye wha's in yon toon	Trad	Johnson 1796
	O, let me in this ae night	Trad	Currie 1800
	O, bony was yon rosy briar	Trad	Currie 1800
	O, wat ye wha that loes me	Trad	Thomson 1799
	Does haughty Gaul invasion threat?	*Push about the jorum*	Currie 1800
	Forlorn, my love, no comfort near	*Let me in this ae night*	Currie 1800
	Why, why tell thy lover?	*Caledonian Hunt's Delight*	Currie 1800
	The braw wooer	*The Lothian lassie*	Currie 1800
	O this is no my ain lassie	*This is no my ain house*	Currie 1800

Date Written	Title	Tune	Published
	Their groves o sweet myrtle	*Humours of Glen*	Currie 1800
	I'll ay ca in by yon toon	*I'll gang nae mair to yon toon*	Johnson 1796
	Had I the wyte?	*Come kiss with me*	Johnson 1796
	The lass that made the bed to me	*The Cumberland Lass*	Johnson 1796
	The cooper o Cuddy	*Bab at the bowster*	Johnson 1796
	The lass o Ecclefechan	*Jack o Latin*	Johnson 1796
	Mark yonder pomp	*Deil tak the wars*	Johnson 1796
	How cruel are the parents	*John Anderson, my jo*	Johnson 1796
	On Chloris being ill	*Ay wauken-O*	Johnson 1796
	A man's a man, for a' that	*For a' that*	Johnson 1796
	There's news, lasses, news	*Captain Mackenzie's Reel*	Johnson 1803
	Mally's meek, Mally's sweet	*Deil flee oer the water*	Johnson 1803
	Jockey's taen the parting kiss	*Bonie lass, tak a man*	Johnson 1803
	To the woodlark	*Loch Erroch Side*	Thomson 1798
	The cardin o't, the spinnin o't		
		Queensbury's Scots measure	Johnson 1796
	Twasna her bonie blue e'e	*Laddie, lie near me*	Thomson 1800

1796

EPISTLE	To Colonel de Peyster		Currie 1800
VERSICLES	To Jessie Lewars		Cunningham 1834
INSCRIPTION	To Jessie Lewars		Currie 1800
GRACE	After meat at the Globe Inn		Thomson 1796
FRAGMENT	Leezie Lindsay		Johnson 1796
BALLADS	The Dean of the Faculty	*The Dragon of Wantley*	Cromek 1808
	The Trogger		Cunningham 1834
SONGS	Here's a health to ane I loe dear		Trad Currie 1800
	O, lay thy loof in mine, lass	*The Shoemaker's March*	Johnson 1803
	A lass wi a tocher	*Ballinnamona Ora*	Thomson 1799
	O wert thou in the cauld blast	*Lennox love to Blantyre*	Currie 1800
	Fairest Maid on Devon banks	*Rothiemurchie*	Currie 1800

Of Doubtful Authorship

FRAGMENT   A revolution song
A TALE   The Vowels
POEMS   The Tree of Liberty
            To the owl
            On the illness of the Poet's child
            On the death of the Poet's daughter
            Verses written under a violent grief
SONGS   Come rede me, Dame (The Quaker's Wife)
            There grows a bonie, briar bush
            Before I saw Clarinda's face
            The Hermit of Aberfeldy
            When first I saw fair Jeanie's face

Of Spurious Authorship

EPIGRAM   Johnie Peep
ADDRESS   To a potato
EPITAPH   On the Poet's daughter
LAMENT   For Mary (also Prayer for Mary)
SONGS   As I was wandering on a midsummer evening
            Donald Brodie met a lass
            Evan Banks
            Farewell to Ayrshire
            Gie my love brose, brose
            Gala Water
            Happy we are a' thegither
            I met a lass, a bonie lass
            Jennie McCraw, she has ta'en to the heather
            Katherine Jaffrey
            Lass, when your mither is frae hame
            O wat ye what my minnie did?
            O blaw, ye westlin winds, blaw saft
            Shelah oNeil
            The last, braw bridal I was at
            There came a piper out o Fife
            The ruined maid's lament
            The Thorn
            To thee, loved Nith
            The auld man, he came oer the lea
            To my bed
            When I think on the happy days
            Will ye go and marry, Katie?
            When clouds in skies do come together
            Ye hae lien a' wrang, lassie
            Your rosy cheeks are turned sae wan

APPENDIX V

Editions of Complete Works

1786 KILMARNOCK
Also in 1867, 1868, 1869,
1871, 1876, 1877, 1886,
1889, 1909, 1913 and 1923,

1787 EDINBURGH
Also in 1793, 1794, 1798,
1800, 1801, 1802, 1805,
1806, 1807, 1808, 1811,
1813, 1814, 1815, 1816,
1817, 1818, 1819, 1820,
1821, 1823, 1824, 1828,
1831, 1832, 1834, 1835,
1836, 1837, 1838, 1839,
1843, 1847, 1851/52,
1856/57, 1859, 1860, 1862,
1864, 1865, 1867, 1868,
1869, 1872, 1875, 1876,
1877/79, 1881, 1883, 1884,
1886, 1888, 1890/91, 1891,
1892, 1893, 1895, 1896,
1986/97, 1897, 1901, 1902,
1911, 1913, 1923, 1932,
1945, 1951, 1959, 1990,
2000.

1787 LONDON
Also in 1793, 1800, 1801,
1802, 1804, 1806, 1807,
1808, 1809, 1810, 1811,
1812, 1813, 1814, 1815,
1816, 1817, 1819, 1820,
1821, 1822, 1823, 1824,
1825, 1826, 1827, 1828,
1829, 1830, 1831, 1833,
1834, 1834, 1834/35, 1835,
1836, 1837, 1838, 1839,
1840, 1841, 1842, 1843,
1844, 1845, 1846, 1847,
1848, 1850, 1851, 1853,
1854, 1855, 1856, 1857,
1858, 1859, 1860, 1861,
1862, 1863, 1864, 1865,

1866, 1867, 1868, 1870,
1871, 1872, 1873, 1875,
1876, 1879, 1880, 1881,
1882, 1883, 1884, 1885,
1886, 1886/87, 1887, 1888,
1889, 1890, 1891, 1892,
1893, 1895, 1896, 1897,
1898, 1901, 1902, 1903,
1904, 1905, 1906, 1908,
1911, 1912, 1913, 1919,
1921, 1923, 1924, 1925,
1926, 1927, 1928, 1929,
1930, 1931, 1943, 1944,
1949, 1950, 1953, 1954, 1956
and 1958, 1995.

1787 DUBLIN
Also in 1789, 1790, 1803,
1816 and 1819.

1789 BELFAST
Also in 1790, 1793, 1800,
1805, 1806, 1807, 1814,
1816, 1818 and 1837

1798 PHILADELPHIA
Also in 1804, 1809, 1818,
1823, 1831, 1835, 1836,
1842, 1857 and 1886/87.

1800 GLASGOW
Also in 1801, 1802, 1804,
1807, 1816, 1820, 1821,
1822, 1825, 1828, 1831,
1834/36, 1836, 1841,
1843/44, 1845, 1846, 1847,
1850, 1852, 1857, 1858,
1859, 1862, 1865, 1866,
1867, 1870, 1871, 1874,
1875, 1877, 1878/80,
1879/80, 1881, 1887, 1888,
1892, 1894, 1895, 1896,
1901, 1902, 1903, 1906,
1907, 1911, 1919, 1927,

1928, 1930, 1938, 1940,
1947, 1950, 1954, 1955 and
1959.
1801 BERWICK
1801 MONTROSE
Also in 1816, 1819 and 1823.
1801 PAISLEY
Also in 1802 and 1907.
1802 DUNDEE
Also in 1834, 1904 and 1905.
1802 KIRKCALDY
Also in 1817.
1802 NEWCASTLE-UPON-TYNE
Also in 1811, 1812, 1814,
1816, 1818, 1819, 1821 1841.
1803 ARBROATH
1804 CORK
1807 STIRLING
1808 ALNWICK
Also in 1812, 1815 and 1828.
1808 MUSSELBURGH
1812 BALTIMORE
Also in 1816.
1813 PERTH
1818 DUNBAR
Also in 1834
1818 DURHAM
1819 AYR
1819 FALKIRK
1820 NEW YORK
Also in 1824, 1826, 1830,
1832, 1843, 1855, 1856, 1857,
1867, 1869, 1877, 1892, 1901,
1909, 1920 and 1926.
1824 ABERDEEN
Also in 1848.
1826 PARIS
Also in 1843, 1853 and 1865.
1834 LIVERPOOL
1835 LEIPSIG
Also in 1840, 1845, 1859 (with
Heidleberg), 1878, 1889, 1893
and 1895 (with Wein).
1836 HALIFAX
Also in 1837, 1838, 1840,
1843, 1850, 1851, 1852, 1853,
1859, 1862, 1865, 1866 and
1868.

1836 HARTFORD
1838 HOWDEN
1839 STUTTGART (AND TUBINGEN)
1840 BRUNSWICK. Also in 1846.
1841 BERLIN
Also in 1860, 1869 and 1877.
1844 DERBY
Also in 1867.
1844 MANCHESTER
Also in 1845, 1847, 1848 and
1858.
1848 BOSTON
Also in 1853, 1857, 1863,
1897, 1898 and 1908.
1855 MAUCHLINE
1859 NUREMBERG
1870 CINCINNATI
1870 NEWPORT, RHODE ISLAND
1870 TORONTO
1873 WAKEFIELD
1874 ROUEN
1889 OXFORD
Also in 1913.
1892 PRAGUE
1893 MODENA
1896 HALLE
1906 HEIDLEBERG
1922 BUFFALO, NY
1923 OSLO
1925 CLUJ (RUMANIA)
1925 WALTHAM ST LAWRENCE
1934 TOKYO
Also in 1935.
1937 HAMBURG
1942 CHAPEL HILL, NORTH
CAROLINA
1945 FAROE ISLANDS
1946 HARMONDSWORTH
1950 MOSCOW
Also in 1954 and 1961.
1951 ODENSE
1952 BUDAPEST
1953 FLORENCE
1954 BARCELONA
1956 WARSAW
1986 ALLOWAY (BURNS
FEDERATION)

Poems and Songs in Translation
(In chronological order)

French (1826, 1843 and 1874).
German (1839, 1840, 1846, 1859, 1860, 1869, 1872, 1877, 1878, 1889, 1893, 1896 and 1937).
Latin (1862, 1892 and 1899).
Bohemian, (1892).
English (William Corbett, 1892 and W. K. Seymour, 1954).
Italian (1893 and 1953).
Gaelic (1910).
Icelandic (1922).
Norwegian (1923).
Rumanian (1925).
Esperanto (Montagu C. Butler, 1926).
Welsh (1931).
Swedish (1933, 1942 and 1954).
Japanese (1934 and 1935).
Faroese (1945).
Russian (1950 and 1952).
Danish (1951).
Hungarian (1952).
Portugese (1952).
Greek (1953).
Spanish (1954).
Polish (1956).
Hebrew (1956).
Dutch (ND).

(See also: *Robert Burns in Other Tongues, a critical review* by William Jacks, Glasgow, 1896)

APPENDIX VI

Miscellaneous Editions
and Manuscript Collections

Stewart and Meikle Edition	1799
Stewart	1799, 1801
Currie	1800, 1801
Cromek	1808
Morrison	1811
Hamilton Paul	1819
Gilbert Burns	1820
John Gibson Lockhart	1828
William Clark	1831
Cunningham	1834, 1835, 1840
Hogg and Motherwell	1834, 1835, 1845
Aldine	1834, 1839
Chambers	1838, 1851, 1852, 1856
Alex Smith	1865
Scott Douglas	1877
William Henley	1896
James Barke	1955, 1985
William Wallace	1958
James Kinsley	1971
Bicentenary	1986
and	
Johnson Musical Museum	1787, 1788, 1789, 1790, 1792, 1796, 1803
Thomson Collection	1792, 1793, 1794, 1798, 1799, 1800
also	
Glenriddel MS	1874
with	
Grose's Antiquities	1791
Clarinda Correspondence	1843

Biographies and Burnsiana

Angellier, Auguste	Paris, 1893.
Blackie, John Stuart	Great Writers, 1888.
Brown, Hilton	There Was A Lad (Essay), 1949.
Carswell, Catherine	London, 1930, 1936 (2nd edition 1951).
Chambers, Robert	Biographical Dictionary of Eminent Scotsmen, Glasgow, 1813 (Burns by Robert Heron)
Crichton-Browne, Sir James	Burns From a New Point of View, 1926.
Cunningham, Allan	Life and Land of Burns, 2nd edition, 1835. New York, 1841, and London (ND).
Currie, James	Liverpool, 1800/1/2/3 and London, 1820 with additions. Dove's English Classics 1826. Also Edinburgh, 1838.
Dakers, Andrew	New York, 1923.
Daiches, David	London, 1952. Robert Burns and His World London, 1971.
Douglas, Sir George	Bookman Biography (with Rev W. S. Crocket), 1904.
Dove, Patrick Edward	Glasgow, 1859.
Ferguson, John de Lancey	Pride and Passion, New York, 1939.
Froding, Gustaf	Stockholm, 1909.
Gilfillan, George	Edinburgh, 1856.
Grimble, Ian	London, 1986.
Hecht, Hans	Heidleberg 1919 (Translated Jane Lymburn, 1936).
Henderson, Thomas	Little Biographies, 1904.
Henley, William Ernest	The Centenary Burns, 1896/97.
Hepburn, Thomas N.	Gabriel Setoun, Famous Scots, Edinburgh, 1896.
Heron, Robert	Memoir of the Late Robert Burns, 1797.
Higgins, James C.	Edinburgh 1893 and Kilmarnock, 1928.
Hogg, James	The Ettrick Shepherd, Memoir of Burns, 1834/36.
Irving, David	Lives of the Scottish Poets, 1804.
Ishebashi Magoichiro	Osaka, 1952.

Kinsley, James   Poems and Songs of Robert Burns in 3
                                  Volumes. Oxford University Press, 1968
                                  and also one volume, Oxford Paperbacks,
                                  1969
Lang, Andrew   Select Biography, Newcastle-upon Tyne.
Lindsay, John Maurice   The Ranting Dog, 1938. (Robert Burns,
                                  1954).
Lockhart, John Gibson   Constable's Miscellany, Edinburgh, 1828
                                  (Corrected 1830). 'Improved' by A.
                                  Murray 1872. Revised by W. S. Douglas
                                  882 and by J. H. Ingram 1890. Notes
                                  added by M. Sloan 1904. Essay by Sir
                                  Walter Raleigh, Liverpool, added 1914.
Mackay, James A.   Edinburgh, 1992.
Mackintosh, John   Paisley, 1906.
Mackenzie, James   Edinburgh, 1924.
Mackenzie and Dent   Select Biography, Newcastle, c.1827.
Marshall's   Catalogue of 500 Celebrated Authors of
                                  Great Britain now living, 1788.
McIntyre, Ian   The Dirt and the Deity, London.
Miller, Hugh   Recollections of Burns (from Tales and
                                  Sketches, 1886).
Oliphant, Margaret O.W.   Literary History of England, Vol 1, 1882.
Peterkin, Alexander   Edinburgh, 1815.
Rossetti, Wiiliam M.   Lives of Famous Poets, 1878.
Russell, William   Extraordinary Men, 1853.
Shairp, John Campbell   English Men of Letters, 1879 and 1897.
Shanks, Henry   Peasant Poets of Scotland, Bathgate, 1881.
Stewart, William   Robert Burns and the Common People,
                                  Glasgow, 1910.
Thomson, Arthur A.   The Burns We Love (Foreword by G. K.
                                  Chesterton), 1931.
Tillotson, John   Lives of Eminent Men, 1856.
Tyler, Samuel   Dublin, 1849.
Waddell, Peter H.   A Spiritual Biography, 1867.
Walker, Josiah   Edinburgh, 1811.
White, James   A Memoir, 1859.
Will, William   Robert Burns as a Volunteer, Glasgow,
                                  1919.
Wilson, John   New York 1845.
Wright, Dudley   Robert Burns and his Masonic Circle,
                                  Paisley, 1921/1929.

BURNSIANA

Barke, James	Editor, Complete Poems and Songs of Robert Burns, 1955, 1960, 1991, 1995 (Intro. by John Cairney) With Sydney Goodsir Smith – Editor – The Merry Muses of Caledonia. Preface by J. De L. Ferguson, London 1965.
Bold, Alan	A Burns Companion (1991) Robert Burns – a pictorial profile (1992) Rhymer Rab, an Anthology of the Prose and Poetry of Burns (1993).
Burns Chronicle	Index of Articles, 1892/1925 and 1926/45 by J. C. Ewing.
Burns Encyclopaedia	London, 1959 (Edited by Maurice Lindsay).
Burnsiana	Alloway Publishing, 1988 (Compiled by James A. Mackay).
Burns Information and Quiz Book	(Compiled by Harold Thomas) Edinburgh 1988.
Dictionary of National Biography	Vol 7 1886 (Entry by Sir Leslie Stephen).
Encyclopaedia Britannica	Vol 4 1876 (Entry by John Nichol).
Esslemont, Peter	Brithers A' – A Miscellany, Aberdeen, 1943.
Fisher, W.D.	Burns and the Bible, Glasgow, 1927.
Hazlitt, William	Lectures on English Poets (No.7) Surrey Institution.
Henley, W.E.	Editor (with T. F. Henderson) of Centenary Edition of the Poetry of Robert Burns (4 Vols), London, 1896.
Hepburn, Anthony	Editor, Robert Burns – Poems and Selected Letters, London, 1959. (Preface by Editor and Introduction by David Daiches)
Hill, John C.	The Love Songs & Heroines of Robert Burns, London, 1961
Hunter, Clark	Let Burns Speak – An Edited Autobiography, Paisley, 1961
Irving, Gordon	The Wit of Robert Burns, London, 1972.
Keith, Christina	The Russet Coat, London, 1956.
Kinsey, James	Burns Poems and Songs, Oxford University Press, 1971.

Low, Donald A.   Critical Essays on Robert Burns, London,
                                    1975.
Mackay, James A.   The Burns Federation 1885–1985.
                                    Kilmarnock, 1985.
                                    The Complete Letters of Robert Burns,
                                    Alloway, 1987.
                                    Burns A – Z , The Complete Word Finder,
                                    Dumfries, 1990.
Montgomerie, William   Editor, Robert Burns – Essays by
                                    Contemporary Authors, Glasgow, 1947.
Munro, Archibald   Burns and Highland Mary, Edinburgh,
                                    1896.
McNaught, Duncan   The Truth About Robert Burns, Glasgow,
                                    1921.
Pearl, Cyril   Bawdy Burns – The Christian Rebel,
                                    London, 1958.
Ross, John D.   Burns' Clarinda, Edinburgh, 1897.
Smith, Grant F. O.   Editor, The Man Robert Burns, Toronto,
                                    1940.
Stevenson, R. L.   Essay – Some Aspects of Robert Burns.
Stirling, James Hutchison   Editor, Burns in Drama (1878), Murison
                                    Collection.
Stirling, L. M.   Scotland's Sons (Burns Chronicle 1956),
                                    Mitchell Library.
Wallace, William   Bicentenary Edition of Poetical Works of
                                    Robert Burns, Edinburgh, 1958.
Wood, J. Maxwell   Burns and the Riddell Family, Dumfries,
                                    1922.

BURNS – RELATED FICTION

Barke, James   The Song in the Green Thorn Tree,
                                    London, 1947.
                                    The Wonder of All the Gay World,
                                    London, 1949.
                                    The Crest of the Broken Wave, London,
                                    1953.
                                    The Well of the Silent Harp, London,
                                    1954.
                                    Bonnie Jean, London, 1959.
                                    (This sequence of novels forms a work
                                    entitled The Immortal Memory.)

Campsie, Alistair	The Clarinda Conspiracy, Edinburgh, 1989.
Legge, Clayton Mackenzie	Highland Mary, a romance, Boston, 1906. Highland Mary, a romance (1796–1896), Glasgow, 1896.
Steuart, John A.	The Immortal Lover, London, 1930.

ORIGINAL BURNS-RELATED WRITING BY
JOHN CAIRNEY

1968   BURNS
A six-part television serial (55-minute episodes) for Scottish Television.

1969   THE ROBERT BURNS STORY
Two-hour solo play in two parts for Shanter Productions.

1975   THE HOLY FAIR
A musical play with traditional songs for Burns Festival, Ayr.

1976   THE LINGERING STAR
A play with songs based on the Mary Campbell story. Burns Festival.

1977   THE THOMSON LETTERS
Duologue for actors with song illustrations.

1978   THE CLARINDA CORRESPONDENCE
Dramatisation of letters between Burns and Nancy McLehose with original song-settings by Geoff Davidson. Featuring John Cairney as Sylvander and Alannah O Sullivan as Clarinda at St Cecilia's Hall, Edinburgh.

1979   A DRUNK MAN LOOKS AT ROBERT BURNS
A reading in two parts linking the works of Burns and Hugh MacDiarmid. Performed by John Cairney and Russell Hunter at the Burns Festival.

1980   AS OTHERS SAW HIM
A group reading with songs from accounts of Burns by his contemporaries.

1986   A MOMENT WHITE
Aspects of Burns with original drawings by Irene Dickson. Research by Alannah oSullivan. A *Glasgow Herald* publication with Outram Press to mark the bi-centenary of the 1786 Kilmarnock Edition.

1987   THE MAN WHO PLAYED ROBERT BURNS
        A book of the author's travels on theatrical world tours playing
        Robert Burns on stage between 1965 and 1979. Mainstream
        Publishing and HarperCollins.

1988   BURNSANG
        Reader and Singers in an Entertainment based on the songs of
        Burns.

        BURNSPEAK
        Readers and actors in an Entertainment based on the words of
        Burns.

1989   A TOAST TO THE LASSIES
        A scenario for Narrator, Singer and Dancers (USA) and featuring
        Jean Redpath and Alisair Fraser (violin).

1990   THERE WAS A LAD
        Full length musical based on the Robert Burns story with original
        music by Geoff Davidson. Presented in the City Halls as part of
        Glasgow's Year of Culture. Featuring John Cairney and Anne
        Lorne Gillies.

1994   INTRODUCTION
        To Complete Works – Harper-Collins, Glasgow, 1995.

1996   TAM O SHANTER
        Recording with music by Sir Malcom Arnold. Directed by John o
        Leary for Word Pictures, Auckland, New Zealand. Winner of Silver
        Medal, New York Festival Of Radio, 1997.

2000   ON THE TRAIL OF ROBERT BURNS
        A biography of Burns related to the place-names associated with
        him. Luath Press, Edinburgh, 2000.

Some other books published by **LUATH** PRESS

On the Trail of Robert Burns
John Cairney
ISBN 0 946487 51 0 PBK £7.99

Is there anything new to say about Robert Burns?

John Cairney says it's time to trash Burns the Brand and come on the trail of the real Robert Burns. He is the best of traveling companions on this convivial, entertaining journey to the heart of the Burns story.

Internationally known as 'the face of Robert Burns', John Cairney believes that the traditional Burns tourist trail urgently needs to find a new direction. In an acting career spanning 40 years he has often lived and breathed Robert Burns on stage. *On the Trail of Robert Burns* shows just how well he has got under the skin of Burn's complex character. This fascinating journey around Scotland is a rediscovery of Scotland's national bard as a flesh and blood genius.

Immortal Memories [of Robert Burns]: the best ever
John Cairney
ISBN 1 84282 009 5 HBK £20.00

A compilation of toasts to the immortal memory of Robert Burns as delivered at Burns Suppers around the world together with other orations, verses and addresses 1801–2001.

The annual Burns Supper, held on or around his birthday, 25 January, has become something of a cult in virtually every country in the world where 'Scottish' is spoken – and even where it is not. This is an occasion when people gather around a dinner table to give tribute to a Scottish poet who died more than 200 years ago. It really is an extraordinary phenomenon.

Thus begins John Cairney's latest work focusing on Scotland's national bard, Robert Burns. To be asked to deliver the 'Immortal Memory', the chief toast and centerpiece of the traditional Burns Supper, is recognised as a privilege and cherished by Burns enthusiasts the world over. *Immortal Memories* is an extensive collection of these toasts, spanning 200 years from the first Burns Supper in Alloway in 1801 to the Millennium Burns Suppers of 2001.

Luath Press Limited

committed to publishing well written books worth reading

LUATH PRESS takes its name from Robert Burns, whose little collie Luath (*Gael.*, swift or nimble) tripped up Jean Armour at a wedding and gave him the chance to speak to the woman who was to be his wife and the abiding love of his life. Burns called one of 'The Twa Dogs' Luath after Cuchullin's hunting dog in Ossian's *Fingal*. Luath Press was established in 1981 in the heart of Burns country, and now resides a few steps up the road from Burns' first lodgings on Edinburgh's Royal Mile.

Luath offers you distinctive writing with a hint of unexpected pleasures.

Most bookshops in the UK, the US, Canada, Australia, New Zealand and parts of Europe either carry our books in stock or can order them for you. To order direct from us, please send a £sterling cheque, postal order, international money order or your credit card details (number, address of cardholder and expiry date) to us at the address below. Please add post and packing as follows: UK – £1.00 per delivery address; overseas surface mail – £2.50 per delivery address; overseas airmail – £3.50 for the first book to each delivery address, plus £1.00 for each additional book by airmail to the same address. If your order is a gift, we will happily enclose your card or message at no extra charge.

Luath Press Limited
543/2 Castlehill
The Royal Mile
Edinburgh EH1 2ND
Scotland
Telephone: 0131 225 4326 (24 hours)
Fax: 0131 225 4324
email: sales@luath.co.uk
Website: www.luath.co.uk